Collins

Children and Young People's Workforce

Mark Walsh and
Janet Stearns

Level 2 Certificate

Candidate Handbook

Published by Collins Education
An imprint of HarperCollins Publishers
77-85 Fulham Palace Rd
Hammersmith
London
W68JB

Browse the complete Collins Education catalogue at
www.collinseducation.com

10 9 8 7 6 5 4 3 2 1

ISBN 978 00 0 741599 1

Mark Walsh and Janet Stearns assert their moral rights to be identified as
the authors of this work

British Library Cataloguing in Publication Data.
A Catalogue record for this publication is available from the British Library.

Commissioned by Charlie Evans
Project Managed by Jo Kemp
Design and typesetting by Joerg Hartsmannsgruber and Q2A
Cover design by Angela English

Index by Indexing Specialists Ltd

Printed and bound by L.E.G.O.S.p.a

Contents

Chapter 1   Introduction to communication in health and social care or children's and young people's settings (SHC 21) — 2

Chapter 2   Introduction to equality and inclusion in health and social care or children's and young people's settings (SHC 23) — 32

Chapter 3   Introduction to personal development in health and social care or children's and young people's settings (SHC 22) — 58

Chapter 4   Contribute to children and young people's health and safety (MU 2.4) — 86

Chapter 5   Child and young person development (TDA 2.1) — 120

Chapter 6   Safeguarding the welfare of children and young people (TDA 2.2) — 134

Chapter 7   Maintain and support relationships with children and young people (TDA 2.7) — 156

Chapter 8   Support children and young people's positive behaviour (TDA 2.9) — 174

Chapter 9   Contribute to the support of child and young person development (CCLDMU 2.2) — 190

Chapter 10   Contribute to the support of the positive environments for children and young people (MU 2.8) — 206

Chapter 11   Understand partnership working in services for children and young people (MU 2.9) — 228

Chapter 12   Paediatric emergency first aid (PEFAP 001) — 246

Chapter 13   Managing paediatric illness and injury (MPII 002) — 274

Acknowledgements

Alamy: 9, 10, 14, 16, 21, 22, 25, 27, 32, 39, 47, 48, 50, 55, 58, 60, 68, 72, 76, 82, 86, 92, 95, 97, 99, 100, 110, 120, 125, 126, 130, 137, 139, 140, 141, 158, 160, 162, 164, 168, 176, 177, 179, 182, 184, 190, 194, 196, 197, 200, 203, 208, 212, 219, 228, 255, 256, 259, 260, 264, 276, 291, 293, 296

Changing Faces: 37

Department for Education (Crown copyright): 138

Food Standards Agency (Crown copyright): 222

Getty Images: 63, 149, 151, 174, 180, 199, 220, 265, 266, 283, 284, 292, 294

Image Bank: 159, 172

iStockphoto: 2, 4, 12, 19, 26, 34, 42, 43, 51, 52, 61, 65, 74, 78, 88, 90, 93, 102, 107, 108, 115, 116, 127, 155, 156, 166, 170, 185, 192, 198, 207, 214, 223, 224, 232, 240, 242, 253, 255, 268, 269, 277, 282, 298

Rex: 135

Science Photo Library: 270

Shutterstock: 38, 40, 41, 103, 104, 105, 112, 113, 117, 123, 124, 129, 133, 147, 148, 153, 161, 186, 202, 210, 216, 217, 218, 230, 231, 234, 236, 238, 243, 245, 246, 248, 250, 252, 254, 261, 262, 263, 265, 267a, 267b, 268, 270, 271, 274, 277, 278, 280, 281, 285, 287, 289, 297a, 297b, 298

Introduction

Welcome to the Level 2 Certificate for the Children and Young People's Workforce.

The material in this book covers all 13 mandatory units of the Level 2 certificate, which combine to give you 31 credits towards your qualification. You need a total of 35 credits to achieve the full qualification and your tutor or assessor will help you to choose relevant optional units in order to do this.

Each chapter of the book covers a specific Level 2 unit. You will see that the chapters are divided into different sections, which are exactly matched to the specifications for the Level 2 qualification. Each section provides you with a focused and manageable chunk of learning and covers all of the content areas that you need to know about in a particular unit.

In order to achieve your Level 2 qualification, you need to provide evidence of your knowledge and understanding as well as your practical competence in the real work environment. Each chapter in this book begins with a summary of 'What you need to know' and 'What you need to do' in order to successfully complete the unit. The checklist at the end of each chapter will help you to keep track of your progress.

The suggested assessment tasks in each chapter will help you to gather the evidence you need for each unit. Your tutor or assessor will help you to plan your work in order to meet the assessment requirements.

There is a strong work-related focus to the materials in this book, using case studies, activities and realistic examples to develop your interest in and understanding of professional practice within the Children and Young People's Workforce.

We hope that the material in this book is accessible, interesting and inspires you to pursue a rewarding career with children and young people. Good luck with your course!

Janet Stearns and Mark Walsh

1 | Introduction to communication in health, social care or children's and young people's settings (SHC 21)

Assessment of this unit

This unit highlights the central importance of communication in work with children and young people. It focuses on the reasons why people communicate in childcare settings, the methods they use and the importance of ensuring that communication in care settings is effective.

You will be assessed on both your knowledge of effective communication and your ability to apply this in practical work with children and young people. In order to successfully complete this unit, you will need to produce evidence of your knowledge, as shown in the 'What you need to know' chart opposite, and evidence of your practical competence, as shown in the 'What you need to do' chart, also opposite. Your tutor or assessor will help you to prepare for your assessment and the tasks suggested in the chapter will help you to create the evidence that you need.

CHAPTER 1

AC   What you need to know

1.1	Different reasons why people communicate
1.2	How effective communication affects all aspects of your work
1.3	Why it is important to observe an individual's reactions when communicating with them

AC   What you need to do

2.1	Find out an individual's communication and language needs, wishes and preferences
2.2	Demonstrate communication methods that meet an individual's communication needs, wishes and preferences
2.3	Show how and when to seek advice about communication
3.1	Identify barriers to communication
3.2	Demonstrate how to reduce barriers to communication in different ways
3.3	Demonstrate ways to check that communication has been understood
3.4	Identify sources of information and support or services to enable more effective communication
4.1	Explain the term 'confidentiality'
4.2	Demonstrate confidentiality in day to day communication, in line with agreed ways of working
4.3	Describe situations where information normally considered to be confidential might need to be passed on
4.4	Explain how and when to seek advice about confidentiality

This unit also links to some of the other mandatory units:

TDA 2.7	Maintain and support relationships with children and young people
CCLDMU 2.2.	Contribute to the support of child and young person development

Some of your learning will be repeated in these units and will give you the chance to review your knowledge and understanding.

Understand why communication is important in the work setting

Your assessment criteria:

1.1 Identify different reasons why people communicate

What is communication?

People who work with children and young people need to develop effective communication skills in order to make and maintain relationships. Childcare workers communicate with both children and adults for a number of different reasons. This unit will help you appreciate the importance of this aspect of your own work with children and young people. You must understand:

▶ what communication involves

▶ the different reasons for communication

▶ the way communication affects how practitioners work.

Communication is about making contact with others *and* being understood. When communicating, people send and receive 'messages'. We all communicate continuously by sending messages. Figure 1.1 describes how this happens through a communication cycle.

The communication cycle is a way of showing that communication involves a two-way process of sending and receiving messages. These messages can be in the form of:

▶ **verbal communication**, using spoken or written words

▶ **non-verbal communication**, using body language such as gestures, eye contact and touch.

Over to you!

How would you explain what 'communication' is if a child asked you to explain this idea?

Key terms

Non-verbal communication: ways of communicating without using words (for example, through body language)

Verbal communication: forms of communication that use (spoken or written) words

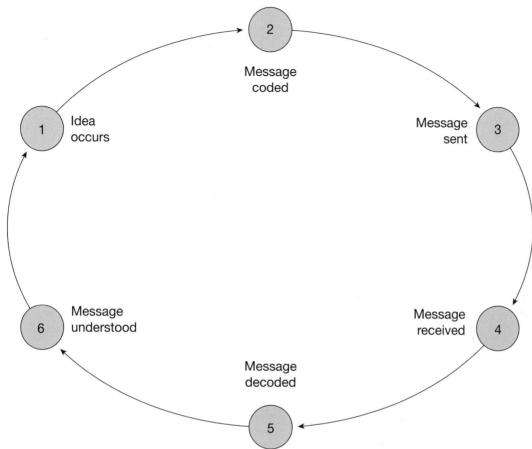

Figure 1.1 The communication cycle

People who work in children and young people's settings may need to communicate for a variety of reasons with different people: with the children they are caring for, with parents, with colleagues and with workers from other care agencies.

Case study

Joseph is 2 years of age. He enjoys helping his mum in the kitchen when she is making a meal. When she says, 'Can I get some fruit for you Joe?' he puts his arms in the air, says 'me, me' and smiles at her. His mum responds by picking him up and saying, 'Okay, you take something yourself this time'.

1. How does Joseph's mum communicate with him in this example?

2. How does Joseph communicate non-verbally with his mum in response to her question?

3. Describe how a cycle of communication occurs in this example.

Why do people communicate in work settings?

A lot of communication happens in children and young people's care settings: many different kinds of conversations occur, as well as a variety of singing, drawing, painting and imaginative play activities that also involve communication. A closer look at these activities will show you that children, young people and adults **interact** and communicate with each other for a variety of different reasons (see Figure 1.2).

Your assessment criteria:

1.1 Identify different reasons why people communicate

Key terms

Interact: relating to another person

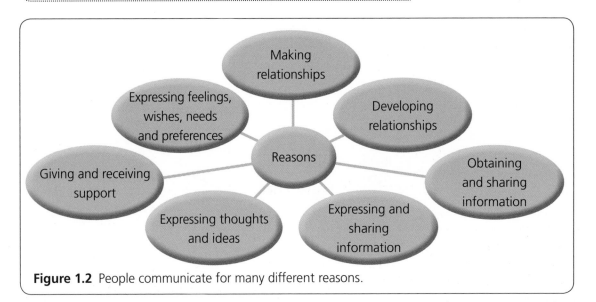

Figure 1.2 People communicate for many different reasons.

Making relationships

People communicate to make new relationships. In children and young people's care settings, these relationships may be with parents, carers, children or colleagues. Positive verbal and non-verbal communication skills, such as being friendly, smiling and shaking hands when greeting the person, are needed to make a good first impression in a relationship.

Developing relationships

Early years practitioners develop relationships with children and young people, their parents or carers and colleagues by maintaining a friendly and supportive approach, and by being interested in what other people are doing and feeling. This enables service users to feel comfortable and secure, and that they can trust and rely on professionals.

Obtaining and sharing information

Early years practitioners may need to obtain and share information about children and young people with colleagues and other

Over to you!

Can you think of four different reasons why you communicated with others when you were last in your work or placement setting?

professionals to ensure the team is fully informed. A practitioner may also need to communicate with a child, young person or family member about the care and support they receive, or about the kinds of services and facilities that are available in a care setting.

Expressing thoughts and ideas

An early years practitioner may need to share their thoughts about care issues or about aspects of practice with colleagues. Effective communication skills are also needed to encourage children and young people to talk about what they have learnt, say what they think or to express themselves imaginatively.

Giving and receiving support

Children and young people often seek reassurance from practitioners as a way of developing their self-confidence. In response, practitioners use praise and touch, and give time and attention as a way of rewarding a child or young person's efforts and achievements. Some care settings also use support groups, staff meetings and appraisals as ways of providing early years practitioners with support and reassurance about their work performance.

Expressing feelings, wishes, needs and preferences

Early years practitioners need to find ways of encouraging children and young people to express their feelings and to talk about how they wish to be treated, as well as to say what they like and dislike. Children and young people will communicate in this way if they trust and have a secure relationship with a practitioner.

Over to you!

How do you use your communication skills to give support to children and your colleagues? Think about your use of verbal and non-verbal communication skills.

Knowledge Assessment Task   1.1

You will communicate with children, parents, carers and colleagues in the setting where you work or are on placement in a number of different ways and for a variety of different reasons. Complete a summary sheet like the one below to show that you can identify the different reasons why people communicate.

Who took part in this example of communication?	What happened? Describe the communication you observed.	What were the reasons for this episode of communication?

How does effective communication impact on your work?

Effective communication is a central part of the work that happens in care settings. You will need to develop a range of communication skills and be able to use them effectively to carry out the various aspects of your work role. You will need to be able to communicate effectively with children, their parents and your colleagues as well as colleagues from other agencies.

Your assessment criteria:

1.2 Explain how effective communication affects all aspects of own work

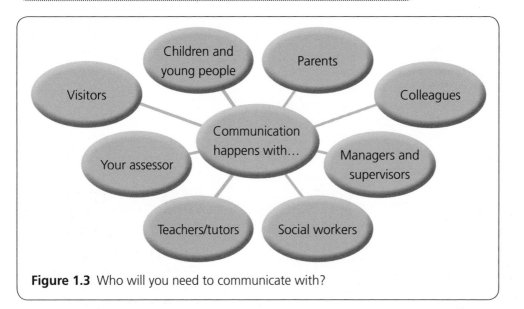

Figure 1.3 Who will you need to communicate with?

Figure 1.3 identifies a variety of people with whom you may need to communicate in your care setting. Knowing about the communication cycle and being able to send and receive messages appropriately is the key to communicating well. In general, you will use communication effectively as part of your work role if you:

▶ get the other person's attention before you begin talking to them

▶ speak clearly and directly so that you get your message across

▶ adapt the way you talk so that the child or adult you are talking to is able to understand you

▶ use **empathy** to try and understand the other person's point of view or the way they might be affected by what you are saying to them

▶ listen carefully to what the child or adult says to you

▶ use your own non-verbal communication skills effectively

▶ summarise what the other person has said as a way of checking your understanding of what they mean.

Over to you!

Are any of your work colleagues particularly good at using empathy? Reflect on what it is they do that enables them to do this well.

Key terms

Empathy: understanding another person's feelings as if they are your own

Your communication skills will develop and become more effective as you gain experience in your work role, learning by observing more experienced colleagues. Learning from others, seeking advice and using support are all part of this process.

Effective communication with children

People who work in childcare settings are expected to be able to communicate effectively with children. This is not always easy or straightforward. Communication with the children is more likely to be effective if you:

▶ get the child's attention before you start talking

▶ make eye contact at the child's level

▶ use simple age-appropriate language, short sentences and a friendly tone of voice

▶ give the child time to understand what you are saying and enough time to respond

▶ be patient and attentive when a child is talking to you, giving them time to express themselves

▶ don't rush the child or interrupt to speed things up

▶ listen carefully and use simple questions to clarify what the child is telling you

▶ be aware of your own body language and take note of what the child's body language is communicating

▶ use your facial expression in an active, positive way to support what you are saying and as a way of responding to what the child is saying to you

▶ use pictures, colourful posters or displays to express ideas or to communicate information in a way that is easy to understand.

Over to you!

In a small group or with a colleague, discuss the strategies you use to encourage children or young people to express their own thoughts and ideas when you are communicating with them. Note any ideas other people suggest that you could try yourself.

Being respectful, consistent in your approach and patient in the way you listen and respond to children in your work setting will encourage them to trust you and communicate with you.

Effective communication with parents

Parents need to be able to trust you and have confidence in your ability to support and care for their children. Communication with parents is more likely to be effective if you:

▶ establish a good rapport with each child's parent(s)

▶ show parents respect by using their preferred names (for example, 'Mrs Griffiths' or 'Jenny', depending on how the person wishes to be known)

▶ acknowledge that, as the main carers, they should always be consulted about anything that affects their child

▶ speak directly and clearly, using positive body language and good eye contact

▶ give each individual enough time to understand what you are saying and listen carefully to what they say to you

▶ respond quickly and in an appropriate way to a parent's communication by phone, email or in person

▶ respect **confidentiality** by communicating personal, sensitive or private information about their child in an appropriate area of the care setting

▶ adapt your communication skills to meet the needs of parents who have hearing or visual impairment, for example, or whose first language is not English.

Parents will trust and respect you if you adopt a consistent, professional and respectful approach when you communicate with them. They need to be confident that you value their child and that you are able to communicate with them about their child's learning and development.

Effective communication with colleagues

Effective communication with colleagues is an essential part of your work role; you will be working in a team. Communication with colleagues is more likely to be effective if you:

Your assessment criteria:

1.2 Explain how effective communication affects all aspects of own work

Key terms

Confidentiality: ensuring information is only accessible to people who are authorised to know about it

Over to you!

Can you think of reasons why parents may be sensitive about the way you deal with confidential information relating to them, their child or their family?

▶ establish an appropriate work-related rapport with each of your colleagues

▶ show that you respect your colleagues' skills, abilities and professional approach

▶ talk clearly and directly, using positive body language and giving them enough time to absorb what you are saying

▶ always listen to your colleagues' point of view, making sure you are polite and constructive if you disagree

▶ check that colleagues understand what you are trying to communicate, especially if you are passing on important information

▶ clarify any points by asking questions if you don't fully understand what you have been told or are being asked to do

▶ demonstrate that you understand confidentiality and respect the feelings of your colleagues by communicating about sensitive, personal or private issues in an appropriate place

▶ ask someone to check any emails, letters or notes that you write on behalf of the care setting to ensure that your language and presentation is professional.

Effective communication with work colleagues is based on establishing a friendly but professional working relationship, which allows you to give and receive support. Communication with colleagues should revolve around your shared goal of promoting children's learning and development.

Over to you!

Do you communicate effectively with your colleagues or the staff at your placement setting? What could you do to improve this area of your communication?

Knowledge Assessment Task   **1.2**

You will need to communicate with children and adults on a one-to-one basis and in groups as part of your early years work role. You should understand and be able to explain how effective communication affects all aspects of your work. Complete a table like the one below to explain how effective communication with children, parents and colleagues affects aspects of your work role.

Focus of communication	Identify a reason why you need to communicate	Explain how effective communication affects your work role
Communication with children		
Communication with parents		
Communication with colleagues		

Why is it important to observe feedback?

Your assessment criteria:

1.3 Explain why it is important to observe an individual's reaction when communicating with them

Effective communication is a two-way process: when you are listening you are not just waiting for your turn to speak! To be an effective communicator, you have to notice how other people *respond* to your communication. People react non-verbally to both the *way* that you are communicating with them and to the *content* of your communication (see Figure 1.4). So, being able to read non-verbal feedback is very important. Indeed, this may be the only kind of response you receive from some children who are not confident enough to speak to you. Observing feedback is a way of assessing:

▶ whether the person has understood your communication

▶ the person's feelings about what you said to them

▶ the effectiveness of your method of communication

▶ the appropriateness of the language you used.

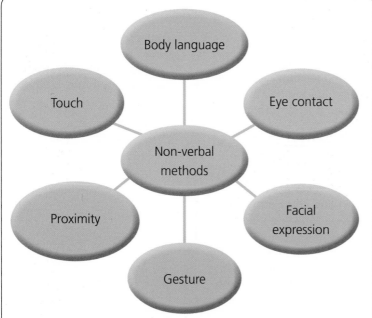

Figure 1.4 Non-verbal forms of communication feedback.

Bear in mind that an individual's cultural background, disabilities, religious beliefs, stage of development and personality may affect the way they react to you and use non-verbal methods of feedback.

Visual impairment may affect the way a person reacts to you and their methods of non-verbal feedback.

Case study

Sam, aged 17, had a work placement at a local nursery school last year. She says that she learnt a lot about how (and how not) to communicate during the two weeks she spent there. After a couple of days, she was asked to do some work on the phone. This involved answering early morning calls from parents whose children were unable to attend (because of illness) and also phoning a group of parents to tell them about the arrangements for a Forest School trip.

Sam was quite confident about her telephone skills but quickly got into difficulties. She was greeting one parent and their child in reception when she heard the phone ring. She apologised and quickly ran to answer it. When she picked up the receiver she said 'Yep, Nursery, who is it? What's your child called?' without pausing for breath. The parent who was calling asked Sam to speak more slowly and in a friendlier tone. Sam felt told off and lost some confidence.

1. Which aspects of Sam's speech made her communication less effective than it should have been?

2. How could Sam have improved her approach when answering the phone?

3. What advice would you give to Sam to ensure that she communicates the information about the Forest School trip as effectively as possible?

Knowledge Assessment Task   1.3

As an early years practitioner you need to develop the ability to observe the reactions of others to your communication in one-to-one and group situations. These reactions may be expressed verbally (what the other person says in reply) or non-verbally (through their body language). Complete a table like the one below to explain why it is important to observe an individual's verbal and non-verbal reactions when you are communicating with them.

Focus of observation	What should you observe?	Why is it important to observe this?
Verbal response		
Non-verbal response		

How can you find out about individual's communication and language needs and preferences?

Effective communication happens when the right method is used to send a message so it can be received and understood. Early years practitioners need to know about a range of communication methods. They should also be skilled at identifying the communication and language needs, wishes and preferences of children and adults in the setting.

Children and young people's care settings are used by people from a diverse range of backgrounds who will want to communicate in different ways. Finding out about each individual's language needs, wishes and preferences is an important part of your role. You can do this by:

▶ asking parents whether their children have particular language or communication needs

▶ reading reports and notes that provide information on a child's speech and language development, learning difficulties, disabilities (such as hearing or visual impairment) or physical conditions that affect communication abilities (for example, cleft palate)

▶ being aware that an adult or child's culture, ethnicity and nationality may affect their language preferences and needs

▶ observing the children and adults who use your setting to see how they use their communication and language skills

▶ asking your supervisor or mentor, senior staff and specialist professionals (such as speech and language therapists and **SENCO**s) for information, advice and support when communicating with children or adults who have special communication needs.

Key terms

SENCO: Special Educational Needs Co-ordinator

You may need to communicate with adults (parents, work colleagues, visitors or other professionals) who have special communication needs as a result of a hearing or visual impairment, or because English is not their first language. General guidance on communicating with children and adults with hearing and visual impairments is provided in Figure 1.5.

Figure 1.5 Adapting to meet special communication needs.

Advice on communicating with hearing-impaired people	Advice on communicating with visually-impaired people
• Make sure that your face can be seen clearly.	• Speak in the same way as you would to a sighted person – not louder or more slowly!
• Face the light and the person at all times.	• Say who you are in your greeting even if you have met the person before (they may not recognise your voice).
• Speak clearly and slowly – repeat and rephrase if necessary.	• Always introduce other people who are with you and explain what is going on.
• Minimise background noise.	• Let the person know when you are about to do something that will affect communication (such as leave the room or move away).
• Use your eyes, facial expressions and gestures to communicate where appropriate.	• End conversations clearly – do not just walk away.
• Do not be tempted to shout.	• Ask the child or adult if they need any particular help (to sit down or to move about, for example) but do not assume that this is always necessary or wanted.

Case study

Tanya Williams' son Dylan attends a local preschool nursery 3 days a week. Tanya is a shy person but is willing to talk about Dylan when she collects him. Dylan's Key person is a bit frustrated with Tanya. She doesn't understand why Tanya doesn't respond to the notes sent to her home about special events or to the requests to arrange a meeting. Tanya always seems surprised and embarrassed when she's reminded about things like this.

1. Can you think of any reasons why Tanya doesn't respond to the notes or requests?
2. How could Dylan's key person find out about Tanya's communication needs, wishes and preferences?
3. What would you do to make your communication with Tanya more effective if you were Dylan's Key person?

How can you use verbal and non-verbal communication?

Your assessment criteria:

2.2 Demonstrate communication methods that meet an individual's communication needs, wishes and preferences

Early years practitioners use two main types of communication in their work roles: verbal and non-verbal communication. Verbal communication is based on the use of words (see Figure 1.6). Early years practitioners need effective verbal skills to:

▶ obtain information from colleagues, parents and children

▶ respond to questions

▶ contribute to team meetings

▶ give feedback and report observations about children

▶ provide support to children parents and colleagues

▶ deal with problems and complaints

▶ write notes and reports

▶ create word-based pictures and displays.

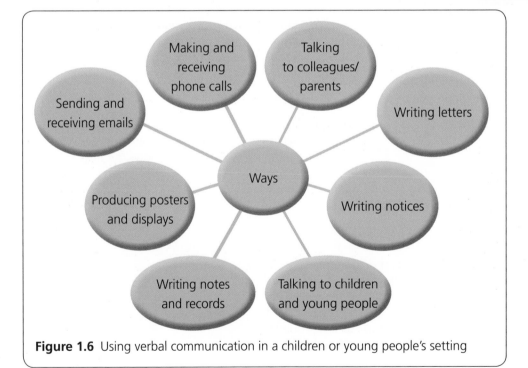

Figure 1.6 Using verbal communication in a children or young people's setting

Non-verbal communication occurs when a child or adult uses their body, behaviour and appearance to communicate with others. For example, a child's body language may tell an early years practitioner that they are uncomfortable or need to go to the toilet even when they say they're okay. Important forms of non-verbal communication are outlined in Figures 1.7 and 1.8.

Figure 1.7 Forms of non-verbal communication

Non-verbal communication	What does it involve?	Examples
Eye contact	Looking another person directly in the eyes	• Short or broken eye contact can express nervousness, shyness or mistrust. • Long unbroken eye contact can express interest, attraction or hostility.
Touch	Physically touching or holding a person	• Holding someone's hand. • Placing a hand on a person's arm or shoulder to reassure them.
Physical gestures	Deliberate movements of the hands to express meaning	• Using a thumbs-up gesture to show agreement or pleasure. • Shaking a fist to show anger or aggression.
Facial expression	Movements of the face that express a person's feelings	• Smiling • Frowning
Proximity	The physical closeness between people during interactions	• Being very close may be reassuring. • People need less personal space (proximity) when they have a close, trusting relationship. • Alternatively, unwelcome proximity can feel uncomfortable and threatening.

Over to you!

When you have a chance to watch some group activity in your workplace, observe the way children and adults use their bodies to communicate. Try to work out what different people are 'saying' non-verbally.

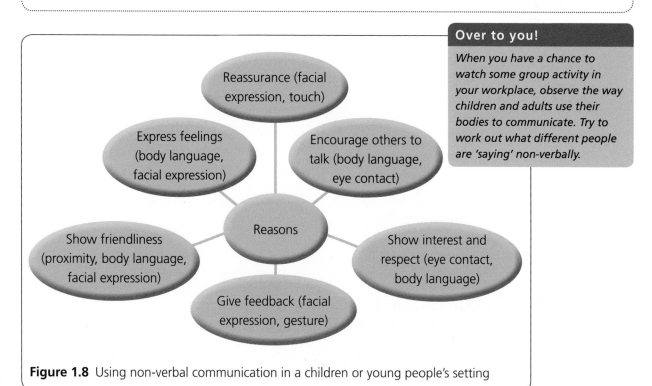

Reassurance (facial expression, touch)

Express feelings (body language, facial expression)

Encourage others to talk (body language, eye contact)

Reasons

Show friendliness (proximity, body language, facial expression)

Give feedback (facial expression, gesture)

Show interest and respect (eye contact, body language)

Figure 1.8 Using non-verbal communication in a children or young people's setting

How can you choose the right communication method?

To be an effective communicator in your work setting, you need to be able to use communication methods that meet each individual's needs, wishes and preferences. Your goal is to ensure that the messages you send can be received and understood. To achieve this, you may sometimes need to change or adapt the form of communication you are using. Figure 1.9 identifies some of the issues you might consider when choosing the best way to communicate with a child or adult.

Your assessment criteria:

2.2 Demonstrate communication methods that meet an individual's communication needs, wishes and preferences

Figure 1.9 Thinking about communication methods

Method	When might you use it?	Questions to ask
Talking face-to-face	• Asking or answering questions • Providing information or feedback • Receiving information or feedback • Making and maintaining work relationships • Providing support for children or colleagues	• Does the child or adult understand English? • Is my choice of words age appropriate? • Does the person have any hearing impairment? • Will we need support from an interpreter or signer? • Have I chosen an appropriate place to talk? • Are there any cultural, religious or gender issues that might affect our communication?
Talking on the telephone	• Asking or answering questions • Providing information or feedback • Receiving information or feedback • Ordering resources • Arranging meetings	• Does the other person have any hearing impairment? • Are their English language skills strong enough for a telephone conversation? • What is the best time to call? • Would it be okay to leave a message? Consider whether this might breach confidentiality.
Writing	• Writing letters, notes or notices for parents to read • Writing letters, reports, memos or minutes of meetings for colleagues or other professionals to read • Writing notices, displays or signs for children to read	• Is the language I'm using age appropriate, clear and direct? • Will the intended audience be able to read and understand what I've written? • Does the reader have dyslexia, learning difficulties or other problems with reading? • How will I make sure the adult or child actually receives or sees what I'm writing?

continued...

Method	When might you use it?	Questions to ask
Email, text message	<ul><li>Writing replies or brief notes to parents or colleagues</li><li>Sending newsletters or information to parents, colleagues or other professionals</li></ul>	<ul><li>Do I have the email or phone details for everybody who wants or needs the information?</li><li>Is the language I'm using appropriate and easy to understand?</li><li>Have I removed any confidential information, including email addresses, from emails sent to groups of people?</li></ul>
Non-verbal communication	<ul><li>Using appropriate eye contact, body language, proximity and facial expression when talking face-to-face</li><li>Using appropriate gestures and touch when explaining or providing support</li><li>Using appropriate tone of voice and pitch when talking face-to-face or on the telephone</li></ul>	<ul><li>Is my non-verbal communication appropriate to the situation?</li><li>How can I use non-verbal communication to support what I am saying?</li><li>Are there any cultural, religious or gender issues that might affect the way others understand my non-verbal communication?</li><li>Does the child or adult have a visual impairment or learning difficulty that might mean they don't notice my non-verbal communication?</li></ul>

Early years practitioners who use their communication skills effectively are able to think about the different ways in which they might communicate with individual. The key is to choose the method of communication that is most suited to the situation.

When should you seek advice about communication?

Your assessment criteria:

2.3 Show how and when to seek advice about communication

There may be situations in which you feel unsure about how you should communicate with a child or adult. Perhaps you will be aware that you are struggling to communicate effectively with somebody. In situations like these, you should seek advice and obtain support (see Figure 1.10). You can do this by:

▶ talking to your supervisor, mentor or line manager about the difficulty – ask for their advice about how to deal with the problem

▶ talking to communication or language support specialists (teachers, psychologists or speech and language therapists) who work at or spend time in your work setting.

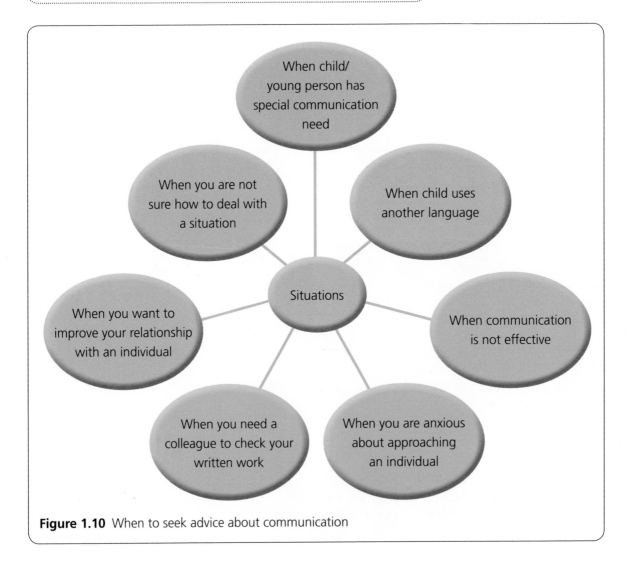

Figure 1.10 When to seek advice about communication

Parents are often a good source of information and guidance on how best to communicate with their children.

Practical Assessment Task   2.1   2.2   2.3

The first time you meet a child, perhaps with family members, is the best time to find out about their communication and language needs, wishes and preferences. To complete this assessment task you need to demonstrate that you are able to do this competently. You will need to produce evidence based on your practice at work which demonstrates that you:

1. can find out about an individual's communication and language needs, wishes and preferences

2. can use communication methods (verbal and non-verbal) that meet the individual's communication needs, wishes and preferences

3. know how and when to seek advice about communication.

Your evidence must be based on your practice in a real work environment and must be witnessed by or be in a format that is acceptable to your assessor.

How can barriers reduce the effectiveness of communication?

Your assessment criteria:

3.1 Identify barriers to effective communication

Despite your best efforts, you may sometimes find that you are unable to communicate effectively with a child or adult in your work setting. There are a number of possible reasons why this might happen. Knowing about different **barriers** to effective communication will enable you to avoid potential difficulties and adapt your communication approach when this is necessary. Barriers to communication are things that interfere with a person's ability to send, receive or understand a message (see Figure 1.11).

Key terms

Barrier (to communication): something that prevents a person from communicating effectively

▶ *Environmental factors* – noise impairs listening and concentration. Poor lighting can prevent a person from noticing non-verbal communication and could reduce a hearing-impaired person's ability to lip read. Environments that are too hot or cold cause discomfort and those that lack privacy discourage people from expressing their feelings and problems.

▶ *Developmental stage* – a child's developmental stage could limit their ability to communicate and may be a barrier to effective communication if you don't take this into account when choosing your words or way of talking to them. Don't use long sentences, complex words or unusual phrases with young children.

▶ *Sensory deprivation and disability* – visual impairment may reduce a person's ability to see faces, written signs and leaflets. Hearing impairment may limit conversation. Conditions such as Cerebral Palsy, cleft palate, Down's syndrome and autism tend to limit a child's ability to communicate verbally and non-verbally, and difficulties interpreting non-verbal communication are typical of autism.

▶ *Language and cultural differences* – the UK is a multicultural country with a mix of different ethnic groups and a range of language communities. English may be a second or even third language for some children and adults, and may not be spoken or understood at all by others. Communication in written and spoken English may not be easy or even possible for people in this situation. Similarly, people from different cultural groups may interpret non-verbal behaviour in different ways, misunderstanding messages.

Over to you!

Can you think of any occasions when your ability to communicate was affected because you were upset or unwell? Did other people recognise this and adapt their communication approach in any way?

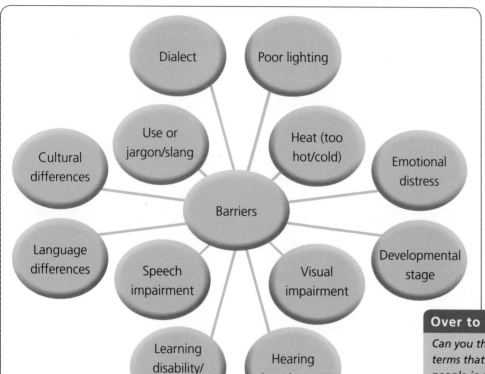

Figure 1.11 Barriers to communication.

Over to you!
Can you think of any slang terms that are used by young people in your local area? Do you think that adults or other young people from a different area would know what these terms mean? What about jargon used in your workplace? Would someone from another profession understand?

▶ *Jargon, slang and use of acronyms* – these forms of language only make sense to people with specialist knowledge. A person who doesn't have this specialist knowledge won't understand the message. Practitioners working in children and young people settings sometimes use jargon and acronyms to communicate quickly with each other. Teenagers sometimes use forms of slang to communicate with each other in ways their parents and teachers don't understand.

▶ *Dialect* – people who speak English using a dialect (for example, Glagwegian or Liverpudlian) pronounce words in different ways. They may also use some words that are specific to the local area. A child or adult who isn't from the same area may not understand a local dialect.

▶ *Distress, emotional difficulties and health problems* – some conditions, depression and stroke, for example, may affect an individual's ability to send and receive messages effectively. Illness and injuries can also cause people to withdraw from communication situations. Similarly, when a person is angry, aggressive or upset they may find it difficult to communicate, resulting in their own their own communication being misunderstood by others.

Key terms

Acronym: an abbreviation that stands for a longer phrase, such as 'NHS' for National Health Service

Dialect: a localised version of a language

Jargon: technical language that is understood by people in a particular industry or area of work

Slang: an informal type of language that is used by a particular group of people

23

How can you overcome communication barriers?

Barriers to communication can often be overcome, or at least reduced, by making changes to the environment, adapting your approach or by using support services.

Adapting the environment

Environmental changes might include:

▶ replacing poor lighting with brighter lighting

▶ reducing background noise or creating some quiet areas

▶ putting up multilingual posters and displaying signs clearly

▶ fitting electronic devices such as **induction loop systems** for hearing-impaired people.

Adapting your approach to communication

In order to improve communication, early years practitioners can adapt their approach by:

▶ making sure they can be seen clearly, facing both the light and the person they are talking to

▶ making sure their mouth is visible when speaking

▶ minimising background noise

▶ using eyes, facial expressions and gestures to communicate as necessary and appropriate.

Timing

Speaking clearly and slowly, and repeating or rephrasing what you say can make communication more effective for some children and adults. The speed or pace of communication may need to be slower if a person has a hearing or visual impairment, a learning disability or is anxious and confused. It is also important to allow time for the person to digest your communication and to respond. This can mean making silences comfortable while the person works out how to reply.

Using support services and specialist devices

Early years practitioners should understand the language needs and communication preferences of the children and adults with whom they work. If a child or adult has difficulty communicating in English or has sensory impairments or disabilities that affect their communication skills, specialist communication support may be needed. Learning a few words of another person's language or developing some basic sign language skills can really help an early years practitioner to establish a positive, supportive relationship with a child and their parents.

Key terms

Induction loop system: a system that boosts sound for hearing aid users

Over to you!

Visit the websites of the Royal National Institute for the Deaf (www.RNID.org.uk) and the Royal National Institute for the Blind (www.RNIB.org.uk). Find out about the range of services that these groups provide for people who have sensory impairments. Produce a summary of the different forms of communication support that are available to people with visual or hearing impairments.

A range of electronic devices exist to help children and adults overcome communication difficulties. These include hearing aids, text phones, telephone amplifiers and hearing loops, for example. Electronic devices can be used both to send and receive messages. It is important to give the person using a communication device enough time to use it properly.

This symbol tells hearing aid users that a special communication loop is available for them to use.

Case study

Helena is a 26-year-old Polish woman. Her 3-year-old son Radek attends Puddle Duck Nursery on three mornings a week. Radek often cries when his mum leaves him. Sophie, Radek's key worker, struggles to comfort him but tries to give him reassurance and a cuddle. Helena has given the nursery manager a letter from Radek's hospital consultant; he has a hearing impairment which will be corrected with an operation next month to fit grommets. Sophie is wondering how she can communicate more effectively with Radek during his time at the nursery.

1. What are the barriers to effective communication with Radek in this situation?
2. How could these barriers be overcome to make communication with Radek more effective?
3. What are grommets and why do some children need them?
4. Identify four other barriers that can reduce the effectiveness of communication in early years settings.

Key terms

Grommets: small tubes that are surgically inserted into the ear drum, helping to prevent infections (such as 'glue ear') which can cause partial hearing loss

Practical Assessment Task   3.1   3.2

What kinds of barriers to effective communication occur in the early years setting where you work or are on placement? Complete the table below by identifying three examples of barriers to effective communication that you are aware of and then demonstrate ways of overcoming each barrier.

Barrier to communication	How does this make communication less effective?	How have you tried to overcome this barrier?
Example 1		
Example 2		
Example 3		

Your evidence for this task must be based on your practice in a real work environment and must be witnessed by or be in a format that is acceptable to your assessor.

How can you check that communication is effective?

Your assessment criteria:

3.3 Demonstrate ways to check that communication has been understood

3.4 Identify sources of information and support or services to enable more effective communication

Effective communication in early years settings helps practitioners, parents and children to form good relationships and to work well together. Children and adults communicate most effectively when they:

▶ feel relaxed

▶ are able to **empathise** with each other

▶ experience warmth and genuineness in relationships.

There are a number of ways of checking that your communication is effective. You need to know that your message has been received and understood correctly. You can check this by using active listening and clarifying or repeating techniques.

Active listening

Active listening involves paying close attention to what the other person is saying, while also noticing their non-verbal communication. People who are good at active listening also tend to be skilled at using **minimal prompts**. These are things like nods of the head, 'Mm' sounds and encouraging words like 'Yes, I see' or 'Go on'. Skilful use of minimal prompts encourages the person you are communicating with to keep speaking or to say a little more.

Clarifying or repeating

You can ensure that your communication has been understood by clarifying (repeating back, summarising or rephrasing) aspects of what the person has said during the conversation. You could say something like, 'Can I just check that you meant …?' or, 'Do you mean …?' You should try not to clarify too often in a conversation as this will interrupt the speaker's flow; it might also make them think you are 'parroting', which may appear insincere.

Key terms

Empathise: understand another's feelings

Minimal prompt: unobtrusive sounds and behaviours that encourage the other person to talk

How can you obtain communication support and assistance?

You should always seek support and assistance if you encounter communication problems with any children, parents or practitioners. You may be able to obtain help from:

- ▶ your supervisor, line manager or mentor
- ▶ senior and experienced colleagues
- ▶ the child's parents
- ▶ specialist practitioners such as speech and language therapists, psychologists or special needs teachers
- ▶ interpreting services and organisations who work with recent immigrants and asylum-seeking families whose use of English is a barrier to effective communication
- ▶ specialist organisations that provide support for children with sensory impairments, disabilities and language problems.

Interpreters can help to make communication more effective where language is a barrier.

Practical Assessment Task

3.3 **3.4**

How do you ensure that your communication with children and adults has been understood? Are you able to use the checking techniques described opposite?

1. Working with a child or young person who attends your workplace, demonstrate that you are able to use ways of checking that your communication with them has been understood.

2. Make notes on sources of information and support or services that you could use to enable more effective communication with this or another child or young person if the need arose.

Your evidence for this task must be based on your practice in a real work environment and must be witnessed by or be in a format that is acceptable to your assessor.

Principles and practices relating to confidentiality at work

What is confidentiality?

Confidentiality is not about keeping secrets; it is about protecting an individual's right to *privacy*. You may obtain private, personal information from children or parents as part of your work role. As an early years practitioner you have a duty to:

► keep personal information about children and families private

► only share information about children and families with those who have a right to know or when a parent has given permission.

Your workplace will have a confidentiality policy that sets out the rules and procedures on sharing confidential information. You should read this and make sure that you follow it in your practice. You may be asked to sign a confidentiality agreement as part of your employment contract. Again, you should have a clear understanding of what this means in practice.

How can you demonstrate confidentiality?

There will be many occasions in your day-to-day work when you will need to share information about children. This information can be shared with your work colleagues without breaching confidentiality because everybody in the team needs to know about each child. However, you can promote and demonstrate confidentiality by:

► only talking about children in areas of the setting where you cannot be overheard by non-staff members

► not revealing confidential information about one child to another child who may remember and pass it on

► using children's first names or initials when discussing or writing up your observations about them

► storing written records about children and families in locked cupboards or cabinets and making sure you put them back in the correct place after using them

► using a secure password to access computers that contain information about children and families

► making sure parents only have access to their own child's personal and developmental records

► referring parents to their child's key person when they need information relating to their child.

You should not talk, gossip or complain about the children or families you work with when you are at home or when you are socialising with your friends. This is a serious breach of confidentiality and might lead to disciplinary action by your employer.

Your assessment criteria:

4.1 Explain the term 'confidentiality'

4.2 Demonstrate confidentiality in day-to-day communication, in line with agreed ways of working

4.3 Describe situations where information normally considered to be confidential might need to be passed on

4.4 Explain how and when to seek advice about confidentiality

Key terms

Confidentiality: ensuring information is only accessible to people who are authorised to know about it

Over to you!

Obtain a copy of the confidentiality policy written for your workplace. Identify the main points and how they affect your work role. What are you expected to do to protect confidentiality in your workplace?

When should confidential information be passed on?

There may be times when you have to reveal what you have been told, or have seen, to a more senior person at work or to an external organisation. A parent, child or colleague's request that you maintain confidentiality can be overridden if:

▶ what they say suggests that a child may be at risk of harm

▶ they reveal information that can be used to protect another person from harm

▶ a court or a statutory organisation, such as OFSTED, asks for specific information about a child.

When should you seek advice about confidentiality?

It is best to treat everything you learn about children and their families in your workplace as confidential information; it is advisable to check with your supervisor before you pass on confidential information. Similarly, it is always best to tell your supervisor if you receive any information that concerns you. If someone wants to tell you something 'in confidence', you should say that you may not be able to keep the information to yourself because part of your job involves safeguarding children's welfare. It is then up to the person to decide whether to tell you or not.

Practical Assessment Task   4.1   4.2   4.3   4.4

Practitioners in children and young people's settings should communicate with others (children and young people, families and colleagues) in ways that apply and protect the principle of confidentiality. Using your knowledge of confidentiality and what you have learnt from the confidentiality policy written for your workplace, produce evidence that:

1. explains the term 'confidentiality', illustrating your explanation with two examples of situations when it is important to keep information confidential in your workplace

2. demonstrates how you protect confidentiality and follow the confidentiality procedures of your work setting in your day-to-day communication with others

3. describes two situations that could occur, or which have happened, in your workplace when information normally considered confidential needs to be passed on

4. explains how and when you would seek advice about the confidentiality issues involved in question 3.

Your evidence for this task must be based on your practice in a real work environment and must be witnessed by or be in a format that is acceptable to your assessor.

Are you ready for assessment?

AC	What do you know now?	Assessment task	✓
1.1	Different reasons why people communicate	Page 7	
1.2	How effective communication affects all aspects of your work	Page 11	
1.3	Why it is important to observe an individual's reactions when communicating with them	Page 13	

Your tutor or assessor may want to observe you actually doing this in your placement or work setting.

AC	What can you do now?	Assessment task	✓
2.1	Find out an individual's communication and language needs, wishes and preferences	Page 21	
2.2	Demonstrate communication methods that meet an individual's communication needs, wishes and preferences	Page 21	
2.3	Show how and when to seek advice about communication	Page 21	
3.1	Identify barriers to communication	Page 25	
3.2	Demonstrate how to reduce barriers to communication in different ways	Page 25	
3.3	Demonstrate ways to check that communication has been understood	Page 27	
3.4	Identify sources of information and support or services to enable more effective communication.	Page 27	
4.1	Explain the term 'confidentiality'	Page 29	
4.2	Demonstrate confidentiality in day to day communication, in line with agreed ways of working	Page 29	
4.3	Describe situations where information normally considered to be confidential might need to be passed on	Page 29	
4.4	Explain how and when to seek advice about confidentiality	Page 29	

2

Introduction to equality and inclusion in health, social care or children's and young people's settings (SHC 23)

Assessment of this unit

This unit introduces you to the concepts of equality and inclusion and their importance in work with children and young people. It focuses on the meaning of key words and ideas relating to equality and inclusion, forms of discrimination that can occur in care settings for children and young people and legal aspects of work with children and young people. You will also develop your knowledge of ways of working with children and young people in an inclusive, anti-discriminatory way and the sources of information, advice and support that you could use to develop your practice in this area.

To successfully complete this unit you will need to produce evidence of your knowledge of concepts, practices and the law relating to equality and inclusion as shown in the 'What you need to know' chart opposite. You also need to produce evidence of your practical ability to promote equality and work in an inclusive way in your workplace, as shown in the 'What you need to do' chart, also opposite. These criteria must be assessed in a real work environment by a vocationally competent assessor.

Your tutor or assessor will help you to prepare for your assessment and the tasks suggested in the chapter will help you to create the evidence that you need.

CHAPTER 2

AC   What you need to know

1.1	What is meant by diversity, equality, inclusion and discrimination
1.2	Ways in which discrimination may deliberately or inadvertently occur in the work setting
1.3	How practices that support equality and inclusion reduce the likelihood of discrimination
3.1	A range of sources of information, advice and support about diversity, equality and inclusion
3.2	How and when to access information, advice and support about diversity, equality and inclusion

AC   What you need to do

2.1	Identify which legislation and codes of practice relating to equality, diversity and discrimination apply to your own role
2.2	Show you can interact with individuals in ways that respect their beliefs, culture, values and preferences
2.3	Describe how to challenge discrimination in a way that encourages change

This unit also links to some of the other mandatory units:

TDA 2.7	Maintain and support relationships with children and young people
TDA 2.2	Safeguarding the welfare of children and young people

Some of your learning will be repeated in these units and will give you the chance to review your knowledge and understanding.

Equality and inclusion are key principles in all children and young people's settings.

Your assessment criteria:

1.1 Explain what is meant by diversity, equality, inclusion and discrimination

Over to you!

Think about the different forms of diversity within your local population. Are there different ethnic communities, groups of people who speak languages other than English or different religious communities, for example?

What are diversity, equality and inclusion?

Diversity

As a children's or young people's practitioner you will meet children and adults from a wide range of social, cultural, language and ethnic backgrounds. You will work with boys and girls, children of different ages, children with different abilities and disabilities, children who speak different languages and who have different cultural traditions, as well as children who could be described as middle class, working class, as 'black', 'white' or of mixed heritage. You should value and treat each child fairly and equally.

The **diversity** in the United Kingdom population is vast; if you think about the local area where you live, you can probably identify a number of different sub-groups within the community (see Figure 2.1). This means that the population consists of individuals with a huge range of different characteristics. These differences impact on people's needs. As a result, you have a responsibility to value difference as a way of meeting people's individual needs.

Equality

You will probably know from your own experience of children, and from being a child yourself, that children want to be treated equally and fairly. This doesn't always mean that all children should be treated *the same*. **Equality** in children and young people's settings is about giving each child the appropriate opportunities to achieve to the best of their ability and in line with their own interests. Valuing children as individuals is a very important first step in promoting this kind of **equality of opportunity**.

Key terms

Diversity: the range of differences (social, cultural, language, ethnic, ability and disability) within a population

Equality: treating a person fairly or in a way that ensures they are not disadvantaged

Equality of opportunity: a situation in which everyone has an equal chance

Figure 2.1 Ethnic diversity in the UK

Ethnic group	Population	Proportion of total UK population
White	54,153,898	92.1%
Mixed race	677,177	1.2%
Indian	1,053,144	1.8%
Pakistani	747,285	1.3%
Bangaldeshi	283,063	0.5%
Other Asian (non-Chinese)	247,644	0.4%
Black Caribbean	565,876	1.0%
Black African	485,277	0.8%
Black (others)	97,585	0.2%
Chinese	247,403	0.4%
Others	230,615	0.4%

Over to you!

How is the individuality of each child acknowledged and celebrated in the care setting where you work or where you are on placement? Find out about the way in which a child's background, abilities and achievements are assessed and documented, for example. You might also think about the ways in which practitioners talk to children, and talk about children to others, providing feedback on their particular abilities, achievements or needs.

Inclusion

Any children's or young people's service must promote **social inclusion** in order to offer equality of opportunity to those who use it. An inclusive service works hard at:

▶ identifying and removing barriers to access and participation

▶ enabling children and families to use the full range of services and facilities

▶ welcoming, valuing and supporting everyone who uses the care setting.

Inclusion doesn't happen by chance. The people who work in children and young people's care settings have to:

▶ be honest and reflective about how their workplace operates

▶ be critical in a constructive way, so that positive changes can be made

▶ work at identifying *actual* barriers to access and participation

▶ remain alert to *potential* barriers that may exclude some people

▶ act in practical ways to remove actual and potential barriers.

Key terms

Social inclusion: the process of ensuring that all members of society have access to available services and activities

Over to you!

How diverse is your setting? Do children and families from a diverse range of social and cultural backgrounds use the services? Are members of some social or cultural groups noticeably less well represented or absent altogether?

What is discrimination?

Diversity is not welcomed or celebrated by everyone, despite the fact that the UK has been a multicultural society for many years. Diversity and difference frightens some people, leading to a view of people as either 'them' or 'us'. This can result in unfair treatment or **discrimination** against those who are different from the majority (see Figure 2.2). Children and young people can suffer discrimination due to:

▶ skin colour and other physical characteristics

▶ disability or health status

▶ gender (as a boy or a girl)

▶ social background and family circumstances

▶ culture, traditions and way of life.

Unfair discrimination that is obvious and deliberate is known as **overt discrimination**. Unfair discrimination that happens inadvertently or which is carried out in a secretive, hidden way is known as **covert discrimination**.

Prejudice is at the root of discrimination. A prejudice is an opinion, feeling or attitude of dislike concerning another individual or group of people. Prejudices are typically based on inaccurate information or unreasonable judgements.

Key terms

Discrimination: unfair or less favourable treatment of a person or group of people in comparison to others

Overt discrimination: obvious and deliberate unfair treatment

Covert discrimination: secret and hidden unfair treatment, either deliberate or inadvertent

Prejudice: an unreasonable or unfair dislike or preference towards a person or a group of people

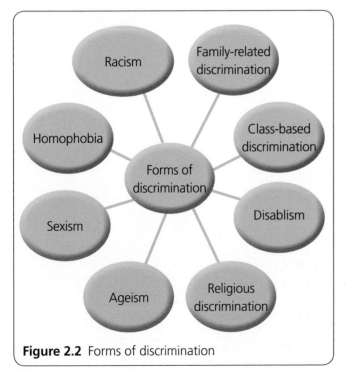

Figure 2.2 Forms of discrimination

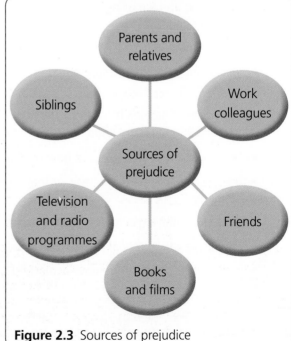

Figure 2.3 Sources of prejudice

When a person acts on a prejudice, they become involved in discrimination. People are not born with prejudices – these have to be learnt (see Figure 2.3). However, children can be quick to pick up these views if they hear others talking in a prejudiced way. Acknowledging diversity, challenging prejudices and tackling all forms of discrimination are important elements of anti-discriminatory practice in early years and youth work.

The *Changing Faces* campaign challenges discrimination against those with facial disfigurement.

Case study

In 1963 Jane Elliot, a teacher in a small primary school in the USA, carried out an experiment. She divided the children in her class into two groups based on their eye colour. On the first day of the experiment the blue-eyed children were told that they were the better group and were treated more favourably. They had more privileges such as second helpings at lunchtime and extra playtime. Jane Elliot also ridiculed the brown-eyed children and continually put them down. On the second day, she made the brown-eyed children the favoured group. This time they had all of the advantages and the blue-eyed children were told they were the bottom group.

Imagine that you were one of the children in Jane Elliott's class.

1. How would you have felt on the day you were in the less favoured group?

2. How do you think you would have felt when you were told you weren't as good as other children because of the colour of your eyes?

3. How do you think you would have reacted towards your friends when they were in the favoured group?

4. How do you think you would have felt when you were in the favoured group?

The results of Jane Elliot's experiment were startling. Children of different eye-colour who had previously been friends fought and put each other down. When children were in the favoured group, they did better in maths and word tests than the children who were not. The same children performed badly when they were in the other group. Jane Elliot concluded that self-esteem and self-image was adversely affected when children experienced discrimination.

Knowledge Assessment Task 1.1

You have been asked by your workplace manager to produce a leaflet or a poster as part of an inclusion campaign. The aim is to raise parents' awareness of equality and inclusion issues in children and young people's settings. Your leaflet or poster should explain what *diversity*, *equality*, *inclusion* and *discrimination* mean in relation to practice in your setting; use words and images to communicate the meaning of each term as clearly as possible. Keep the work you produce as evidence towards your assessment.

Why does discrimination happen in some settings?

Your assessment criteria:

1.2 Describe ways in which discrimination may deliberately or inadvertently occur in the work setting

As Jane Elliot's experiment showed, discrimination can damage a child's self-esteem and self-confidence, and is a barrier to equality of opportunity. So, discrimination should always be avoided in children and young people's settings. Where discrimination does occur, practitioners should be able to recognise and challenge it.

Practitioners and children and young people's organisations generally aim to be inclusive and welcoming to all children and families who wish to use their services. Despite this, overt discrimination does sometimes occur. This can be the result of:

▶ individual staff members favouring some children and families or treating others in a less favourable way because of prejudices that they hold

▶ organisations deliberately setting out to attract children, young people and families from particular backgrounds or areas, while making it difficult for others to obtain places

▶ members of staff expressing their prejudices, values and beliefs in the way they talk to children and families

▶ presenting children with equipment, resources or visual images that reflect the lifestyle, culture and experiences of a particular social group, rather than mirroring the more diverse range of cultures within UK society

▶ employment policies that result in staff being recruited from a narrow range of backgrounds and age groups

▶ having a gender-biased approach to providing different learning and development opportunities for boys and girls

▶ not adapting or providing facilities and services for children who have disabilities or special learning and development needs.

Spending time with some children but not others can be a form of discrimination.

Deliberate discrimination within children and young people's settings is relatively unusual. Where discrimination does occur it usually happens inadvertently or by accident. Practitioners may not be aware that the way they practice, talk or operate the service favours some children and families but disadvantages others. This can happen because:

▶ some practitioners lack cultural awareness and knowledge about the lifestyles of different groups

▶ some practitioners promote gender or cultural **stereotypes** by encouraging children and young people to play with particular toys or engage in particular activities (construction or football for boys, dolls or crafts for girls, for example), or by responding to children's behaviour in a stereotypical way

▶ resources have become outdated, gender or culture-specific

▶ admissions policies and practices in the setting impose conditions that some people are unable to meet

▶ diversity and difference is not celebrated through different cultural festivals or the telling of stories from a wide range of cultural traditions

▶ the recruitment process results in the selection of applicants who will 'fit in' because they are 'people like us'.

Key terms

Stereotypes: set and often ill-informed generalised ideas, for example, about the way people from certain backgrounds behave or feel

Case study

A new member of staff at a children's centre has introduced the children to the rhyme, 'Tinker, tailor, soldier, spy, rich man, poor man, beggar man, thief', which she sings at snack time as the children count the pips or stones in their fruit. The children like this rhyme and now join in. However, Oliver, aged 4, has started to ask what each term means. When the new member of staff explained that 'tinkers are like gypsies', Oliver replied, 'My mummy says tinkers are dirty'. The two children from gypsy families who attend the children's centre then started to cry.

1. Is this an example of direct or indirect discrimination?
2. What stereotype is being used in this situation?
3. Do you think nursery rhymes like this are harmless fun, or should they be avoided?

Over to you!

How socially and culturally diverse is the staff group in the setting where you work or are on placement? Is the staff group representative of the local community?

Over to you!

Look at and review the range of resources available for children in the care setting where you work or are on placement. Do the toys, equipment and visual images reflect a diversity of lifestyles, traditions and social backgrounds?

39

How can you promote equality and inclusion?

Seeing each child as an individual with unique qualities and particular needs is an important way of avoiding the stereotyping that sometimes leads to inadvertent discrimination. As a practitioner, you should be able to support the learning and development of each child in ways that are appropriate to their abilities, interests and needs. Strategies for promoting equality and inclusion include:

▶ valuing children equally while acknowledging their individuality and differences

▶ using effective communication skills to develop strong and trusting relationships with all children and families

▶ adapting your approach to each child's particular needs so that they obtain the support and assistance required to enjoy equality of opportunity

▶ ensuring that people from diverse backgrounds are represented in the range of images and resources (e.g. posters, books, toys, displays, leaflets, DVDs, photographs) that children and families see in the setting

▶ using resources that challenge stereotypes by showing both men and women in caring, employment and leadership roles, disabled people undertaking a full range of activities and people from a variety of cultural backgrounds in everyday life situations.

Your assessment criteria:

1.2 Describe ways in which discrimination may deliberately or inadvertently occur in the work setting

1.3 Explain how practices that support equality and inclusion reduce the likelihood of discrimination

Mixed-sex football games are a way of promoting equality and inclusion.

The way in which gender, ethnicity, culture and social background are portrayed in a child's early years has an impact on the expectations they develop about their future. All children and families should be encouraged and supported to believe that everyone can:

▶ take an active role in society

▶ achieve success in a variety of ways

▶ aspire to valued, responsible and influential positions in life.

Over to you!

How are children and families who use English as an additional language included and supported in the setting where you work or are on placement? Do you think anything else could be done to improve the inclusion of people with language support needs?

What are the benefits of having both male and female staff working in children and young people's settings?

Knowledge Assessment Task 1.2 1.3

You have been asked to produce an information leaflet that could be included in the Induction Training materials given to new employees at your workplace. Your manager has asked you to produce an informative leaflet that:

▶ describes ways in which discrimination may deliberately or inadvertently occur in the work setting

▶ explains how promoting equality and inclusion reduces the likelihood of discrimination occurring.

Your leaflet should include practical examples and suggestions relevant to the children and families who use your setting. It can include images, words, diagrams and tables but should focus on how discrimination occurs and how it can be prevented through equality and inclusion strategies. Keep your written work as evidence towards your assessment.

Your assessment criteria:

2.1 Identify which legislation and codes of practice relating to equality, diversity and discrimination apply to own role

What is the legal framework for practice with children and young people?

Practitioners have to work within a framework of **legislation**, **codes of practice**, **policies** and **procedures** that are designed to promote equality and inclusion and prevent discrimination.

The legal framework promotes diversity and protects the rights of individuals (children, families and practitioners) in children and young people's settings. You need to be able to identify examples of legislation, codes of practice and policies and procedures relating to equality, diversity, discrimination that affect your role. You should also know about the legal responsibilities early years and young people's service employers and employees have for promoting diversity and rights.

In children and young people's settings, the main statutes promoting diversity and equality and protecting children and adults from discrimination are:

▶ The Convention on the Rights of the Child (1989)

▶ The Children Act (1989) and (2004)

▶ The Care Standards (2000)

▶ The Race Relations Act (1976) and the Race Relations (Amendment) Act (2000)

▶ The Public Order Act (1986) and the Racial and Religious Hatred Act (2006)

Key terms

Code of practice: a document setting out standards for practice

Legislation: another term for written laws, such as Acts of Parliament

Policies: plans of action

Procedures: documents that specify ways of doing something or dealing with a specific issue or problem

▶ The Disability Discrimination Act (1995) and (2005)

▶ The Special Educational Needs and Disability Act (2001)

▶ The Equality Act (2006)

▶ The Education Act (1981), (1993) and (1996)

These laws influence the rights of individuals and standards of quality in care provision. Every early years, childcare and educational organisation needs to have policies and practices that put these laws into action.

The Convention on the Rights of the Child (1989)

This Convention introduced rights for children and young people under 18 years of age. It is based around the principles that:

▶ decisions about a child should be based on what is in the child's best interests

▶ children should not be discriminated against

▶ children should be free to express themselves

▶ children have the right to survive and develop.

Over to you!

List five 'rights' that you think all children who use your workplace should enjoy. Why do you think the idea of children having 'rights' is controversial and rejected by some people?

Promoting and protecting a child's rights is a key part of a practitioner's role.

The Children Act (1989) and (2004)

The Children Act (2004) updated the Children Act (1989) following an inquiry into the death of Victoria Climbié in 2000. The Children Act (1989) established that care workers should see the needs of the child as **paramount** when making any decisions that affect a child's welfare. Under the 1989 Act, local authorities are required to provide services that meet the needs of children who are identified as being 'at risk'. The goal of the Children Act (2004) is to improve the lives of all children who receive informal or professional care. It covers all services that children might use, such as schools, day care and children's homes, as well as health care services. The Children Act (2004) now requires care services to work together so that they form a protective team around the child.

The Children Act (2004) resulted from a report called *Every Child Matters*. This led to significant changes in the way services for children and young people are provided in the UK. The aims of *Every Child Matters* (www.everychildmatters.gov.uk) are that all children should:

▶ be healthy

▶ stay safe

▶ enjoy and achieve

▶ make a positive contribution

▶ achieve economic wellbeing.

The ongoing *Every Child Matters* programme of children's service development ensures that **safeguarding** remains the key priority for everyone who is part of the children's workforce. People who work or volunteer with children, young people and vulnerable adults now have to have their background checked by the Criminal Records Bureau (CRB). Since 2009, a Vetting and Barring Scheme that is administered by the **Independent Safeguarding Authority** and the Criminal Records Bureau has required all adults who work with children to register. Equivalent agencies called Disclosure Scotland and Access Northern Ireland operate in other parts of the UK.

The Care Standards Act 2000

The Care Standards Act (2000) established legally required national minimum standards of care provision that early years, young people's services, and health and social care organisations must achieve. The aim of this law is to ensure that everyone who uses such services receives fair and equal treatment. Care organisations are now inspected by the **Care Quality Commission** to check whether they meet the current national minimum standards of care.

Key terms

Care Quality Commission: the body that regulates health and social care services in England

Independent Safeguarding Authority: the body responsible for protecting children by monitoring and vetting all practitioners in the children and young people's workforce

Paramount: most important

Safeguarding: the process of providing protection

Case study

Beverley, aged 15, suffered neglect and abuse at the hands of her mother and stepfather for 6 years before the local authority and police became aware of the situation. From the time her mother remarried, Beverley was forbidden to play with her two half-brothers. She was also locked in her room at night, given very little to eat and made to do all the household chores.

Beverley's parents deliberately excluded her from family life. They made her use an outside toilet, always made her stay at home on family days out and starved her of love and affection, even though she could see her siblings being hugged and cuddled. Beverley was frightened of her mother who shouted at and hit her.

Because she was shabbily dressed, underweight and often unkempt, Beverley was bullied at school. Eventually, she told a teacher what her life was like at home. A doctor who examined her said that she was underweight, had eyesight and teeth problems and had suffered emotional abuse and neglect. Beverley and her half-brothers were removed from the family home by social workers. Her parents admitted charges of cruelty and neglect and were given community sentences.

1. In what ways was Beverley subjected to ill-treatment?

2. Identify examples of legislation that could be used to protect Beverley and promote her rights.

3. How did care practitioners intervene to safeguard Beverley's interests and wellbeing?

The Race Relations Act (1976) and Race Relations (Amendment) Act (2000)

The Race Relations Act (1976) made racial discrimination unlawful. The Act defined racial discrimination as 'less favourable treatment on racial grounds'. The Race Relations (Amendment) Act (2000) extended and strengthened the 1976 law by making racial discrimination by public authorities, such as the Police, NHS and local authorities, unlawful. These Race Relations Acts aim to eradicate racial discrimination and to promote equal opportunities for members of all ethnic groups.

The Public Order Act (1986) and the Racial and Religious Hatred Act (2006)

The Public Order Act (1986) made it an offence to use words or behaviour or to display written material that is intended to stir up racial hatred. The Racial and Religious Hatred Act 2006 also made it an offence to engage in acts intended to stir up religious hatred.

Over to you!

Do you know what the equality policy of your work setting says about racial and religious hatred? Find out and reflect on the ways in which racial equality is promoted in your workplace.

The Disability Discrimination Act (1995)

This Act safeguards the rights of disabled people; 'less favourable treatment' of disabled people in employment, the provision of goods and services, education and transport is unlawful. The aim of the Acts is to ensure that disabled people receive equal opportunities and that employers, traders, transport and education providers make 'reasonable adjustments' to their premises and services to allow access.

The Special Educational Needs and Disability Act (2001)

This Act was created to help establish legal rights for disabled children and those with special educational needs in compulsory and post-16 education, training and other student services. It extended the Disability Discrimination Act (1995) and sought to prevent unjustified discrimination against disabled learners of all ages.

Your assessment criteria:

2.1 Identify which legislation and codes of practice relating to equality, diversity and discrimination apply to own role

Case study

'Cathy was 7 years old when we first tried to get her into a mainstream primary school. The health and social care professionals and teachers at her special school were set against this. We thought that the special school was damaging her development because her disability was being used to define who she was and who she could become. We had to argue, cajole and plead for Cathy to be accepted at our local primary school where her friends attend. We had to deal with all the usual excuses that parents of disabled children hear from local education authority staff: no disabled toilet; not accessible for a wheelchair; other children will suffer; other parents will object; the professionals know what is in her best interest. In the end we persuaded the head teacher that, like any other child who was keen to learn, Cathy should be able to attend her local school.'

1. Explain how Cathy's experience provides an example of discrimination against disabled children.

2. What were Cathy's parents' reasons for wanting her to attend mainstream primary school?

3. Which laws now protect the rights of disabled children such as Cathy to fair and equal treatment in educational settings?

The Equality Act 2006

This Act created the Equality and Human Rights Commission, outlawed discrimination relating to religion, belief and sexual orientation and placed a duty on public bodies to promote gender equality.

The Education Act (1981), (1993) and (1996)

The Education Act (1981) placed a duty on local education authorities (LEAs) to educate disabled children in mainstream schools. If the parents of a disabled child wished:

▶ the disabled child could be educated in the ordinary school

▶ other children's education would not be adversely affected

▶ the child's integration should involve an efficient use of resources.

The Education Acts of 1993 and 1996 improved the rights of disabled children and their families to have their needs and wishes regarding inclusion taken into account.

Codes of practice

Codes of practice provide guidelines on implementing the often complicated legislation that affects practice when dealing with children and young people. Examples of codes of practice relevant to your work include:

▶ the Code of Practice for Children with Special Educational Needs (SEN Code of Practice)

▶ the Early Years Foundation Stage (EYFS) guidance on implementing the requirements of the EYFS curriculum.

Codes of practice provide guidance and rules on ways of implementing legislation and policy, as well as guidance on professional standards of behaviour and standards of practice. They identify what practitioners should do in specific situations.

Over to you!

Use the Equality and Human Rights Commission website (www.equalityhumanrights.com) to find out about the rights of disabled children and adults.

Practical Assessment Task   **2.1**

How do legislation and codes of practice influence the ways in which you practice in your work setting? Create a table identifying the ways in which the legal framework affecting work with children and young people influences the way you promote equality and diversity and challenge discrimination through your work role.

Your evidence for this task must be based on your practice in a real work environment and must be presented in a format acceptable to your assessor.

Over to you!

What does the inclusion policy in the setting where you work or are on placement say about the integration of disabled children? Find out and make some notes on how this affects your role as a practitioner.

How can you show respect in your interactions?

Interacting with children and families in ways that clearly demonstrate respect is a very important part of inclusive practice in children and young people's settings. Everybody who uses your setting should be valued and respected for who they are, whatever their physical characteristics or their social or cultural background. People feel respected when you:

Respect for difference and identity needs to be part of a practitioner's way of communicating with others.

▶ treat them as an equal while recognising their individual needs, wishes and preferences

▶ acknowledge and recognise that their beliefs, culture and traditions are an important part of who they are

▶ use inclusive, non-discriminatory language that avoids stereotypes, prejudices and **stigmatised** terms

▶ are open-minded and prepared to discuss needs, issues and concerns in a way that recognises the unique qualities of each child, as well as the characteristics they share with others

▶ show interest in their cultural and religious traditions and take part in an appropriate way in celebrating festivals and events that are significant for them and their children.

Key terms

Stigmatised: disapproved of socially

Practical Assessment Task   2.2

How do you use your interactions with children and families to show respect for their culture, beliefs, values and preferences? Complete an interaction diary over the next week, recording when your approach and behaviour showed respect for a child or family's:

▶ beliefs and culture
▶ values
▶ preferences.

You should use examples that were witnessed by a senior colleague, your workplace assessor or manager; ask that person to confirm that you did show respect during the interactions you describe. Your evidence for this task must be based on your practice in a real work environment and must be witnessed by or be in a format acceptable to your assessor.

How can you challenge discrimination and encourage change?

Equality and inclusion for all children and families requires that everyone in a children and young people's setting is committed to anti-discriminatory practice. You can ensure that your own practice is inclusive and non-discriminatory by:

▶ showing equal concern for all children and families

▶ valuing difference and individuality

▶ valuing the personal beliefs of everyone you work with

▶ developing your knowledge and awareness of the lifestyles, beliefs and traditions of people from a variety of cultures, but particularly those represented in your local community

▶ organising and taking part in activities and events that celebrate the religious and cultural traditions of the local communities

▶ using non-discriminatory language

▶ promoting positive images of a diverse range of people and cultures

▶ showing that you have high expectations of yourself and others

▶ providing each child with challenging, varied and engaging opportunities to learn and develop, whatever their gender, ethnicity, cultural or family background

▶ adapting the physical environment of the setting so that children and adults of all ages, abilities and disabilities can use the facilities easily

▶ asking questions, raising concerns and contributing to discussions about inclusion, discrimination and equality of opportunity

▶ becoming familiar with the inclusion and equal opportunities policies and procedures of the setting

▶ intervening if you witness children or adults using discriminatory language, stereotypes, prejudices or discriminatory behaviour

▶ pointing out that such language or behaviour is not acceptable and can be hurtful to others, being clear that you object to the language or behaviour but are not rejecting the child or adult who uses it

▶ providing an example of appropriate language to enable the child or adult to avoid making the same mistake again

▶ providing appropriate support for children or adults who have been subjected to discriminatory behaviour or hurtful language.

You may witness discriminatory behaviour or notice that the practices or procedures of colleagues in your workplace discriminate against some children or families. It is always necessary to draw attention to discrimination – challenging it in a calm, constructive and clear way will help all those involved to learn from the situation and to promote changes in their thinking and behaviour so that it is less likely to occur again. Turning a blind eye to discriminatory practices allows it to continue and will compromise your own standards of practice. You should not let this happen.

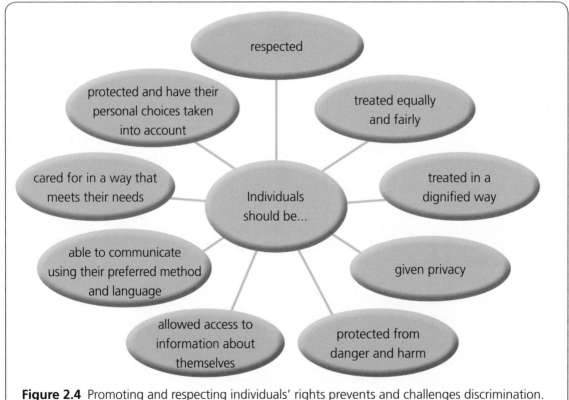

Figure 2.4 Promoting and respecting individuals' rights prevents and challenges discrimination.

Case study

Ella is 4-year-old girl with Down's syndrome. She enjoys coming to her pre-school foundation stage class on 3 afternoons each week. However, she has recently been seen crying and now seems afraid of two boys in her class. This afternoon, Heather, a student on work placement, witnessed the two boys teasing her by pulling faces and repeatedly saying 'belm, belm' to her. Ella was upset by this and sat on the floor crying while the boys circled around her.

1. Do you think that the boys behaviour is an example of discrimination
2. Describe how Heather could intervene in this situation to challenge what is happening in a way that promotes change.

Practical Assessment Task   2.3

Discrimination can be deliberate or inadvertent, overt or covert. Practitioners in children and young people's settings have a responsibility to challenge discrimination and to try and encourage people to adopt more positive, non-discriminatory ways of behaving and talking.

▶ Describe how you have challenged, or would try to challenge, an instance of discrimination that occurred in your work setting.

▶ Describe how your approach to challenging discrimination would encourage others to change their behaviour or way of talking so that they did not discriminate in future.

Your evidence for this task must be based on your practice in a real work environment and must be witnessed by or be presented in a format that is acceptable to your assessor.

Experienced colleagues can be a good source of information, advice and support on equality issues.

Your assessment criteria:

3.1 Identify a range of sources of information, advice and support about diversity, equality and inclusion

Where can you find information, advice and support?

You should now be aware of the need to take diversity, equality and inclusion issues seriously and will know that you should do your best to protect children's rights, promoting equality for every child. While you may be committed to inclusive practice, it can sometimes be challenging. You may be uncertain about the best way of dealing with some situations that arise. This is where accessing information, advice and support is necessary.

As you gain experience in early years or youth practice, your ability to deal with the variety of situations and challenges that can occur will improve. However, even the most experienced practitioners sometimes face unexpected situations and find themselves needing to seek information and advice about inclusion, diversity or equalities issues.

Practitioners can obtain information, advice and support about inclusion and equality issues from a variety of sources (see Figure 2.5).

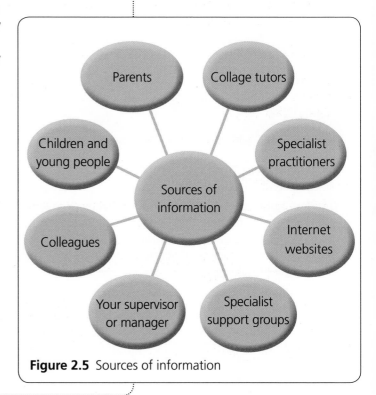

Figure 2.5 Sources of information

Parents

Experienced practitioners recognise that a child's parents are usually the most accurate source of information or advice about the needs, wishes and preferences of their child. Whenever possible you should seek to include a child's parents in discussions and decisions relating to diversity, equality and inclusion issues. As well as being good inclusive practice, this may also be the quickest and most effective way of finding out how you can best provide the kinds of support or assistance that a child needs.

Senior staff and colleagues

Your manager and other colleagues may be very good sources of information, advice and support when you are faced with difficult situations. They will almost certainly have greater experience and more training than you; it is a good idea to seek information, advice and support from more experienced people in your workplace whenever you can. You can do this by:

▶ asking questions during meetings or when chatting informally

▶ discussing issues you are unsure about with your supervisor or your manager

▶ identifying and discussing areas of practice that you find difficult with your supervisor, manager or a specialist practitioner, such as a **SENCO** or social worker, who spends time in your workplace.

Written resources

Information can also be obtained from a variety of resources that may be available in your setting, college resource centre or local library. These include:

▶ the policies and procedures written for your workplace

▶ codes of practice that provide guidance on professional standards and the implementation of laws

▶ framework documents for educational programmes, such as the Early Years Foundation Stage curriculum

▶ books, magazines and journals that focus on early years practice or youth work and which regularly cover diversity, equality and inclusion issues

▶ the internet, particularly the websites of specialist early years and youth work organisations, organisations focusing more generally on diversity, inclusion and equality issues, and reliable information providers such as the BBC.

Key terms

SENCO: Special Educational Needs Coordinator

Over to you!

Can you think of an instance where you have needed additional information, advice or support in relation to a diversity, equality or inclusion issue? What did you do? Did you recognise you needed help and seek it? If you did not, think about whether getting assistance would have been more beneficial both to you and to the children and families involved.

When should you seek information, advice and support?

It is impossible to produce a **definitive** list of all of the situations in which you may need to obtain additional information, advice and support. To ensure that you are well prepared for any challenges you might face, you could reflect on your knowledge and understanding of issues relating to:

▶ the cultural and religious needs of children and families

▶ identity issues concerning ethnicity and race

▶ ways of including and supporting children and families with English as a second language

▶ gender differences, issues and equality

▶ forms of disability and how these impact on children's inclusion and equality

▶ the health and illness experiences of children and families

▶ the use of inclusive language

▶ ways of challenging incidents of unfair treatment or discrimination

▶ how to deal with bullying or other discriminatory behaviour by children or young people within the setting

▶ ways of helping children to learn from situations where discrimination or exclusion has occurred

▶ strategies for supporting children and families who have been subjected to discrimination or unfair treatment.

You may already have some experience of inclusion and equality issues in these types of areas. It is also possible that you can think of other inclusion and equality issues that are not mentioned here. In either case, once you are aware of an issue, the next step is to find ways of responding to it. It is at this point that you may need to access sources of additional information, advice and support.

Your assessment criteria:

3.1 Identify a range of sources of information, advice and support about diversity, equality and inclusion

3.2 Describe how and when to access information, advice and support about diversity, equality and inclusion

Key terms

Definitive: a final or complete list

Over to you!

Who or where would you go to obtain information, advice or support about diversity, equality or discrimination issues that occurred in your work setting?

Feedback and advice from others can be a useful way of developing an inclusive approach your practice with children and young people.

Knowledge Assessment Task — 3.1 3.2

Imagine that you are about to take part in a performance and development review with the manager of your setting. The review will focus on your learning and development needs in relation to your current role.

1. In preparation for the review, you have been asked to produce a short description of a diversity, equality or inclusion situation in which you needed additional information, advice or support. Ideally, your example should refer to a situation that you have already experienced or which you witnessed in your workplace. Alternatively, it could be a situation that you have thought about but which has not yet occurred.

2. How did you (or would you) demonstrate that you know how and when to access information, advice and guidance about this situation? Provide a brief explanation of what you did or would do.

Keep your written work as evidence towards your assessment

Are you ready for assessment?

AC	What do you know now?	Assessment task	✓
1.1	What is meant by diversity, equality, inclusion and discrimination	Page 37	
1.2	Ways in which discrimination may deliberately or inadvertently occur in the work setting	Page 41	
1.3	How practices that support equality and inclusion reduce the likelihood of discrimination	Page 41	
3.1	A range of sources of information, advice and support about diversity, equality and inclusion	Page 55	
3.2	How and when to access information, advice and support about diversity, equality and inclusion	Page 55	

Your tutor or assessor may want to observe you actually doing this in your placement or work setting.

AC	What can you do now	Assessment task	✓
2.1	Identify which legislation and codes of practice relating to equality, diversity and discrimination apply to your own work role	Page 47	
2.2	Show you can interact with individuals in ways that respect their beliefs, culture, values and preferences	Page 48	
2.3	Describe how to challenge discrimination in a way that encourages change	Page 51	

3 | Introduction to personal development in health, social care or children's and young people's settings (SHC 22)

Assessment of this unit

This unit introduces you to the concepts of personal development and reflective practice, and the key part they play in work roles with children and young people.

You will be assessed on both your knowledge of personal development and reflection, and on your ability to apply this in relation to your own development as a practitioner. The 'What you need to know' chart opposite identifies the knowledge-based criteria you must cover in your assessment evidence. You also need to produce evidence of your practical ability to assess and plan for your own learning and development as a practitioner. The 'What you need to do' criteria listed opposite must be assessed in a real work environment by a vocationally competent assessor.

Your tutor or assessor will help you to prepare for your assessment and the tasks suggested in the chapter will help you to create the evidence that you need.

CHAPTER 3

AC — What you need to know

1.1	The duties and responsibilities of your own work role
1.2	The standards that influence the way your work role is carried out
1.3	Ways to ensure that your personal attitudes and beliefs do not obstruct the quality of your work

AC — What you need to do

2.1	Explain why reflecting on work activities is an important way to develop knowledge, skills and practice
2.2	Assess how well your own knowledge, skills and understanding meet standards
2.3	Demonstrate the ability to reflect on work activities
3.1	Identify sources of support for your own learning and development
3.2	Describe the process for agreeing a personal development plan and who should be involved
3.3	Contribute to drawing up a personal development plan for yourself
4.1	Show how a learning activity has improved your own knowledge, skills and understanding
4.2	Show how your reflecting on a situation has improved your own knowledge, skills and understanding
4.3	Show how feedback from others has developed your own knowledge, skills and understanding
4.4	Show that you can record progress in relation to your personal development

This unit also links to some of the other mandatory units:

TDA 2.9	Support children and young people's positive behaviour
CCLDMU 2.2	Contribute to the support of child and young person development

Some of your learning will be repeated in these units and will give you the chance to review your knowledge and understanding.

Understand what is required for competence in own work role

Your assessment criteria:

1.1 Describe the duties and responsibilities of own role

Key terms

Collaborate: work together with others to achieve a shared goal

Duty: something a person is expected or required to do

Job description: a written outline of the duties and responsibilities of a work role

Person specification: a written outline of the qualifications, experience and qualities needed to perform a particular work role

Responsibility: what a person is expected to do

Do you understand your work role?

Here we focus on ways in which you can develop the knowledge, skills and values needed to perform your work role effectively. A clear understanding of the requirements of your work role is needed for this. You should understand:

▶ what you need to do as part of your work role

▶ the aspects of your work role you do well or carry out competently at the moment

▶ the areas of practice you need to improve on through further training or by gaining more experience.

Understanding your duties and responsibilities

Everybody who is employed or working voluntarily in early years, childcare or young people's settings should have a **job description**. Your job description should be written for your particular work role and should clearly outline your work-related **duties** and **responsibilities**. Typically, during the recruitment process, employers also produce a **person specification** that identifies the qualifications, experience and qualities or abilities that a person requires for a particular job. If you are a student on placement, your school or college and the placement organisation should **collaborate** to produce guidelines relating to your role.

The duties and responsibilities associated with your work role will depend on the kind of setting you work in, and the priorities and focus of the organisation that employs you. For example, if you work as an early years assistant in a pre-school nursery for younger children (3–5 year olds), your practical duties and responsibilities are likely to be different to those of a person who works as a classroom assistant with disabled teenagers or older children.

Over to you!

What does your job description say about the duties and responsibilities associated with your work role? Ask your employer for a copy of your job description, if you don't have one. If you are a student on placement, check your placement guidelines to identify the duties and responsibilities associated with your work role.

Aptitude and skills

Work with children and young people is varied. It can be physically and mentally demanding. You may have fantastic enjoyable days filled with positive experiences. You may also have very challenging, tiring and distressing days when your patience is really tested. Whatever kind of day you are having, you must always work to meet the needs of the children who use your care setting. These needs will be diverse, so you will need to be flexible in your approach.

At interview, you will need to demonstrate that you have the aptitude for the kind of day-to-day work that a particular role involves. You will also need to show that you have the skills needed for a particular role or that, because of your aptitude and willingness to learn, you have the potential to develop the necessary skills.

Teamworking skills are central to any early years or youth worker's practice; in this sector people don't usually work as individual practitioners, they work in teams. You must be able to co-operate and collaborate in order to provide a safe, stimulating environment for children and young people.

Starting a new job

When anyone starts a new job, they need clear guidance on what is expected of them. When you start at a new setting, your manager should ensure that you have an **induction** covering:

► practical issues such as the layout of the work setting and the normal routines

► any special ideas and values that underpin the work of the setting

► the **policies** and **procedures** used in the setting, especially in relation to health and safety

► an introduction to your colleagues and other support workers

► an introduction to the children and parents who use the setting.

The induction phase of a new job can feel overwhelming – there is so much new information to take on board. It is okay to ask questions about things you don't understand, can't remember or are not sure about. Not asking questions can result in mistakes being made. Don't worry about looking silly; it shows professionalism and maturity to clarify issues.

Your supervisor and work colleagues will expect you to ask questions and to seek their help when you start your job or placement. It is a good idea to make use of their greater experience and the assistance they are able to offer.

Your assessment criteria:

1.1 Describe the duties and responsibilities of own role

Key terms

Induction: a period of basic training

Policies: written documents that set out an organisation's approach towards a particular issue

Procedures: documents that set out in detail how a particular issue should be dealt with or how particular tasks should be carried out

Case study

Roz, aged 16, has three younger brothers. They are aged 2, 5 and 11. She looks after them from time to time when her mum has to go out shopping and her dad is at work. Roz likes being 'in charge' of her brothers and feels that she is good managing them. She says that the key is to be strict with them about their behaviour. Roz would like to apply for a job at a local nursery school. She thinks that her experience of looking after her brothers and her caring personality, together with the fact that she 'loves playing with children', should be enough to get her an interview and hopefully the job.

1. Identify one way in which your work role and responsibilities are similar to and one way in which they are different from those Roz describes in relation to caring for her brothers.

2. Do you think that Roz has the right kind of aptitude for working with children in a nursery?

3. Describe the kinds of skills that Roz would need to develop or demonstrate in order to get a job like the one that you do at the moment.

What are the standards that influence your role?

All early years and young people's settings have to operate within a legal framework, and should follow the guidance and rules of **regulatory bodies**. Health and safety laws and childcare practice standards are very important elements of this framework. Examples of standards that affect your role can be found in:

▶ codes of practice
▶ internal policies and procedures
▶ legislation (such as the Health and Safety at Work Act, 1974)
▶ National Minimum Standards (found in the **EYFS** documents)
▶ National Occupational Standards.

Internal policies and procedures

Your employer should have produced and made you aware of a range of policies and procedures that cover the standards of practice you need to achieve. Policies and procedures are usually explained during induction training and many settings have additional training sessions or staff meetings where practitioners have the opportunity to learn more.

You need to know how the different policies and procedures used in your work setting impact on your work role. Following them carefully should ensure that you are working to the expected legal and regulatory standards. Your senior colleagues and the manager of your workplace should be able to explain any of the workplace's policies and procedures to you, so it is worth asking about any that you are unsure of or which you don't understand.

Your assessment criteria:

1.2 Identify standards that influence the way the role is carried out

Key terms

EYFS: Early Years Foundation Stage

Regulatory body: an organisation that sets standards and rules for care practitioners to follow

Over to you!

Did you have an opportunity to find out about and discuss the policies and procedures of your work setting when you started your job or placement? Where would you find a copy of the policies and procedures if you wanted to check something today?

The Health and Safety at Work Act (1974)

The Health and Safety at Work Act (1974) is the key law affecting the health and safety rights and responsibilities of employers and employees in your workplace (see Figure 3.1). Employers are responsible for providing:

▶ a safe and secure work environment

▶ safe equipment

▶ information and training about health, safety and security.

To meet their legal responsibilities, employers must:

▶ carry out health and safety risk assessments

▶ develop health and safety procedures, such as fire evacuation procedures

▶ provide health and safety equipment, such as fire extinguishers, fire blankets and first aid boxes

▶ ensure that the workplace has built-in safety features, such as smoke alarms, fire exits and security fixtures (electronic pads on doors and window guards, for example)

▶ train their employees to follow health and safety procedures, use health and safety equipment correctly and safety features appropriately

▶ provide a range of health and safety information, including warning signs to alert people to safety features such as fire exits and first aid equipment and to warn them about prohibited areas and not smoking, for example.

Employees (practitioners and students) have a responsibility to:

▶ work safely within the care setting

▶ monitor their work environment for health and safety problems that may develop

▶ report and respond appropriately to any health and safety risks.

Your assessment criteria:

1.1 Describe the duties and responsibilities of own role

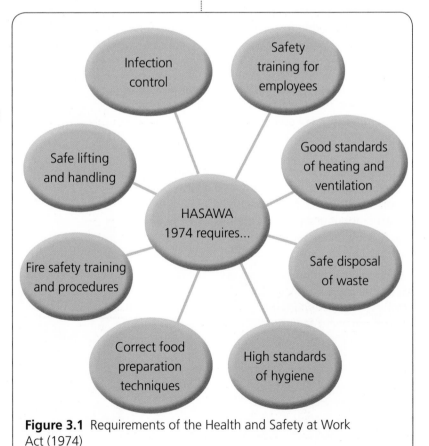

Figure 3.1 Requirements of the Health and Safety at Work Act (1974)

Practitioners and students carry out their legal responsibilities by:

▶ developing an awareness of health and safety law

▶ working in ways that follow health and safety guidelines, policies and procedures

▶ monitoring the work environment for health and safety hazards

▶ dealing directly with hazards that present a health and safety risk, where it is safe to do so

▶ reporting health and safety hazards or the failure of safety systems or procedures to a supervisor or manager.

Your employer's health and safety policy should cover the key points of this legislation. You should have a good understanding of what it says and how this affects your work role.

Case study

Hamza Khan is a student taking a childcare course at a local college. He has never worked in an early years setting before and is very excited to be starting a placement at Chadderton Primary School. Hamza is going to spend time with Foundation Stage children and may also get the chance to work in the main primary school. He has just visited the school to meet Mrs Lloyd, the class teacher and his supervisor. He is feeling a bit frustrated and grumpy because she gave him a folder containing information about the school and about the policies and procedures that apply in the Foundation Stage area. He doesn't really want to read this but has been told that he will need to show that he understands the health and safety policy and procedures before he can spend time with the children.

1. Identify the main piece of health and safety legislation that is likely to be covered by the Chadderton Primary School policies and procedures.

2. Describe the health and safety responsibilities Hamza will have when he starts working at Chadderton Primary School.

3. Give two reasons why Hamza needs to understand what the policies and procedures say about health and safety.

Children Act (2004)

This piece of legislation updated the Children Act (1989). It places a legal duty on local authorities (councils) to improve the wellbeing of children and young people; **safeguarding** is a key part of this (see also page 000). Local authorities work with Local Safeguarding Children's Boards to protect the welfare of children. The report *Every Child Matters*, which focuses on safeguarding, has the aim of ensuring that children:

▶ are healthy

▶ stay safe

▶ enjoy and achieve

▶ make a positive contribution

▶ achieve economic wellbeing.

Welfare requirements

The Early Years Foundation Stage statutory framework applies to all early years settings. All early years settings must satisfy five wellbeing requirements:

1. safeguarding and promoting children's welfare
2. suitable people
3. suitable premises
4. environment and equipment
5. organisation and documentation.

These welfare requirements are not a statutory requirement in settings for older children and young people. However, they do focus attention on key issues and areas of work that are important in providing a suitable care, learning and development environment for children and young people of all ages.

National Occupational Standards

The aim of the National Occupational Standards (NOS) for children and young people's practice is to:

▶ raise the quality of care provision in children and young people's settings

▶ identify the knowledge, skills and understanding needed by competent practitioners for work with children and young people.

National Occupational Standards are also used to develop care qualifications (such as this one!) and courses that seek to improve practice in the sector. Employees and students are responsible for working to the NOS. Your employer or placement provider should provide you with ongoing support and suitable training opportunities to enable you to achieve and maintain acceptable standards of practice. You have a duty to make the most of these opportunities.

Your assessment criteria:

1.2 Identify standards that influence the way the role is carried out

1.3 Describe ways to ensure that personal attitudes or beliefs do not obstruct the quality of work

Key terms

Safeguarding: protecting or keeping safe

Over to you!

The website of the Children's Workforce Development Council (www.cwdcouncil.org.uk) provides a range of information on standards that apply to work with children and young people. You can also find copies of the National Occupational Standards on this website.

How can you keep personal views and work separate?

There must be some separation between your personal views and the way you relate to others in the workplace. You need to accept differences, avoid challenging the beliefs of others and should not get into conflict over attitudes and beliefs in general. You can do this by:

▶ discussing issues openly and by contributing your thoughts and ideas to meetings and discussions

▶ listening to the ideas, views and opinions of others in an open-minded way

▶ allowing people to work in ways that suit them if the outcome is acceptable – people don't always have to do things your way!

▶ avoiding confrontation as this creates hostility and may damage the confidence of individual colleagues and the morale of the team in general.

Case study

Carrie has to get her three children up, dressed and fed before taking them to nursery and school. She often arrives fifteen minutes after the morning session has begun at the nursery because she has to take her daughter to school first. Debbie, one of the nursery staff, isn't impressed by this regular lateness and has made comments about the children 'looking half-dressed today'. Carrie feels criticised and is going to make a complaint if Debbie says anything else.

1. What mistake is Debbie making in relation to Carrie and the boys?

2. What does Debbie say or do that suggests she is being judgemental towards Carrie?

3. What do you think Debbie could do to deal with this situation in a more constructive way?

Knowledge Assessment Task   1.1   1.2   1.3

You have been asked to take part in a vocational studies day at a nearby secondary school. The pupils at the school are interested in the 'World of Work' and have been told that there will be a poster display with information about a range of local jobs. You should produce a poster that could be used on the day. You will need to:

1. Describe the duties and responsibilities of your own role.

2. Identify standards that influence the way your work role is carried out.

3. Describe how you ensure that your personal attitudes and beliefs do not obstruct the quality of your work.

Keep your written work as evidence towards your assessment.

Be able to reflect on own work activities

Why use reflection?

Reflection is an important skill for children and young people's practitioners. Reflection involves:

▶ looking inward (contemplating)

▶ examining your own practice

▶ thinking about what you have done and the reasons why.

Reflection can lead you to consider your actions and practice from new angles. Being able to look critically at particular experiences or areas of your own practice is now accepted as an important way of learning and developing. You should be able to reflect on both positive and negative aspects of your practice as a care worker. If things are not going so well, or you feel you need support in a particular area, you could follow up your reflections by talking through issues with your colleagues or supervisor. It is this kind of action that helps us to learn from our mistakes and from difficult experiences. Similarly, if a situation has gone extremely well, you can learn from it by reflecting on just how and why it went right. Learning the lessons of success is as important as learning lessons from failure.

Reflection will help to make you more self-aware and your practice more effective. It ensures that you consider:

▶ how best to meet children's or young people's needs

▶ what your own skills and knowledge are

▶ how to adapt in different circumstances.

Your assessment criteria:

2.1 Explain why reflecting on work activities is an important way to develop knowledge, skills and practice

2.2 Assess how well own knowledge, skills and understanding meet standards

Key terms

Reflection: thinking carefully about something in an open-minded way

Self-evaluation: assessing your own skills, abilities, achievements or professional development needs

There are lots of opportunities for reflection during the working day, as well as afterwards. For example, opportunities for reflection arise:

- ▶ in appraisals or supervision sessions
- ▶ during team meetings
- ▶ on training courses
- ▶ when talking to colleagues or parents
- ▶ when thinking about work incidents or events that have happened.

In addition to clarifying your own thoughts, these opportunities may give you the chance to receive feedback, to hear others' perspectives and to see how they deal with issues, problems and challenges.

How can you meet the standard?

Reflection will help you to assess your own development and the extent to which you meet expected standards of performance for your work role. You could look at the guidance on reflection provided by the Early Years Foundation Stage in England and try completing the **self-evaluation** form produced by OFSTED. These may give you an insight into areas where you need guidance and support and areas where you may benefit from further development.

The process of appraisal

Your regular supervision sessions and annual **appraisals** provide ideal opportunities to assess the extent to which you meet expected standards of practice. You should be able to discuss the strengths and weaknesses of your performance and skills with your supervisor or manager (see Figure 3.2). To benefit from appraisal, you will need to be totally honest with yourself, without being overly self-critical. The aim of your appraisal is to discuss your past and present performance in your work role and to plan for your future development.

Figure 3.2 What is appraisal?

Appraisal is time to:	Appraisal is *not* time to:
• listen	• be disciplined or told off
• discuss	• moan or complain
• plan.	• be surprised or shocked by what is said.

Key terms

Appraisal: an assessment of an individual's skills, achievements, learning and professional development needs

Self-evaluation: assessing your own skills, abilities, achievements and professional development needs

Over to you!

Obtain a copy of the OFSTED self-evaluation form for your work setting. Find out how well your setting meets national standards. What is being done or is planned to develop this further? Think about how your own work role contributes to this process.

How do you reflect on your work?

Reflection involves being able to stand back and think objectively about:

- your past and current work performance
- whether you are meeting your goals
- whether you are achieving the standards of practice expected of someone in your work role.

Reflection is not always easy as you must be totally honest with yourself, and a little bit self-critical. As well as reflecting on your own views, you should also take into account feedback from other people about your work performance. As part of your reflective approach, you will need to be able to think about alternative approaches, activities, strategies and solutions to the opportunities, problems and challenges that exist in your work setting. Figure 3.3 illustrates the reflective process and identifies the kinds of questions that you may ask in order to reflect on an issue, incident or experience.

Using a reflective journal

It is a good idea to record your reflections, perhaps in a diary or journal, so that you can look back and consider how things have changed over time. This can also help to focus your attention on areas where you need to develop your knowledge, skills or practice.

It is best to see reflection as an ongoing process of learning and development. You can learn both from your successes and from the situations that haven't gone quite so well. It is important to take a variety of perspectives, including peer observations and parent feedback, into account when reflecting on your performance and practice development.

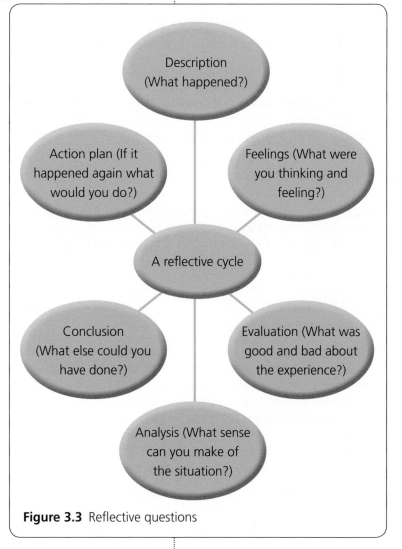

Figure 3.3 Reflective questions

Case study

Kelly is an experienced classroom assistant; she has worked in a primary school for 3 years, mainly with children aged between 9 and 10 years. At the start of term, she moved to work in the reception class with 4-year-old children. Kelly struggled to adapt to the different ways of working in the reception class. At first she felt overwhelmed by the amount of practical help that the younger children needed. She wasn't used to helping children with coats and shoes, and didn't always notice when they needed to use the toilet. This led to several accidents and Kelly became cross and impatient with some of the children. Jane, the class teacher, asked Kelly to reflect a bit more on her approach to her new role. Kelly wrote down her thoughts and feelings a couple of times a week. This really seemed to help, as Kelly became more aware of the children's needs and realised that her role should involve providing more hands-on physical assistance. As a result, Kelly felt much happier in her new job and became a more effective team member.

1. What did Kelly need to do in order to reflect on her work role and practice?

2. What do you think were the benefits for Kelly of becoming a more reflective practitioner?

3. How do you think others may have benefited from Kelly's ability to reflect on her practice?

Practical Assessment Task   2.1   2.2   2.3

Reflection is an important part of practice in work with children and young people. Using an appropriate method to record your reflections (such as a written or audio diary or journal), spend some time thinking about aspects of your practice with children or young people. Your assessor will ask you some questions about your reflections in order to assess whether you are able to reflect effectively on your own work activities. You should be able to:

1. Explain why reflecting on practice is an important way of developing knowledge, skills and practice.

2. Assess how well your own knowledge, skills and understanding meet the standards associated with your job and work setting.

3. Demonstrate the ability to reflect on your work activities.

Your evidence for this assessment activity must be based on your practice in a real work environment.

Be able to agree a personal development plan

Key terms

Objectives: aims or goals that a person seeks to achieve

What support is available for your learning and development?

Your personal development plan

A personal development plan is a document where you record:

▶ **objectives** for your development

▶ activities to meet these objectives

▶ timescales for achieving objectives

▶ timescales for reviewing progress.

A personal development plan should help you to focus your efforts on developing your professional knowledge, skills and practice. You will benefit from the help and support of others when you are completing your personal development plan.

Learners can be supported in a number of different ways (see Figure 3.4) to achieve their learning and development goals.

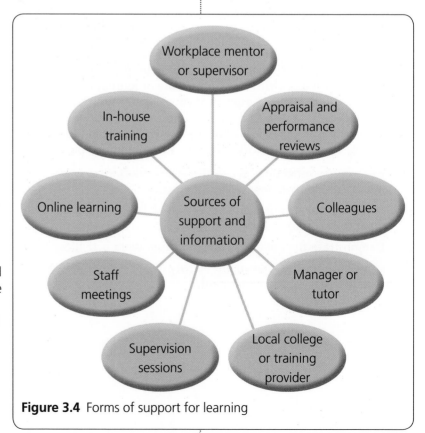

Figure 3.4 Forms of support for learning

The relevance of each form of support will depend on an individual's particular development needs.

You will probably benefit from several forms of support during your course; you should use all the sources of support that are available to help you address any weaknesses and develop your practice. It is important to know how you can access different sources of support, and to seek help when you need it. Tutors and workplace supervisors see asking for support as a sign of maturity rather than as an indication of incompetence or lack of ability.

Using training opportunities

You may be able to meet your development goals by attending a formal training course or a less formal information study day held at your setting, at a local college or set up by external training providers. If you are thinking about taking this approach, you need to ensure that the training opportunities you choose are:

▶ accessible

▶ suitable for your development needs

▶ affordable

▶ achievable within your time constraints.

Larger employers in the children and young people's workforce sector may offer in-house training during or after work hours. You should try to make the most of these opportunities as they have the added benefit of being based in your workplace around the specific needs of staff in your setting. In addition to any training benefits, participation also contributes to teamwork effectiveness.

Staff meetings

Team members usually meet regularly at staff meetings. Practitioners can discuss practice issues, sharing information about policies and procedures, and good practice solutions. Managers and senior colleagues may also impart information about future developments in the setting. Some settings use staff meetings to allow practitioners to report on training events and courses they have attended. This enables other staff members to share the key learning points, to consider how they may incorporate them into their practice, and to assess whether they too would benefit from attending the course.

Over to you!

How do you contribute to staff meetings in your work setting? Do you use them as learning and development opportunities? Think about ways in which you could increase your participation to get more out of the meetings you attend.

73

How do you create a personal development plan?

Agreeing a personal development plan

To create a personal development plan you need to:

- ▶ assess your skills and abilities at a **baseline** point

- ▶ develop your understanding of the knowledge, skills and standards of practice that are expected for your work role

- ▶ construct a plan that will enable you to progress from where you are now to the point you would like to be.

Personal development planning involves collaboration between you and your supervisor. You will need time and support to create your personal development plan. You will certainly have to discuss your training and development needs over the next year or so with your supervisor before you begin writing your plan.

Contributing to your personal development plan

Remember that your personal development plan is a way of addressing your development needs and of achieving progress towards being a more effective care practitioner. So, your personal development plan should specify a range of objectives that are quite specific about how you intend to achieve them.

Identifying development objectives and creating a plan to achieve them is a valuable exercise in breaking down your goals into achievable chunks. Establishing achievable objectives is very important. When people do not achieve their objectives or feel stressed by them, it is often because they are overwhelmed by the size of the task.

The objectives that you set are the destination point in a development journey. They should fill in the knowledge and skills gaps, or address the development needs you identified during the initial self-assessment process. Using the SMART approach is a good way of ensuring that you set development goals you can achieve.

Key terms

Baseline: the starting point or point at which something is first measured

Over to you!

Can you think of any particular development goals that you would like to achieve in the next six months? Consider goals in relation to your knowledge, skills, practice, values, beliefs and career aspirations, for example.

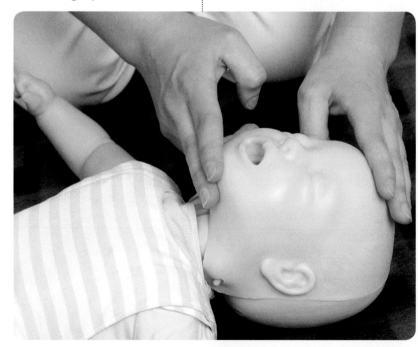

Training should meet your development needs in a SMART way.

Using the SMART approach, each objective should be:

▶ **S**pecific (clear and detailed)

▶ **M**easurable (so you'll know when you've done it)

▶ **A**chievable (realistic)

▶ **R**elevant (addresses a need that you've already identified)

▶ **T**ime-limited (you'll do it by a set time, a deadline).

It is important to set dates for achieving goals and to undertake activities that produce evidence, so you can prove that you are developing. See Figure 3.5.

Figure 3.5 An example of a personal development plan (2011–13)

Goals	Actions	Deadline for completion	Review notes	Date completed
1. I want to become a more effective communicator.	• Talk more in class – don't be so shy. • Volunteer to do class presentations. • Be more outgoing in placement setting this year.	30.03.11		
2. I want to get a job working in a care setting in the summer holidays to improve my care practice.	• Identify local care providers who have part-time and temporary work roles. • Create a CV and letter of application and send to local organisations. • Practice and improve my interview technique at college.	30.06.11		
3. I want to do well in my Level 2 CYPW Diploma course.	• Plan study time each week. • Attend all classes and contribute in class. • Complete all assignments on time.	30.12.11		
4. I want to find out about management and teaching careers in the CYPW sector.	• Find out about qualifications needed and course providers. • Research job roles and career pathways in different areas of CYPW work.	30.09.12		

Monitoring and evaluating your plan

To show that you are building up skills and knowledge, you will need to monitor your development and progress; your personal development plan is a good tool for this. It should contain information about your current skills, abilities and achievements (the baseline) and your development objectives (where you want to be). Reviewing your progress towards these objectives is a good way of checking whether you have acquired new skills and knowledge.

Being flexible

It is very important to remember that a personal development plan is only a *plan*. In other words, it is about things that you would like to happen but it is also *flexible*. You should see it as a tool to help you achieve your development objectives, giving direction and guidance. You are advised to look at it regularly and to use it as a central part of your ongoing development as a practitioner. You should arrange to discuss and update your plan on a regular basis, so that it always reflects your needs, achievements and objectives in an up-to-date way. Informally, you can ask yourself a number of review questions to assess your development:

▶ Are you making progress towards your objectives?

▶ Are the actions that you have identified to achieve your objectives working?

▶ Do you have the skills and knowledge you need and are you starting to use them in the workplace?

You should remember that if your work or personal circumstances change, it may not be possible for you to meet all of the objectives in your personal development plan within the original time scale. Some or all of your objectives may need to be modified or rescheduled to reflect your new situation. So, it is essential to review your personal development plan and to check your own progress at regular intervals. Do not wait for your six-monthly appraisal or annual performance review meeting when it may be too late to alter things.

Your assessment criteria:

3.1 Identify sources of support for own learning and development

3.2 Describe the process for agreeing a personal development plan and who should be involved

3.3 Contribute to drawing up own personal development plan

There are reasons why your own development plan needs to be flexible.

Case study

Mia, aged 29, is employed as a classroom assistant at St Thomas's pre-school nursery. She began studying for her Level 2 Children and Young People's Workforce Diploma three months ago. With the support of her supervisor, Sue, Mia is currently trying to write a personal development plan. She has discussed her learning and development needs with Sue on a couple of occasions. Mia is finding it hard to identify what she should focus on as she believes she needs to 'learn everything about children!' Sue has asked Mia to make a list of the childcare skills she believes she has at present and to also bring in her CV and certificates from school or college to their next meeting. The last time they met, Sue asked Mia to list three skills she would like to develop by this time next year. This is the part that Mia is finding difficult. She would like to be 'good at everything I need to do'. Mia sees herself as confident and is always keen to help out and learn by taking part in activities with the children. Sue, on the other hand, is trying to persuade Mia that she needs to 'take one step at a time' and to identify goals or objectives that will enable her to learn and develop her skills in a planned way.

1. Identify two things that Sue is doing to try and 'baseline' Mia's current skills and achievements. Explain why it is important to do this.

2. If you were one of Mia's colleagues and she said to you, 'But why do I need to write a personal development plan? Can't I just get better through doing it?', what would you say?

3. Apart from using the support of Sue, her supervisor, what other sources of support could Mia use to create and monitor her personal development plan?

Practical Assessment Task   3.1 3.2 3.3

Personal development planning is an efficient and effective way of ensuring that you identify and focus on your learning and development needs. You should be able to demonstrate that you know how the personal development planning process works in your workplace. Your assessor will ask you to provide evidence showing that you are able to:

1. Identify sources of support that will promote your own learning and development.

2. Describe the process used in your workplace for agreeing a personal development plan, identifying the people who are involved in this.

3. Contribute to drawing up your own personal development plan.

You may want to make notes to help you to prepare for your assessment. The evidence that you produce for this assessment task must be based on your practice in a real work environment.

Be able to develop own knowledge, skills and understanding

How can you improve your knowledge, skills and understanding?

Having worked through this chapter, you should now understand your own work role, know how to reflect on this, find out about the standards of practice that are expected of you, and you should have agreed a personal development plan. Here we will look at ways of developing your own knowledge, skills and understanding in order to become a better practitioner.

Improvement through learning activities

When you have agreed a personal development plan, the next step is to develop your knowledge, skills and understanding in ways that meet your development needs. As well as increasing your confidence, training and other development activity should:

▶ broaden and deepen your knowledge

▶ improve and extend your range of skills.

Although learning and development can happen without planning, having a personal development plan to reflect on will enable you to achieve your development goals more effectively. However, you should remember that going on courses and attending training events will not automatically result in your development. You need to think and do things differently before you can claim that you have learnt something new.

> **Your assessment criteria:**
>
> **4.1** Show how a learning activity has improved own knowledge, skills and understanding
>
> **4.2** Show how reflecting on a situation has improved own knowledge, skills and understanding

---

Practical Assessment Task   **4.1**

Identify some examples of learning activities (either formal or informal) that you have participated in and which you believe you have learnt from. Your assessor will need to know:

▶ what the learning activities involved

▶ how you participated in the learning activities

▶ how the learning activities improved your knowledge, skills and understanding.

Keep any notes you write as evidence towards your assessment. Your evidence for this assessment activity must be based on your practice and experience in a real work environment.

Improvement through reflection

Reflection should enable you to improve the knowledge, skills and understanding you have in relation to:

▶ interactions with parents

▶ activities you provide for children

▶ relationships with colleagues and visitors to the setting

▶ your input into team activities and meetings

▶ your relationships with children.

Reflection will enable you to build on your achievements and address weaknesses in your performance, always aiming to become a better practitioner. To achieve this you need to be able to:

▶ reflect in action – that is to think on your feet to deal with issues that arise unexpectedly (a child's tantrum, for example)

▶ reflect on action – that is think through issues after the event (perhaps, how an activity could have been managed differently).

Your ability to use reflection should help in your relationships with individual parents as you will often need to think about the best way to report on their child's day. Parents expect you to be able to tell them, in a courteous, respectful and constructive way, how their children are getting on and what benefits they are gaining from the activities you provide. Reflecting on your practice, on your observations of children and on your relationships with parents will help you to become a more professional and effective practitioner.

Practical Assessment Task   4.2

How has the use of reflection helped to improve your practice or promote your learning and development? Your assessor will ask you about your use of reflection in the workplace. He or she will require evidence that shows how reflecting on a situation has improved your own knowledge, skills and understanding. You can produce this evidence by:

1. Identifying and describing a practice situation that you have reflected on

2. describing how the process of reflection helped you to learn from the situation or develop some aspect of your knowledge, skills or understanding.

Keep any notes you write as evidence towards your assessment. Your evidence for this assessment activity must be based on your practice and experience in a real work environment.

How can you use feedback to improve your performance?

Your assessment criteria:

4.3 Show how feedback from others has developed own knowledge, skills and understanding

Being open to feedback is one of the hardest aspects of working and studying, especially if you receive critical comments (see Figure 3.6). When this happens you may be defensive or dismissive as a way of protecting yourself. Instead, you should listen carefully, keep any feedback in perspective and try to respond constructively. Ask for clear examples of any areas of weakness or underperformance, for ideas about how you could improve in these areas and for suggestions about who could help you to improve.

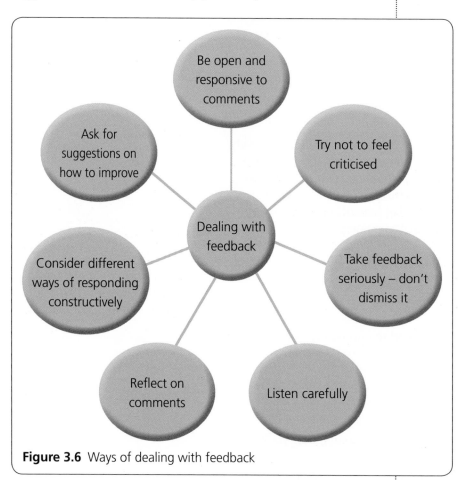

Figure 3.6 Ways of dealing with feedback

Feedback from professional practitioners can help you to develop your knowledge and skills quickly, especially helpful when you are settling into a new role. However, be wary of reading too much into comments from your friends at work and take no notice of anyone who encourages you to take shortcuts to save on time and effort. Possible sources of feedback from colleagues include team meetings, communication books or diaries and informal conversations. Good team spirit, approaches for help or advice, and people wanting to work with you are good indications that you are making a positive contribution to practice.

You may receive feedback formally and informally through, for example:

▶ appraisals

▶ mentoring

▶ team meetings

▶ training opportunities

▶ peer observations

▶ parent questionnaires

▶ conversations with colleagues and parents.

Formal appraisals provide feedback on performance, specifically whether you are meeting expected standards of practice. The aim is to acknowledge competence and indentify areas for improvement, not to criticise you.

Mentors are a good source of feedback; they may be models of good practice, or they may offer you advice and guidance. Colleague feedback from people who often observe you can be constructive. Questionnaire responses from parents and children provide a very important source of feedback. You need to take on board their feelings, observations and comments, even though they may see things very differently from you. Feedback from children and young people can really help you to improve your practice – you will get a better view of how they see you and experience your practice.

You need to be honest when giving feedback to people and open-minded when receiving it.

Over to you!

Who has provided feedback on your performance at work? Reflect on how you have used this feedback. Have you been positive and tried to change or develop your practice, or have you seen it as criticism?

How can you record your personal progress?

You need to collect evidence of your personal development for performance review and appraisal purposes. However, it is also important for you to be able to see what you have achieved compared to your development plan. A portfolio of evidence containing your curriculum vitae (CV), certificates, personal development plan and other evidence of your progress can also be a boost to your confidence and professional self-image. You can record evidence of your progress, development and achievements in:

▶ your CV

▶ your portfolio of achievement

▶ a training folder or file kept at work

▶ other workplace records.

See Figure 3.7.

Your records

Use your CV to demonstrate your knowledge and experience. You should record your school and college qualifications, as well as any other professional development courses that you have undertaken. It is useful to keep your CV on a computer as this makes updating and sending the document easy. Having an up-to-date CV means you can apply for posts that come up unexpectedly.

A portfolio of achievement is typically a file containing your certificates and records of training and development. It can be given to prospective employers to demonstrate what you have done. A training folder or file may contain your personal development plan and appraisal documents, as well as records about training events you have attended.

Your assessment criteria:

4.3 Show how feedback from others has developed own knowledge, skills and understanding

4.4 Show how to record progress in relation to personal development

Over to you!

How are you expected to record your personal development and progress? Find out what your assessor or course provider expects and try to see some examples of other people's portfolios of evidence.

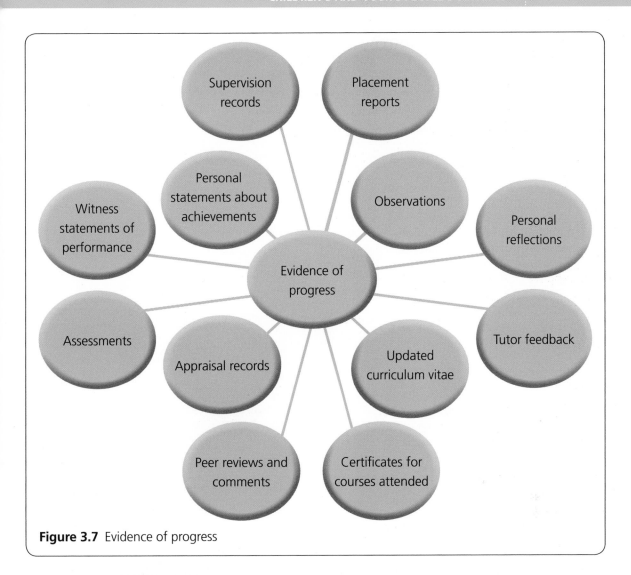

Figure 3.7 Evidence of progress

Practical Assessment Task   4.3   4.4

Feedback from others is an important source of information that
can be used to help you to learn and develop your practice. In this
final activity, you will need to demonstrate to your assessor:

1. how feedback from others (colleagues, parents, children or
   your manager, for example) has enabled you to develop your
   own knowledge, skills and understanding of your work role
   and practice

2. that you are able to record progress in relation to your learning
   and development in an appropriate and effective way.

Keep any notes you write as evidence towards your assessment.
Your evidence for this assessment activity must be based on your
practice and experience in a real work environment.

Are you ready for assessment?

AC	What do you know now?	Assessment task	✓
1.1	The duties and responsibilities of your own work role	Page 67	
1.2	The standards that influence the way your work role is carried out	Page 67	
1.3	Ways to ensure that your personal attitudes and beliefs do not obstruct the quality of your work	Page 67	

Your tutor or assessor may want to observe you actually doing this in your placement or work setting.

AC	What can you do now?	Assessment task	✓
2.1	Explain why reflecting on work activities is an important way to develop knowledge, skills and practice	Page 71	
2.2	Assess how well your own knowledge, skills and understanding meet standards	Page 71	
2.3	Demonstrate the ability to reflect on work activities	Page 71	
3.1	Identify sources of support for your own learning and development	Page 77	
3.2	Describe the process for agreeing a personal development plan and who should be involved	Page 77	
3.3	Contribute to drawing up a personal development plan for yourself	Page 77	
4.1	Show how a learning activity has improved your own knowledge, skills and understanding	Page 78	
4.2	Show how your reflecting on a situation has improved your own knowledge, skills and understanding	Page 79	
4.3	Show how feedback from others has developed your own knowledge, skills and understanding	Page 83	
4.4	Show that you can record progress in relation to your personal development	Page 83	

4 | Contribute to children and young people's health and safety (MU 2.4)

Assessment of this unit

This unit introduces you to health and safety issues, and ways of dealing with non-medical incidents and emergencies in childcare settings. Health and safety policies and procedures are developed and used to promote safe working practices and to safeguard children and adults in early years and young people's settings.

You will be assessed on both your knowledge of health and safety and your ability to apply this in practical work with children and young people. The 'What you need to know' chart below identifies the knowledge-based criteria you must cover in your assessment evidence. You also have to produce evidence of your practical ability to work in a safe way and to follow the health, safety and security procedures of your work setting. The 'What you need to do' criteria listed opposite must be assessed in a real work environment by a vocationally competent assessor.

Your tutor or assessor will help you to prepare for your assessment and the tasks suggested in the chapter will help you to create the evidence that you need.

AC	What you need to know
1.1	The health and safety policies and procedures used in your work setting
1.2	Who is responsible for health and safety issues and how you should report health and safety problems in your work setting
1.3	The meaning of risk management and how this is manged in your work setting
3.1	A range of non-medical incidents and emergencies that may occur in your work setting
3.2	The procedures for dealing with: • fires • security incidents • emergency incidents
4.1	The signs and symptoms which may indicate that a child or young person is injured or unwell
4.2	The circumstances when children or young people may need urgent medical attention
4.3	Your own role and responsibilities in dealing with a child or young person who requires urgent medical attention

AC	What you need to do
2.1	Explain why a safe but challenging environment is important for children and young people
2.2	Identify the differences between a risk and a hazard
2.3	Identify potential hazards to the health, safety and security of children or young people in your work setting
2.4	Contribute to health and safety risk assessment in areas of the work setting and for off-site visits
5.1	Describe how to report an accident, incident, emergency or illness in your work setting
5.2	Complete workplace documentation for recording accidents, incidents, emergencies and illnesses
6.1	Outline the procedures for infection control in your work setting
6.2	Describe personal protective clothing that is used in your work setting to prevent spread of infection
6.3	Demonstrate use of personal protective clothing to avoid spread of infection
6.4	Demonstrate how to wash and dry hands to avoid spread of infection
6.5	Demonstrate safe disposal of waste to avoid the spread of infection
7.1	Identify the procedures of the work setting that affect the management of medication
7.2	Explain how the procedures of the work setting are used to protect both children and young people and practitioners

This unit also links to some of the other mandatory units:

TDA 2.2	Safeguard the welfare of children and young people
MU 2.8	Contribute to the support of the positive environments for children and young people
MP11002	Managing paediatric illness and injury

Some of your learning will be repeated in these units and will give you the chance to review your knowledge and understanding.

Your assessment criteria:

2.2 Identify the differences between risk and hazard

2.3 Identify potential hazards to the health, safety or security of children and young people in the work setting

What are hazards and risks?

Early years and youth workers need to know about and should act in ways that minimise the **risks** to people in their settings. As a safe and effective practitioner you will also need to know how to deal with **accidents**, **incidents** and **emergencies** that occur in your work setting.

Children learn from experience. They don't begin life with a strong awareness of danger or the ability to manage their own safety. You should assume that the children you work with are unaware of the **hazards** and dangers that exist in your workplace. This means that an important part of your job is to **safeguard** them so that they avoid harm.

Understanding hazards and risks

In the health and safety field, there is a basic distinction between a risk and a hazard:

▶ A *hazard* is anything that could be dangerous or which could put a person in danger. Figure 4.1 identifies a number of potential hazards that are present in early years and young people's settings.

▶ A *risk* is the chance of a child or adult being harmed by a hazard. For example, leaving sharp knives (hazards) within reach of young children is a high-risk thing to do. A young child may not understand that touching or playing with a sharp knife could lead to injury.

Key terms

Accident: an event that happens suddenly and unexpectedly or by chance

Emergencies: T/K

Hazard: anything that can cause harm

Incident: an event that may cause disruption or a crisis

Safeguard: protect from harm

Risk: the chance of harm being done by a hazard

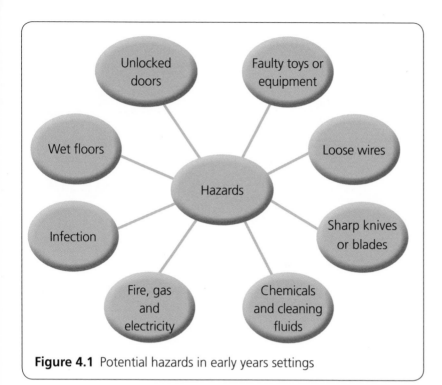

Figure 4.1 Potential hazards in early years settings

Over to you!

Early years and young people's practitioners need to understand and be aware of a range of hazards in the workplace and the risks associated with them. Can you think of two potential hazards to children's health and safety that are present in your workplace? Are all of the children who attend equally at risk from these hazards?

Practical Assessment Task   2.2   2.3

Using Figure 4.1 above and the definitions of *hazard* and *risk*, complete a table like the one below to identify three examples of potential hazards to the health, safety and security of children or young people in your work setting.

Type of hazard	Example of hazard	Why is this hazardous?	Who is at risk?
Health hazard			
Safety hazard			
Security hazard			

Keep any notes you write as evidence towards your assessment. Your evidence for this assessment activity must be based on your practice and experience in a real work environment.

Who is responsible for health and safety in the setting?

Employers, employees and the other adults (for example, parents, carers and visitors) who are present in your workplace all have health and safety responsibilities. These responsibilities are the result of laws and other regulatory requirements that are designed to safeguard children and adults. In general terms, employers are responsible for providing:

▶ a safe and secure work environment

▶ safe equipment

▶ information and training about health, safety and security.

Employers must provide an environment that makes it possible for practitioners to work safely and for children and families to receive safe care and education. Employees have a responsibility to:

▶ work safely within the workplace

▶ monitor the work environment for health and safety issues

▶ report and respond appropriately to any health and safety hazards.

Early Years settings have to comply with the Statutory Framework of the Early Years Foundation Stage. This covers issues including:

▶ safeguarding

▶ suitable people

▶ suitable premises and equipment

▶ organisation

▶ documentation.

Play is never risk free, but needs to be monitored and managed safely.

Your assessment criteria:

1.1 Outline the health and safety policies and procedures of the work setting

1.2 Identify the lines of responsibility and reporting for health and safety in the work setting

Key terms

Policy: a written document that sets out an organisation's approach towards a particular issue

Procedure: a document that sets out in detail how a particular issue should be dealt with or how particular tasks should be carried out

In addition, the standards of provision in early years settings are inspected by Ofsted (England), HMIe (Scotland), ESTYN (Wales) and the ETI (Northern Ireland).

Policies and procedures

Early years and young people's organisations generally produce a range of **policies** and **procedures** to ensure that practitioners work in safe and effective ways. Policies and procedures typically cover issues such as:

▶ health and safety

▶ safeguarding

▶ reporting of accidents

▶ waste disposal

▶ fire prevention and evacuation

▶ security

▶ cleaning and cleanliness

▶ food safety.

You should know all about each of the health and safety policies and procedures used in your workplace. You should always follow them in practice as they are designed to create a safe environment and promote the health and safety of everyone in the setting. Ignoring or not following health and safety policies increases the risk of children and adults experiencing harm, and may put you in breach of the law.

Lines of responsibility and reporting

The health and safety policy used in your workplace will identify the person who has overall responsibility for health and safety issues in the setting, probably the setting manager or headteacher. There may also be information in the policy, in the health and safety folder or on a poster in the staffroom about the specific health and safety responsibilities of other staff members. For example, a room leader may have health and safety responsibility for their particular room or area of the setting.

You should always report any accidents, incidents or hazards to the person who is identified as having health and safety responsibility for the area where this occurs. If you are unsure who to report to, it is best to report your concerns or observations to your supervisor or directly to the person with overall responsibility for the workplace.

Over to you!

Do you know where the health and safety policy for your setting is kept? What kinds of issues or topics are covered by the policy? Make sure that you have a look at it soon and that you understand the main points, especially the responsibilities it gives you for maintaining health and safety standards.

Over to you!

If one of the children in your care fell over and hurt themselves in your workplace tomorrow morning, who would you report this incident to? Is this the person who, according to the Accident Policy, you should report to? Make sure that you check the appropriate workplace policies to ensure that you understand the reporting procedure correctly.

What legislation affects the policies and procedures in the setting?

The Health and Safety at Work Act 1974

This Act is the main piece of health and safety law in the UK. It affects everyone in an early years or young person's setting, but focuses mainly on employers and employees. Under the Act, practitioners share responsibility for health and safety with the organisation that employs them. To meet their legal responsibilities, care and education organisations:

▶ carry out health and safety risk assessments

▶ develop health and safety procedures, such as fire evacuation procedures

▶ provide health and safety equipment, such as fire extinguishers, fire blankets and first aid boxes

▶ ensure that settings have built-in safety features, such as smoke alarms, fire exits and security fixtures (electronic pads on doors and window guards, for example)

▶ train their employees to follow health and safety procedures and use health and safety equipment and safety features appropriately

▶ provide a range of health and safety information and warning signs to alert people to safety features such as fire exits and first aid equipment, and to warn them about prohibited areas and activities (no smoking, for example).

All toys and play equipment used in children's settings must be safe, clean and non-toxic.

Practitioners carry out their legal responsibilities by:

▶ developing an awareness of health and safety law

▶ working in ways that follow health and safety guidelines, policies and procedures

▶ monitoring the care environment for health and safety hazards

▶ where it is safe to do so, dealing directly with hazards that present a health and safety risk

▶ reporting health and safety hazards or the failure of safety systems or procedures to a supervisor or manager.

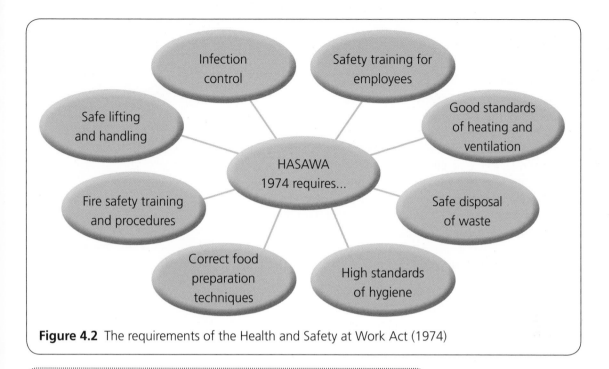

Figure 4.2 The requirements of the Health and Safety at Work Act (1974)

The Manual Handling Operations Regulations (1992)

These regulations cover all manual handling activities, such as lifting, lowering, pushing, pulling or carrying objects or people. You may have to lift babies, children and items of equipment as part of your work; you should learn how to do this properly so that you avoid injury. A large proportion of workplace injuries (fractures, sprains and serious back injuries) are due to poor manual handling skills. Employers have a duty to assess the risk of any activity that involves manual handling. They must put in place measures to reduce or avoid the risk. Employees have a responsibility to follow manual handling procedures and to co-operate on all manual handling issues.

Knowledge Assessment Task   1.1   1.2

Your manager has asked you to contribute to an induction training day for volunteers who are going to help out in your setting. She wants the volunteers to understand that health and safety has a very high priority in the setting. You have been asked to produce a leaflet or poster that:

▶ outlines key points contained in the health and safety policies and procedures of the work setting

▶ identifies the lines of responsibility and reporting for health and safety in the work setting.

Your leaflet or poster should be brief but must communicate key points that the volunteers need to understand about the health and safety policies and procedures that apply in your work setting.

Keep the leaflet or poster that you produce as evidence towards your assessment.

What is risk assessment?

By law, early years and young people's organisations are required to carry out formal risk assessments of their workplaces and of outside settings that children may visit. **Risk assessment** aims to identify potential risks to the health, safety and security of children, practitioners and anybody else who uses the care setting. The aim is to minimise risk by identifying hazards and putting measures in place to protect children and adults. You have an important role to play in contributing to and using risk assessments appropriately.

The risk assessment processes

Risk assessment recognises that play and childcare activities, equipment and the care setting itself can be hazardous. However, steps can be taken to remove or minimise the level of risk to people. All of the activities that take place within your workplace must be risk assessed. Similarly, all of the equipment and facilities have to be checked for hazards. The ultimate aim of a risk assessment is to ensure that people can use care settings without coming to any harm. The **Health and Safety Executive** has identified five stages of a risk assessment. These stages and their purpose are identified in Figure 4.3.

Key terms

Risk assessment: the process of evaluating the likelihood of a hazard actually causing harm

Health and Safety Executive: the government agency responsible for monitoring and enforcing health and safety laws in the workplace

Figure 4.3 The five stages of risk assessment

Stage	Key questions	Purpose
1. Identifying the hazards	• What are the hazards?	• To identify all hazards that could cause a risk
2. Estimating the risk	• Who is at risk?	• To evaluate the risk of hazards causing harm
3. Controlling the risk	• What needs to be done? • Who needs to do what?	• To identify risk control measures and responsibilities for reducing or removing the risk
4. Monitoring risk control measures	• Are the risk control measures being implemented?	• To monitor the implementation and effectiveness of risk control measures
5. Reassess the risk	• Is the risk controlled? • Can the risk be reduced still further?	• To evaluate the effectiveness of current risk control strategies • To identify new risks or changes to risk levels • To consider new strategies for controlling risk

The Management of Health and Safety at Work Regulations (1999)

These regulations place a legal duty on employers to carry out risk assessments in order to ensure a safe and healthy workplace. The risk assessments that are produced should clearly identify:

▶ the potential hazards and risks to the health and safety of employees and others in the workplace

▶ any preventive and protective measures that are needed to minimise risk and improve health and safety.

Many larger organisations employ people as health and safety officers to carry out their risk assessments and manage health and safety issues generally. In smaller organisations this might be the responsibility of one or more of the managers, or of a senior practitioner. Risk assessments must be:

▶ communicated to all practitioners and users of the setting

▶ implemented through the way practitioners work

▶ monitored and reviewed on a regular basis

▶ linked to health and safety policies and to staff training.

You have an important role to play in contributing to health and safety risk assessment, in using the risk assessments that are produced for your workplace and in ensuring that you minimise risk to yourself and others in the way that you work.

Knowledge Assessment Task   1.3

Claudia Kemp recently came to look around your workplace with her daughter Alice, aged 3 years. Claudia has looked after Alice at home until now, but is soon due to go back to work. Health and safety in the setting is one of Claudia's main concerns. She has been told by friends that all early years settings have to produce 'risk assessments' but doesn't understand what this involves or what happens in your work setting. Claudia has asked whether you can send her some information that:

1. explains risk assessment

2. describes how risk assessment is managed in your work setting.

Keep the notes you write for this activity as evidence towards your assessment.

How can you create a safe environment?

Risk assessment needs to be a part of every practitioner's approach to their daily work with children. You should:

▶ be alert to possible hazards

▶ understand the risks associated with each hazard

▶ report any health and safety concerns

▶ find ways of balancing risks with opportunities for children's learning and development.

Planning

Practitioners are responsible for keeping children safe, while also providing them with challenging and fun environments in which to play, learn and develop. Remember that children are less able to identify potential hazards than adults and don't always realise when an activity may be risky. So, the practitioner needs to find ways of promoting safety while also encouraging children to explore, experiment and take appropriate risks. Proper planning and organising of play and learning activities will enable you to identify potential hazards in advance and work out ways of minimising risk. Good planning will take into account the:

▶ developmental abilities and understanding of each child

▶ physical and intellectual demands of an activity or task

▶ potential hazards involved in an activity or task

▶ level of risk an activity or task poses for a particular child.

Your assessment criteria:

2.1 Explain why a safe but challenging environment is important for children and young people

2.4 Contribute to health and safety risk assessment in areas of the work setting and for off-site visits

Figure 4.4 Risk assessment issues when planning an activity

Issues to consider	Risk assessment questions to ask
Space	• Is there a suitable area in which to carry out the activity? • Is the space big enough and appropriate for the type of activity (such as sand and water play)? • Are there any specific hazards within the proposed area?
Equipment and materials	• Does any of the equipment or the materials present a hazard to the children who will use it? • Is there suitable safety equipment available for the planned activity (mats under climbing equipment, for example)?
Participants	• How many children can safely be involved in the activity? • How many adults will be needed to ensure safe supervision?
Support	• Who can provide help and assistance in the event of an accident or incident? • Is assistance needed from people with specific skills or experience? • Do any of the children taking part require extra support to take part safely?

Experienced practitioners become skilled at assessing and managing risk so that they can provide challenging and fun activities. It is important that children do take risks that help them to explore and develop – but in safe, supported environments.

Practical Assessment Task   2.1

The play and learning environments that are provided in children and young people's settings can never be risk free. The hazards within them must be minimised and risks must be assessed and carefully managed. At the same time, a balance needs to be achieved between providing a safe and a challenging environment. To provide evidence for this practical assessment activity, you should:

1. Describe an example of the way in which the environment in which you practise is safe but challenging for the children or young people who use it.

2. Explain why a safe but challenging environment is important for children and young people.

Your evidence for this assessment activity must be based on your practice and experience in a real work environment.

Over to you!

Using a scale of 1 (very low risk) to 5 (very high risk), identify the main hazard in each of the following situations. Estimate the risk and then briefly describe how the risk could be minimised.

1. *The playgroup kitchen floor has just been washed and is still wet.*
2. *A half-full laundry bag has been left in a corridor outside of the nursery toilets.*
3. *Three 4-year-old children have been left playing together in the garden while their babysitter quickly goes to the toilet indoors.*
4. *The scissors have been left out on a table after a craft activity.*
5. *A workman fitting a new security pad to the front door of the nursery has left the door wide open and unattended while he goes to his van for some tools.*

How can you ensure safety during off-site visits?

Taking children on outings is a good way of promoting their development. Trips must be planned carefully and a risk assessment carried out. Parts of the public environment may present particular hazards and risks (see Figure 4.5).

Your assessment criteria:

2.4 Contribute to health and safety risk assessment in areas of the work setting and for off-site visits

Figure 4.5 Hazards in public environments

Public environment	Possible hazards
Retail area	Modern retail developments often have good access and facilities for people with mobility problems. However, hazards include: • large crowds • tables and chairs outside cafes • wet floors • delivery vehicles • boxes of goods and rubbish bags.
Swimming pool	• falling on wet floors • boisterous behaviour • diving in at the shallow end • crowded areas.
Public park	• vehicles (e.g. tractors, grass cutters, refuse collection vehicles) • other users of the park (e.g. joggers, cyclists, people playing sports, people displaying anti-social behaviour) • poorly maintained play equipment, paths and grassy areas • overflowing rubbish pins, broken glass, needles • dog and other animal excrement.
Public transport	A significant number of pedestrians and drivers die in road traffic accidents each year. Other hazards associated with public transport include: • crossing the road too slowly or at an inappropriate place • not wearing a seat belt • standing too close to the edge of a railway platform • falling on the stairs or in the aisle of a bus • getting on the wrong bus or train.
Beach	• crowds, especially on hot days • fast or unpredictable tides, especially in bad weather • vehicles and boats using the beach • strong sunshine • children and vulnerable people may get lost • inexperienced swimmers may get into difficulties.

Visiting the off-site venue before a trip is always a good idea. This will enable you to identify hazards and assess risks, as well as to plan the best way to get to and use the off-site venue. You will have a more realistic idea of the level of supervision that will be needed.

The Health and Safety Executive (www.hse.gov.uk) suggests that you should be able to answer the following 10 questions when planning an off-site visit:

1. What are the main objectives of the visit?

2. What is 'Plan B' if the main objectives can't be achieved?

3. What could go wrong? Does the risk assessment cover the following?

   ▶ the main activity

   ▶ Plan B

   ▶ travel arrangements

   ▶ emergency procedures

   ▶ staff numbers, gender and skill mixes

   ▶ generic and site-specific hazards and risks (including for Plan B)

   ▶ variable hazards (including environmental hazards and those due to participants' personal abilities, and the cut-off points)

4. What information will be provided for parents?

5. What consents will be sought?

6. What opportunities will parents have to ask questions (including any arrangements for a parents' meeting)?

7. What assurances are there of the leaders' competencies?

8. What are the communication arrangements?

9. What are the arrangements for supervision, both during activities and any free time – is there a Code of Conduct?

10. What are the arrangements for monitoring and reviewing the visit?

Practical Assessment Task   2.4

This task focuses on the ways you have contributed to health and safety risk assessment. You will need to demonstrate that you can identify health and safety hazards and contribute to the assessment of risk in relation to:

▶ activities within your workplace

▶ activities that take place off site.

Your contribution to the risk assessment process should be witnessed and verified by your assessor or by a senior colleague whose observations and comments about your risk assessment ability are documented in a way that is acceptable to your assessor. Your evidence for this assessment activity must be based on your practice and experience in a real work environment.

Your assessment criteria:

3.1 Identify non-medical incidents and emergencies that may occur in the work setting

3.2 Outline the actions to take in response to the following situations:
  a. fires
  b. security incidents
  c. emergency incidents

Would you know what to do in an emergency?

Early years and young people's practitioners need to know how to react when a non-medical incident or emergency occurs. An appropriate and timely response can prevent situations from getting worse and should be sufficient to protect children and adults from further harm or injury.

Non-medical incidents and emergencies

Early years and young people's settings should have policies and procedures for responding to non-medical incidents and emergencies. Examples of such situations are identified in Figure 4.6.

Settings have to be prepared for emergency situations and must have appropriate procedures in place so that staff can respond and children can be kept safe. It is important to raise the alarm and to follow the emergency procedure as soon as you realise that a non-medical incident or emergency has happened.

Figure 4.6 Examples of non-medical incidents and emergencies

Getting help

Emergency situations are extremely varied but, fortunately, don't happen very often. However, all members of staff in a setting should know who to call for help and how to contact the emergency services. The names and telephone numbers of first aiders should be displayed on posters or on noticeboards in public areas of the setting. If a situation is serious, a 999 call should be made. The emergency operator will ask for the following information:

▶ which services are required (police, ambulance and/or fire service)

▶ the caller's name and the number of the phone they are calling from

▶ the location of the accident or incident

▶ if relevant, the number of casualties involved

▶ what has happened (including signs, symptoms and state of any casualties)

▶ whether any of the casualties are unconscious.

It is important for the caller to listen carefully to the emergency operator, to provide the information they ask for and to remain as calm as possible, even though this may be difficult in the circumstances.

Fire procedures

Fire emergencies are frightening and can be very dangerous. There should be a detailed fire and evacuation policy for your work setting. You must be familiar with this. You should also take part in all fire drills and know what your role is in any evacuation procedure.

If you are the first person to notice a fire (or smoke), you should raise the alarm, either activating a fire alarm, phoning 999 or instructing someone else to do this. Other actions to take include:

▶ closing doors and windows to prevent draughts fanning the flames

▶ ensuring that all children are moved away from the area and are supervised by adults

▶ evacuating the building and going to the agreed assembly point

▶ reassuring children by staying calm, providing information about what is happening and what they need to do

▶ carrying out a head count of children and adults to ensure that everybody has left the building and is accounted for

▶ tackling the fire, only if it is small, manageable and you have the correct equipment

Over to you!

What do the emergency procedures in your work setting say about the following?

▶ *raising the alarm*

▶ *getting help and assistance from the emergency services*

▶ *evacuating the building*

▶ *the assembly point outside of the building*

▶ *protecting and reassuring children during emergency incidents*

Over to you!

Have you taken part in a fire drill at your workplace in the last 3 months? Can you remember where the assembly point was?

What other types of incidents and emergencies can happen?

Missing children

Carrying out risk assessments, following security procedures and ensuring that you know what each child is doing are important ways of preventing children from getting lost or going missing. However, despite the use of security measures, incidents do happen. A child might wander away or become detached from the rest of their group when walking in a crowded shopping area, playing in the park or on a trip to the beach, for example. Alternatively, a child may wander out through an open door or gate, or may deliberately run away if they are upset about something. Your workplace will have a procedure for dealing with these kinds of situations. You should know what this says and be able to put the procedure into action as soon as you realise what has happened. It is likely that the procedure will involve:

▶ informing the person in charge that the child is lost or missing

▶ searching the care setting or the area where the child was last seen

▶ ensuring that all other children are supervised and remain safe while the search is carried out

▶ informing parents and possibly the police if the child cannot be located quickly

▶ giving the police information about the child's age, appearance, clothing and distinguishing features

▶ reviewing existing risk assessments, policies and procedures after the event to try to prevent a similar incident happening again.

Security incidents

It is important to consider the security of the setting where you work as this affects the safety of children, families and practitioners. Security incidents can occur as a result of:

▶ intruders or unauthorised people entering the building

▶ children leaving the building through unlocked doors or windows.

Early years and young people's organisations can minimise the risk of security incidents by:

▶ having a single entry and exit point that is controlled by staff

▶ using a security system, such as a keypad or locked door, to control entry and exit

Your assessment criteria:

3.1 Identify non-medical incidents and emergencies that may occur in the work setting

3.2 Outline the actions to take in response to the following situations:
d. fires
e. security incidents
f. emergency incidents

- ▶ ensuring that identity badges are worn by staff and visitors, and that only authorised and accompanied visitors are allowed entry

- ▶ training staff members to approach and politely challenge visitors who are not wearing appropriate visitor badges or who appear in the setting (including the outside areas) unexpectedly

- ▶ ensuring that children are only allowed to leave the setting at an agreed pick-up time and are only released to a known, authorised person (parent or other relative, childminder or carer).

You can help minimise the risk of security incidents by:

- ▶ never lending your identity badge to anyone

- ▶ never revealing the keypad code to non-staff members

- ▶ if you are asked, carrying out any checks thoroughly (such as making sure windows and doors are locked)

- ▶ politely challenging any unexpected visitors without a visitor badge (no genuine visitor would be offended by your concern for security)

- ▶ reporting any concerns that you have about visitors or attempts to inappropriately enter your workplace

- ▶ reporting any apparent attempts to break into the building

- ▶ if you have any serious suspicions or become aware of an intruder, seeking help quickly, including calling on-site security staff or the police.

Knowledge Assessment Task   3.1   3.2

Claudia Kemp and her husband, Adam, appreciated the information you sent them about risk assessment (see page 000). They have now arranged a second visit to your setting before deciding whether to apply for a place for their daughter, Alice. Claudia and Adam remain very interested in health and safety issues. In particular, they want to know:

1. What kinds of non-medical emergencies can happen in a setting like yours?

2. What staff at the setting would do in the event of:

    a. a fire

    b. a security incident

    c. an emergency incident that occurs while Alice is at the setting.

You should produce a summary of what staff will do in the event of a non-medical incident or emergency.

Keep any written work that you produce for this activity as evidence towards your assessment.

Know what to do in the event of a child or young person becoming ill or injured

Your assessment criteria:

4.1 Identify the signs and symptoms which may indicate that a child or young person is injured or unwell

4.2 Identify circumstances when children or young people may need urgent medical attention

Key terms

Signs: observable changes associated with illness or disease

Symptoms: a change in normal functioning or feeling that is noticed by a person and which indicates they are, or are becoming, unwell

What should you do if a child is injured or unwell?

Accidents happen unexpectedly in all early years and young people's settings and children can become unwell for a variety of reasons. In either of these situations, a child may need medical help. Part of your work role is to monitor children for signs of illness or injury, and to respond appropriately by getting help when necessary.

Identifying signs and symptoms

The **signs** of illness are those things that you can *see*, such as a visible change in a child's normal appearance and behaviour – becoming pale in colour or not having the energy to play in the usual way. Children often know when they are unwell and will tell you about **symptoms** that they feel, such as feeling sick or having a headache. Observing and talking to children should enable you to identify when they are unwell or have an injury.

When is urgent medical attention needed?

Children and young people can become seriously ill very suddenly. Depending on their age and ability, some children may be unable to tell you that they are feeling unwell, so you must always be alert to changes in their behaviour, indicating pain, nausea or dizziness for example.

In most cases when a child becomes sick or complains of feeling unwell, it is sufficient to look after them until their parent or a carer arrives to collect them. In life-threatening or other serious situations,

Over to you!

Can you think of any recent situations in which you noticed a child exhibiting the signs or symptoms of illness or injury? What was it you noticed and what were the causes of these signs or symptoms?

the emergency services should be contacted immediately. For example, you should call 999 for an ambulance if a child exhibits any, or a combination, of the following signs of acute illness:

▶ difficulty breathing

▶ blueness around the lips

▶ an inability to swallow

▶ high fever

▶ convulsions (fitting)

▶ very cold extremities (hands and feet)

▶ heat exhaustion or severe sunburn

▶ dehydration (not passing urine, lethargy, sunken eyes, dry or cracked lips)

▶ pale and clammy skin

▶ burns or scalds to the skin

▶ becoming floppy, unresponsive or unconscious

▶ an open wound that won't stop bleeding or where the blood pumps out

▶ following a head injury, confusion, headache, vomiting or blurred vision

▶ meningitis symptoms (stiff neck, fever, headache, a rash that doesn't fade when pressed by a glass).

A child should see a qualified medical practitioner if they:

▶ vomit

▶ develop diarrhoea

▶ develop a high temperature

▶ cut themselves or fracture a bone in a fall

▶ develop a large or severe bruise

▶ are bitten by an animal or stung by an insect.

Chronic medical conditions

If you look after children with chronic medical conditions, you need to know how to provide appropriate care for them. This information should be in their records; you can also ask a child's parents or carers what you should look out for and need to do (see Figure 4.7).

What is your role in an emergency?

As a learner or relatively junior member of staff, you will not be expected to take charge in an emergency situation in your workplace. However, you can perform an important role in assisting colleagues who ask for your help and in supporting the children who may be directly or indirectly affected by an accident, incident or emergency.

If you are the first on the scene after an accident or incident has occurred, you should tell other people immediately. You should listen carefully and do as you are asked. They may, for example, ask you to:

▶ call for an ambulance or other emergency service (see page 000)

▶ get the first aid kit or some other equipment (towels, water or protective gloves, for example)

▶ find a trained first aider or a senior member of staff

▶ look after and reassure the other children.

Accidents and unexpected emergencies can cause anxiety for both children and adults. Calming and reassuring others, while keeping them away from the scene, is a vital role.

Your assessment criteria:

4.1 Identify the signs and symptoms which may indicate that a child or young person is injured or unwell

4.2 Identify circumstances when children or young people may need urgent medical attention

4.3 Outline own role and responsibilities in the event of a child or young person requiring urgent medical attention

Over to you!

A senior colleague or qualified member of staff asks you to help during an emergency. What is your role?

Figure 4.7 Signs of crisis associated with chronic conditions

Condition	Look out for...
Allergy	Allergic reactions (in severe cases **anaphylactic shock**): many varied signs depending on the allergy including rashes or hives, swelling of the tongue and difficulty breathing, vomiting, intestinal pain, loss of consciousness and heart attack.
Asthma	Acute asthma attack: inability to breathe normally, failure to respond to inhaler medication.
Diabetes	**Hypoglycaemia**: abnormally low levels of blood sugar that can lead to unconsciousness and seizures. **Hyperglycaemia**: abnormally high levels of blood sugar that can result in frequent hunger, thirst and urination.
Epilepsy	Seizures or fitting: from uncontrolled shaking (convulsions) to a brief loss of consciousness.
Sickle cell anaemia	**Sickle cell crisis**: signs can include pain, fever, pallor, difficulty breathing, fatigue.

Reporting and reviewing an incident

You may need to complete an accident or incident form (or a page in a book used for this purpose) once the accident or incident has been dealt with. You will need to describe what happened as accurately as you can, and how you and others responded. Depending on the severity of the incident, you may also be offered the chance to debrief; this involves talking to your supervisor or manager about what happened, how it affected you and what you learnt from the incident. As well as being a useful learning opportunity, debriefing a situation in a supportive environment will help you deal with lingering anxieties.

Over to you!

Would you know where to find the first aid kit if you were asked to get it as soon as you started work tomorrow morning? Find out where the first aid kit is kept in your workplace and what it contains. You should also find out what the procedure is for checking and restocking the contents.

It can be useful to debrief after an incident.

Knowledge Assessment Task   4.1   4.2   4.3

You need to be aware of the signs and symptoms of illness, particularly those illnesses that can develop quickly into serious health problems.

1. Produce a leaflet or poster for people who work in early years and young people's settings that identifies the signs and symptoms of meningococcal septicaemia (meningitis).

2. When should urgent medical attention be sought for children or young people? Produce a diagram or table identifying a range of circumstances when this might be necessary.

3. Outline what you see as your role and your responsibilities when you notice that a child requires urgent medical attention.

Keep any notes or written work that you produce for this activity as evidence towards your assessment.

Key terms

Anaphylactic shock: a severe, rapid and sometimes fatal hypersensitivity to a substance resulting in tissue swelling that can prevent breathing and which may cause a heart attack

Hyperglycaemia: abnormally high levels of blood sugar

Hypoglycaemia: abnormally low levels of blood sugar

Sickle cell crisis: acute symptoms of sickle cell disease often brought on by physical stress, such as infection, dehydration, extremes of temperature, pregnancy, etc.

Be able to follow the work setting procedures for reporting and recording accidents, incidents, emergencies and illnesses

How do you report an accident, incident, emergency or illness?

All accidents, illness and emergencies that occur in early years and young people's settings must be recorded and reported. The procedure to be followed and the amount of reporting detail needed tends to depend on the seriousness of the accident or incident. In all circumstances, records must be completed accurately as soon as possible after the event.

Reporting procedures

Your work setting should have a set of accident and incident policies and procedures; you should know what these say. You should also know which forms, books or computer-based records are completed when an accident, incident, emergency or illness occurs.

Try to fill out any documentation while your memory is still fresh. Generally, reporting forms ask:

▶ what happened

▶ who was involved

▶ the nature of any injuries or symptoms of illness

▶ the action taken

▶ the outcome.

It is important to complete the documentation even if you think that an injury or illness is relatively minor; serious consequences may only show later. You must always write accurately and objectively – never make up or exaggerate what has happened. If you were not present or did not see exactly what happened, you must state this and you should ask others witnesses to complete a report. The manager of your work setting should review the accident and incident book regularly to assess whether action needs to be taken to minimise the risk of repeat occurrences.

Reporting serious accidents and incidents

If a serious accident or incident happens in your work setting or during an off-site visit, the senior manager has to report this to a range of other people and organisations including:

▶ other people in organisation's management team

▶ any governing body or committee

Your assessment criteria:

5.1 Describe the reporting procedures for accidents, incidents, emergencies and illnesses

5.2 Complete workplace documentation for recording accidents, incidents, emergencies and illnesses

▶ the regulatory body that is responsible for care standards, such as Ofsted (England), Education and Training Inspectorate (Northern Ireland), Care Commission (Scotland) or Estyn (Wales)

▶ in the most serious cases, the Health and Safety Executive (HSC), which may carry out a formal investigation.

In all cases, the child's parents should be informed about what has occurred as soon as possible, either by phone or by sending a note home with the child that day. In some circumstances, parents will need to take their child home early, to a doctor or to hospital. When you speak to a parent remember to be calm and clear, giving them the necessary information. If their child is not badly hurt, reassure them of this at the *beginning* of the conversation. If the situation is more serious, reassure them that everything that should be done is being done, making sure they know where to go and what to do.

Case study

Jan is a nursery nurse working at an infant school. The Year 1 children are being taken on a Forest School trip today. The children are getting off the mini-bus when Terry spots a squirrel scurrying between trees. As he points at it, several of the children run towards it. None of them realise that there is a ditch between them and the squirrel. Four of the children fall head first into the ditch and begin crying loudly. Jan quickly helps the four children out and checks them for cuts and scrapes. Everyone is fine and quickly recovers, except Oliver who seems to have a bump on his forehead. Oliver says that he has a headache and feels 'queasy'.

1. Describe the reporting procedures that Jan would have to follow if she was employed at your work setting.

2. What signs and symptoms suggest that Oliver may be injured or unwell?

Practical Assessment Task   5.1   5.2

This task requires you to demonstrate that you are able to follow the reporting procedures of your work setting. Following an actual accident, incident, emergency or illnesses involving a child or adult in the setting, complete the appropriate documentation to report and record what happened.

Your assessor will need to check that the documentation has been completed correctly and that you have followed the workplace recording procedure. Keep a copy of any records that you complete as evidence towards your assessment. Your evidence for this assessment activity must be based on your practice and experience in a real work environment.

Why is it important to prevent the spread of infection?

Infection control procedures prevent the spread of disease-causing **bacteria** and **viruses** from one person to another. The microorganisms that cause infections are present in everyday life. Usually, children and young people build up **immunity** to common infections, suffering only minor illnesses in the process. However, children can be vulnerable to new and existing strains of infection, and occasionally suffer significant health problems.

Infection control procedures

Early years practitioners should always follow basic infection control procedures. These include:

- maintaining good standards of personal hygiene, relating to dress, hair care, footwear and oral hygiene
- using appropriately personal protective clothing, such as aprons, gloves and masks
- following standard health, safety and hygiene precautions in the workplace
- washing hands regularly and thoroughly (see page 000)
- ensuring that equipment such as nappy changing tables and mats are thoroughly cleaned and disinfected between uses
- safely disposing of waste in the correct bags, bins or containers.

Infection control documentation

There should be a detailed set of infection control policies and procedures relating to your workplace. You should know what these say about:

- hand washing
- use of personal protective equipment
- cleaning standards and procedures
- dealing with spillages (blood, vomit, diarrhoea and other body fluids)
- handling soiled clothes and laundry
- dealing with 'sharps'
- touching and looking after animals (for example, rabbits, guinea pigs, hamsters)
- coughing and sneezing

Your assessment criteria:

6.1 Outline procedures for infection control in own work setting

6.2 Describe personal protective clothing that is used to prevent spread of infection

Key terms

Bacteria: single-celled organisms, some of which can cause disease and others of which are helpful to human beings

Immunity: resistance to disease

Virus: an infectious agent that may cause disease in the human body

- outbreaks of infectious illnesses such as chickenpox, measles and **norovirus**, for example
- infestations of head lice.

Using personal protective clothing

Personal protective clothing and equipment plays an important part in infection control, being a barrier to the transmission of microorganisms from one person to another. Using the personal protective clothing and equipment not only reduces the risk that you will pass on an infection, but reduces the risk that you will contract one. Examples of personal protective clothing and equipment generally available in settings include:

- disposable aprons
- disposable gloves
- face masks
- eye-protector goggles.

Early years practitioners may need to use these items of equipment when:

- changing nappies
- helping children to use the toilet or potty
- caring for children who are injured or unwell (especially bleeding or vomiting)
- picking up and washing soiled clothing or linen
- cleaning up body fluid spillages
- cleaning out animal cages (e.g. rabbits, guinea pigs, hamsters).

You should always dispose of personal protective equipment in the appropriate waste bin – do not reuse aprons, gloves or masks. Remember to wash your hands before and after using them (see page 000).

Over to you!

Go to the Health Protection Agency website (www.hpa.org. uk) and download a copy of Guidance on Infection Control in Schools and other Child Care Settings. This provides more information and guidance on dealing with infection control issues in early years and young people's settings.

Key terms

Norovirus: a virus causing gastroenteritis, sometimes called 'winter vomiting virus' though it may occur at any time of year

Practical Assessment Task   6.1   6.2

The prevention of infection is an important part of every practitioner's role in children and young people's settings. As a safe and competent practitioner you should be able to:

- outline procedures for infection control in your work setting
- describe the range of personal protective clothing that is used to prevent the spread of infection in your workplace.

Keep any notes you write as evidence towards your completion of this assessment activity. Your evidence for this assessment activity must be based on your practice and experience in a real work environment.

How do you wash and dry your hands properly?

Regular, effective hand hygiene is the single most important infection control measure you can undertake in an early years or young people's setting. Washing your hands thoroughly with a decontamination agent and drying them properly prevents growth of bacteria and viruses. You should always wash and dry your hands *before* and *after*:

▶ helping a child to use the toilet or potty

▶ changing a child's nappy or soiled clothes (remember to wear gloves)

▶ using the toilet yourself

▶ preparing or serving food

▶ taking part in messy play or outside activities.

Over to you!

When do you wash your hands at work? Think of the types of activities and tasks you do and reflect on the infection risks that these might pose. Are you protecting yourself and others appropriately through regular and thorough hand washing?

1. Lather hands with soap

2. Rub both palms together

3. Rub each fingers and between fingers

4. Rub palms with finger nails

5. Rub back of hand with finger nails

6. Wash thoroughly and towel dry

You should demonstrate good hand hygiene to the children you care for and encourage them to develop effective hand washing habits too.

Case study

Audrey has been a volunteer nursery assistant at the Elim Preschool group for 2 years. She works at the nursery every Tuesday and sometimes brings Buster, her Labrador dog. The children like Buster a lot and spend time patting and stroking him. Buster is very placid and obedient; he is used to children and seems to enjoy being in the nursery. However, following a visit by an environmental health inspector from the local authority, Audrey has been told not to bring Buster to the nursery. She is quite upset about this as she doesn't understand how Buster could be an infection control risk.

1. Identify reasons why Buster may be an infection control risk at the nursery.

2. Explain how Buster's presence might lead to hygiene problems at the nursery.

3. Suggest how infection control risks can be minimised to allow children to touch and play with animals in early years settings.

How can you dispose of waste safely?

The various kinds of clinical and everyday waste that are produced in early years settings present an infection hazard unless they are dealt with correctly. There should be a detailed waste disposal policy in your workplace and a clear set of procedures relating to waste disposal. You need to know about and must follow the policy and procedures.

If you are unsure about what to do with a certain type of waste, always ask your supervisor or a senior colleague for assistance. The waste disposal policy and procedures should identify how to dispose of different types of waste (see Figure 4.8) and will also give information on how the waste should be stored and removed.

Your assessment criteria:

6.3 Demonstrate use of personal protective clothing to avoid spread of infection

6.4 Demonstrate how to wash and dry hands to avoid the spread of infection

6.5 Demonstrate safe disposal of waste to avoid the spread of infection

Figure 4.8 Methods of disposal for different types of waste

Type of waste	Method of disposal
Body products	Blood, urine, faeces, vomit and sputum should be cleaned up using the spillage procedure and flushed down the toilet or sink, as appropriate. All spillage areas should be disinfected following the local policy and procedures.
Clinical waste	Dressings, plasters, bandages, gloves, aprons, nappies and pads should be put in clinical waste bags in foot-operated bins. This should be stored in a designated area and removed by a specialist waste contractor.
Household waste	Dispose in the domestic rubbish bin using the waste disposal system provided by the local authority.
Leftover food	Put leftovers in the kitchen bin or food bin as soon as the meal is finished.
Linen and clothing	Soiled sheets, towels and clothing should be kept and washed separately from non-soiled linen. They should be washed as soon as possible after soiling.
Recyclable waste	Place recyclable materials in the appropriate recycling bin. In some settings, special packages or bags are provided for clinical equipment that will be sterilised and reused.
Sharps	Needles, blades and other sharps should be disposed of in a special sharps bin. Broken glass or pottery should be wrapped carefully and disposed of in the domestic waste bin or according to the local procedure.

Over to you!

Which of these types of waste do you have to dispose of in your work setting? Do you know the correct method of disposal for each of them?

Case study

Laura Henry recently obtained a job as a Foundation Stage classroom assistant at Redwood Community School. Last week was Laura's first week. An incident occurred while she was working with Doreen, an experienced classroom assistant, and Mrs Phelps, the class teacher. While Doreen was on her lunch break Laura realised that Charlene, a shy 4-year-old girl with Down's syndrome, had wet and soiled her trousers, and needed cleaning and changing. Laura had never dealt with this situation before and wasn't sure what to do. Because she didn't know how to deal with the situation, Laura waited until Doreen returned from her break and then pointed out that Charlene seemed upset about something.

1. Identify reasons why Laura should have asked for help sooner in this situation.

2. Describe the potential hazards that need to be dealt with in order to provide appropriate and safe care for Charlene.

3. What should Laura have done to maximise health and safety and minimise the risk of infection in the situation described?

Practical Assessment Task   6.3   6.4   6.5

Your competence as a practitioner depends on your ability to demonstrate safe practice. For this assessment task you need to demonstrate to your assessor that you are able to:

▶ use personal protective clothing to avoid the spread of infection

▶ wash and dry your hands effectively to avoid the spread of infection

▶ dispose of waste safely to avoid the spread of infection.

You will need to demonstrate these skills in a practical, work-based situation. One way of doing this would be to demonstrate that you are able to apply basic infection control procedures when changing a child's soiled nappy. You may be able to identify another situation in which you can demonstrate these skills but should agree on the suitability of this with your assessor.

Know the work setting's procedures for receiving, storing and administering medicines

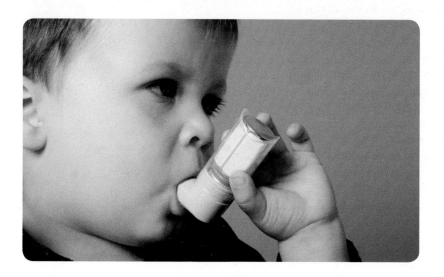

Your assessment criteria:

7.1 Identify the procedures of the work setting governing the receipt, storage and administration of medicines

7.2 Explain how the procedures of the work setting protect both children and young people and practitioners

Why is it important to manage medicines correctly?

Children and young people who use early years and other educational, youth service and childcare settings may require medication because they are recovering from an **acute illness**, have had an operation or because they have a **chronic condition** or health problem. Examples include children who have asthma and need to use inhalers, and children with diabetes who need **insulin**.

It is important to use and store medicine correctly so that the children who need the medication benefit from its effects, and so that there is no risk to other people in the setting.

Medication management

The setting where you work should have a detailed policy and a set of procedures relating to receiving, storing and administering medicines. The policy and procedures will provide detailed guidance on issues such as:

▶ where and how medicines are stored in the setting

▶ who is authorised to administer medicines to children with medical needs

▶ the procedure for administering medicines to children

▶ how and where the administration of medication to children should be recorded

▶ the importance of gaining informed, written parental **consent** before any medicine can be given to a child

▶ when and how to inform parents about the administration of medication to their children.

Key terms

Acute illness: an illness that occurs suddenly and doesn't last very long

Chronic condition: a prolonged or recurring condition requiring ongoing treatment

Consent: permission to do something

Insulin: a hormone that controls blood sugar levels

Over to you!

Do any of the children in your care need to be given medicines while they are attending your workplace? Do you understand why they need to have these medicines?

The importance of procedures

The policy and procedures relating to the receipt, storage and administration of medicine should be adhered to strictly. This aim of the policy is to protect against medication errors; the dose and frequency of medication must be very clearly stated and must always be followed exactly. Children should not be given medicine to pacify them and must never be given medication that has not been specifically prescribed for them by a registered medical practitioner. There is a considerable risk of harming a child if they are given medication that has not been prescribed for them or if the medication that they do need is not given at the times and in the doses prescribed.

Over to you!

Do you know where medicines are stored and administered in your workplace? Who has access to and responsibility for these medicines?

Children should only be given medicine if their parents consent and all workplace procedures are followed.

Knowledge Assessment Task 7.1 7.2

Your workplace is taking part in a 'Safeguarding Children' study day at a local FE college. You have been asked to make a short presentation about the way in which medicines for children are received, stored and administered in your workplace so that children are protected from harm. The college tutor has asked you to produce a leaflet or handout that:

1. identifies the procedures used in your work setting governing the receipt, storage and administration of medicines

2. explains how the procedures of your work setting protect children, young people and practitioners.

Keep any notes you write as evidence towards your assessment. Your evidence for this assessment activity should ideally be based on your practice and experience in a real work environment.

Are you ready for assessment?

AC	What do you know now?	Assessment task	✓
1.1	The health and safety policies and procedures used in your work setting	Page 93	
1.2	Who is responsible for health and safety issues and how you should report health and safety problems in your work setting	Page 93	
1.3	The meaning of risk management and how this is managed in your work setting	Page 95	
3.1	A range of non-medical incidents and emergencies that may occur in your work setting	Page 103	
3.2	The procedures for dealing with: • fires • security incidents • emergency incidents	Page 103	
4.1	The signs and symptoms which may indicate that a child or young person is injured or unwell	Page 107	
4.2	The circumstances when children or young people may need urgent medical attention	Page 107	
4.3	Your own role and responsibilities in dealing with a child or young person who requires urgent medical attention	Page 107	

Your tutor or assessor may want to observe you actually doing this in your placement or work setting.

AC	What can you do now?	Assessment task	✓
2.1	Explain why a safe but challenging environment is important for children and young people	Page 97	
2.2	Identify the differences between a risk and a hazard	Page 89	
2.3	Identify potential hazards to the health, safety and security of children or young people in your work setting	Page 89	
2.4	Contribute to health and safety risk assessment in areas of the work setting and for off-site visits	Page 99	
5.1	Describe how to report an accident, incident, emergency or illness in your work setting	Page 109	
5.2	Complete workplace documentation for recording accidents, incidents, emergencies and illnesses	Page 109	
6.1	Outline the procedures for infection control in your work setting	Page 111	
6.2	Describe personal protective clothing that is used in your work setting to prevent spread of infection	Page 111	
6.3	Demonstrate use of personal protective clothing to avoid spread of infection	Page 115	
6.4	Demonstrate how to wash and dry hands to avoid spread of infection	Page 115	
6.5	Demonstrate safe disposal of waste to avoid the spread of infection	Page 115	
7.1	Identify the procedures of the work setting that affect the management of medication	Page 117	
7.2	Explain how the procedures of the work setting are used to protect both children and young people and practitioners	Page 117	

5 | Child and young person development (TDA 2.1)

Assessment of this unit

This unit is all about the development of children and young people. It covers the major milestones of development and some of the factors that can influence development at different ages and stages. This unit also explores the effect of transitions experienced by children and young people and the potential impact on their development and behaviour.

The assessment of this unit is all knowledge based (things that you need to know about), but it is also very important to be able to apply your knowledge practically in the real work environment.

In order to successfully complete this unit, you will need to produce evidence of your knowledge, as shown in the 'What you need to know' chart opposite. Your tutor or assessor will help you to prepare for your assessment and the tasks suggested in this chapter will help you to create the evidence that you need.

CHAPTER 5

AC   What you need to know

1.1	The expected pattern of development in children and young people from birth to 19 years, including physical, communication, intellectual, social, emotional and behavioural development
1.2	How different aspects of development can affect one another
2.1	The factors that can influence the development of children and young people, including background, health and environment
2.2	The importance of recognising and responding to concerns about the development of children and young people
3.1	Identify the transitions experienced by most children and young people
3.2	Identify transitions that only some children and young people may experience, e.g. bereavement
3.3	How transitions may affect the development and behaviour of children and young people

There is no practical assessment for this unit, but your tutor or assessor may question you about some of the following points:

What you need to do

Apply your knowledge about the development of children and young people to your practice in the real work environment

Apply your knowledge about the effects of transitions on the development of children and young people in the real work environment

This unit also links to some of the other mandatory units:

CCLDMU 2.2	Contribute to the support of child and young person development
TDA 2.9	Support children and young people's positive behaviour
MU 2.8	Contribute to the support of the positive environments for children and young people

Some of your learning will be repeated in these units and will give you the chance to review your knowledge and understanding.

What is development?

Development is a process that every child will progress through in his or her own way. Some children will begin to walk at a very early age and be later learning to talk. Equally, some young people will experience puberty at an earlier age than others.

Development is not about physical growth, but refers to the process of **maturing** and developing skills and abilities. Development norms or milestones provide an average guide for assessing a child's progress, but it is important to remember that there is a very wide range of normal, and every child or young person is an individual.

This unit will examine development in the following areas:

▶ *Physical development:* the development of physical skills, including **gross motor skills** like running, skipping and kicking a ball, and **fine motor skills** like grasping, fastening buttons and using scissors.

▶ *Communication and intellectual (**cognitive**) development:* the development of language and thinking skills, including learning to talk, speaking in sentences and developing knowledge and understanding, imagination, memory and problem-solving skills (like working out what things do and why things happen).

▶ *Social, emotional and behavioural development:* the development of security, confidence and independence, learning how to manage feelings and behaviour and learning how to get along with others.

Aspects of development

All areas of development are linked and influence each other. For example, in using a computer, a child needs the physical, fine motor skills to operate the mouse and the keyboard, but also the intellectual skills to understand the programme and the level of confidence and independence to try things for themselves. Different aspects of development can also affect one another. For example, when learning to walk, a child may have well developed gross motor skills to balance and co-ordinate their movements, but may lack the confidence to let go of their parent's hand in order to walk by themselves.

When studying development, it is important to do so in a **holistic** way and to consider all aspects of development together.

Your assessment criteria:

1.1 Describe the expected pattern of development in children and young people from birth to 19 years, including physical, communication, intellectual, social, emotional and behavioural development

1.2 Describe, with examples, how different aspects of development can affect one another

Key terms

Cognitive: the ability to think and make sense of experiences

Fine motor skills: the use of hand and finger movements

Gross motor skills: the use of large body movements

Holistic: emphasising the importance of the whole child

Maturing: the process of becoming fully developed

Development from birth to 3 years

The first 3 years of life is a period of very rapid development. Children change from being totally dependent infants to active, competent children who can do most things for themselves.

Figure 5.1 Development from birth to 3 years

Area of development	Expected pattern of development
Physical	Children grow and develop at an amazing rate during this time. Their bodies become stronger and they learn to co-ordinate their movements. Most 18 month olds can walk by themselves (although they will often be quite unsteady) and by the age of 3 years, most children can run, jump and pedal a tricycle. Most 2 year olds can scribble with a chunky crayon and by the age of 3 years, most children can thread large beads and build a tower with eight blocks.
Communication and intellectual	Children progress rapidly in both their communication and thinking skills. They change from crying, gurgling babies who rely on reflex behaviour and basic responses, to children who can speak in sentences, ask questions and use problem-solving skills to work out things for themselves. Most 3 year olds can communicate using simple sentences and can usually understand basic concepts like size (e.g. bigger and smaller) and colour (e.g. matching primary colours).
Social, emotional and behavioural	Children make a lot of progress in the first 3 years of life. Babies are totally dependent on adults for all of their care, but by the age of 3 years, most children are confident and independent individuals, although many 3 year olds will still become upset when faced with major separation situations, such as starting nursery.

Key terms

Concepts: ideas that form the building bocks of our ideas and understanding

Over to you!

Make a list of all the different areas of development (physical, communication, intellectual, social, emotional and behavioural) involved in the following activities:

► a 10 month old, sitting with a familiar adult and looking at a picture book together
► a 3 year old, dressing up and 'playing at shopkeepers' with other children
► a 6 year old performing in a school play
► a 10 year old playing football on a team.

Development from 3 to 5 years

Between the ages of 3 and 5, children make great strides in their development. They are physically stronger, their language skills progress very rapidly and they become much more independent and capable. See Figure 5.2.

Figure 5.2 Development from 3 to 5 years

Area of development	Expected pattern of development
Physical	Children develop more body co-ordination of their gross motor skills and learn to control their movements more skilfully. Fine motor skills are also developing as children learn how to use their manipulative skills to complete more complex tasks By the age of 5, many children can hop and skip and most 5 year olds will use a dominant hand (either right or left).
Communication and intellectual	Children are starting to understand more difficult concepts, (like time) and will use problem-solving skills to work things out for themselves. Language skills also progress very rapidly as the child's vocabulary expands and they constantly ask questions! Most 5 year olds have a wide vocabulary and can communicate using complex sentences that are mostly grammatically correct.
Social, emotional and behavioural	Children undergo many changes between the ages of 3 and 5 years and, for most children, this will be the stage of starting nursery and then going on to school. New experiences are challenging for children but help them to learn about managing their feelings and behaviour and develop social skills like sharing and playing together.

Case study

Ross is 2 years old. He can walk sturdily by himself and enjoys going up stairs, lifting both feet onto each step as he goes. He enjoys looking at picture books and can turn the pages one by one. He also enjoys crayoning with chunky wax crayons and creates circular

continued...

scribbling patterns. Ross has started to use some recognisable words, like 'daddy' and 'car' and can sometimes put two words together, like 'all gone'. He can feed himself with a spoon and fork and likes to help in dressing himself. Ross goes to a local parent and toddler group with his mum, where he enjoys playing alongside other children, although he likes his mum to be nearby.

1. Describe the progress in physical, intellectual, communication, emotional, social and behavioural development that you might expect Ross to make over the next year.

2. Give two examples of how different aspects of Ross's development might affect one another.

Key terms

Logical: clear, consistent principles that guide reasoning

Development from 5 to 8 years

Between the ages of 5 and 8, children become much more independent and capable. Friendships are very important at this stage and most children will have a 'best friend', usually of the same gender. In school, children will have new challenges, both socially and academically, as they learn to cope with a wide range of different expectations of their achievement and behaviour. See Figure 5.3.

Figure 5.3 Development from 5 to 8 years

Area of development	Expected pattern of development
Physical	Children have more stamina and better co-ordination of their gross motor skills. Team games like football are very popular and children also become more skilful with their manipulative abilities. Some activities require more practice (like tying shoe laces), but by the age of 8 years, most children can write clearly, using a cursive (joined up) style and draw very detailed pictures.
Communication and intellectual	A great deal of children's learning now takes place in school. Children develop their skills in literacy (reading, writing, speaking and listening) and their understanding of problem-solving and reasoning. By the age of 8 years, children usually understand **logical** thought. Children are also learning more descriptive language. Bilingual children may be learning two systems of communication, one that they use for their learning in school and a different one for communicating at home.
Social, emotional and behavioural	Children are becoming much more mature and independent. Friendships are established and children become much more confident in social situations. With their improved language skills, children are much more capable of expressing their feelings and managing their behaviour. Children are also much more aware of rules at this stage and will be more responsive to the difference between right and wrong.

Development from 8 to 12 years

This period in children's development involves some major transitions. Most children will transfer from primary to secondary school around the age of 11 years. Some children undergo major physical changes at this stage as their bodies start to prepare for adulthood through the process of **puberty**. It can also be a stage in children's lives when they feel pressurised to be like their friends and when they start to rebel against their parents or carers. This can be a very challenging time and children need a great deal of support from caring adults to help them progress confidently into their teenage years.

Your assessment criteria:

1.1 Describe the expected pattern of development in children and young people from birth to 19 years, including physical, communication, intellectual, social, emotional and behavioural development

1.2 Describe, with examples, how different aspects of development can affect one another

Key terms

Abstract: an idea that exists only in the mind and is difficult to understand

Puberty: the process of physical changes resulting in sexual maturity

---

Figure 5.4 Development from 8 to 12 years

Area of development	Expected pattern of development
Physical	The first signs of puberty can start in girls from around the age of 9 and some girls may even start to menstruate around the age of 10 or 11. Puberty usually starts later with boys, often at around 13 or 14 years old and this can lead to some self-consciousness between boys and girls.
Communication and intellectual	Children's thinking skills are maturing and most 10 year olds can now understand abstract ideas (like feelings). Their reasoning and problem-solving skills are becoming more developed and most 10 year olds can complete quite complicated calculations. Children at this stage will enjoy conversing with each other and chatting in friendship groups.
Social, emotional and behavioural	This can be a very challenging time for children. The transition to secondary school can be very demanding and some children will experience intense anxiety and real fear. In some cases, this can lead to problems with self-esteem and some children may become victims of bullying.

Development from 12 to 19 years

During this period of development, young people are maturing into adults. They start to become independent from their parents or carers and are developing their own ideas and individuality. See Figure 5.5.

Figure 5.5 Development from 12 to 19 years

Area of development	Expected pattern of development
Physical	Most girls will complete the process of puberty by the age of 15 or 16 years. For most boys, puberty starts at around the age of 14 years. Some boys grow very rapidly at this stage, which can lead to some degree of clumsiness and poor **spatial awareness.**
Communication and intellectual	Young people will be faced with challenges in school as they prepare for examinations and start to think about their future. This can be a very stressful time for young people as the pressure to achieve and succeed is a powerful force. Communication is increasingly carried out through electronic means such as text messages, email or social networking sites.
Social, emotional and behavioural	Socially and behaviourally, this is a time when young people are experimenting with ideas, feelings and behaviours. Many young people will experience their first romantic relationship at this stage and this can lead to some complicated emotions for them to manage. Boys as well as girls can become overly concerned about their appearance, weight or body image. In some cases, this can lead to eating disorders, low self-esteem and depression.

Knowledge Assessment Task   1.1 1.2

1. Research the expected pattern of all-round development for the following age ranges:

   0–3 years; 3–5 years; 5–8 years; 8–12 years; 12–19 years

   Remember to include physical, intellectual, communication, social, emotional and behavioural development

2. Describe, with examples, how different aspects of development can affect one another at each stage.

Use your research to prepare a presentation and share your findings with the rest of the group.

You can use PowerPoint slides or other visual aids to help you.

Keep your notes as evidence towards your assessment.

Key terms

Spatial awareness: understanding the location of objects in relation to the space around them

Understand the kinds of influences that affect children and young people's development

What can influence the development of children and young people?

There are many different influences that can affect the development of a child or young person at various stages in their life. Some influences can be both positive and negative. For example, a child's background can be a positive influence if it includes caring adults who meet their needs and provide opportunities for them to develop and learn. However, it could be a negative influence if a child's background includes neglect, abuse or harm. Equally, the environment in which a child is brought up can also affect development both positively and negatively. Poor housing conditions, which are damp or overcrowded, can lead to ill health. A lack of safety precautions in the home and limited spaces to play can increase the risk of a child having an accident. A supportive environment with opportunities for play and education will have a positive influence on children's development. A child's health is another major factor that can have an influence on development. For example, if a child suffers from a chronic illness, a physical disability or learning difficulties, then their development can be affected. See Figure 5.6.

Your assessment criteria:

2.1 Describe, with examples, the kinds of influences that affect children and young people's development, including background, health and environment

2.2 Describe, with examples, the importance of recognising and responding to concerns about the development of children and young people

Key terms

Antenatal: happening or existing before birth

Down's syndrome: a condition caused by an extra chromosome in the body's cells, resulting in learning difficulties

Premature: born before the 37th week of pregnancy

Figure 5.6 Some of the influences on development

Influence	Example
Antenatal factors during pregnancy	If a pregnant woman becomes infected with rubella (German measles), the child's development can be affected.
Factors associated with the birth	If the baby is born **prematurely** then development can be delayed.
Family background	Family values, culture and the way a child is encouraged and cared for can all affect a child's development and progress.
The environment	Housing conditions, safety and opportunities for play and education all influence how a child develops.
Health factors	Conditions like asthma or infections such as meningitis can affect a child's development. Hearing difficulties are one of the most common causes of language delay and speech problems in young children. **Down's syndrome** can result in developmental delay, learning difficulties and health problems.

Concerns about development

It is important for everyone who works with children and young people to be aware of the factors that can influence development. The routine monitoring and observation of children and young people's development can often highlight problems or concerns. For example, a child who has had limited opportunities for practising their manipulative skills may really struggle with tasks like using scissors, fastening buttons or writing with a pencil. They may need more time to practise and extra support to boost their confidence.

Being able to recognise and respond to concerns about development is very important in supporting the wellbeing of children and young people. For example, if a young child's language skills are not developing, they will not be able to communicate with others and may not be able to make themselves understood. This will influence their social development, as it will be difficult for them to make friendships or play with other children. It will also affect their emotional development as they will become frustrated at not being able to express themselves. If this is not recognised and responded to, then the child will start to lose confidence and may develop a negative attitude and behaviour pattern.

Equally, if an older child is not developing their literacy skills in reading and writing, then they will fall behind in school. This can lead to problems with behaviour, difficulties in paying attention in class and even truancy. Not doing well compared to their friends can cause children and young people to develop low self-esteem and if this is not recognised and responded to it can have serious consequences for their future.

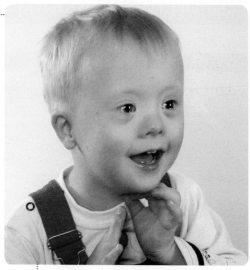

Conditions like Down's syndrome can influence development.

Knowledge Assessment Task   2.1   2.2

Jamil is 3 years old and has just started nursery. He has a small group of friends and is an active boy who loves to run around and play outside. His first language is Urdu, which he speaks at home with his family, and English is his second language. Although he can say several individual words in English, he does not speak in sentences. He also has difficulty pronouncing some words, for example he says 'lellow' instead of yellow.

1. What factors might be influencing Jamil's language development at this stage?
2. Why is it important to recognise and respond to Jamil's language difficulties?
3. What other factors can influence children's development at different stages in their lives?

Keep your notes as evidence towards your assessment.

Over to you!

Think about the influences on your own development. What factors have affected your progress, both positively and negatively?

Some transitions affect most children, like moving from primary to secondary school.

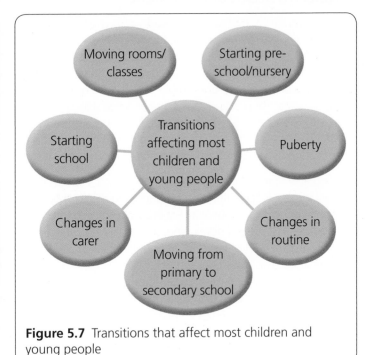

Figure 5.7 Transitions that affect most children and young people

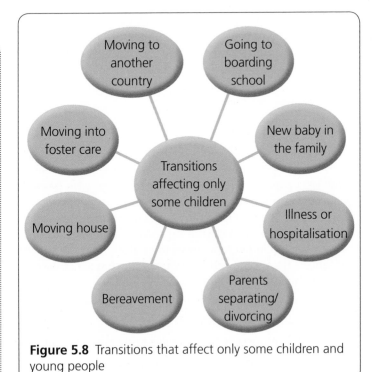

Figure 5.8 Transitions that affect only some children and young people

What are transitions?

Change is a part of life for all children and young people. As they grow and develop, their bodies change, their friendships and relationships change and they will experience a variety of different situations both within and outside of their family (see Figure 5.7). These changes are called transitions and they can affect development in a variety of ways.

Some transitions will affect most children, for example, starting school, moving from primary to secondary school and the process of puberty. However, other transitions will only affect some children and young people, for example, the divorce of their parents, moving home, having a new baby in the family, going into hospital, or the death of a parent or close family member.

The effect of transitions

Children and young people respond to transitions in different ways, both positively and negatively. Transition can affect all aspects of development and behaviour, but in most cases, the effects are short lived and temporary. It is very important that adults who work with children and young people deal sensitively with transition situations and provide support if necessary.

Some of the negative effects of transitions on the development of children and young people include:

▶ *regression* – going back to the development or behaviour of a younger child, for example bed wetting or 'baby talk'

▶ *changes in behaviour* – this can include becoming withdrawn or clingy, but also aggressive or attention-seeking behaviour

▶ *eating disorders* – for example, food refusal, or in some young people, anorexia or bulimia

▶ *sleep disturbances* – including waking up in the night or nightmares

▶ *speech problems* – for example, stuttering or **selective mutism**

▶ *depression* – including extreme sadness, tearfulness and feelings of worthlessness. In some young people this can even lead to suicidal tendencies

▶ *lack of concentration* – difficulties in paying attention and listening, and being easily distracted. This can be a particular problem for children and young people's learning in school

▶ *self-harm* – including cutting, the misuse of alcohol and other drugs, or risky sexual behaviour.

It is very important to be able to support children and young people who are experiencing transitions (see Chapter 9 (Unit CCLDMU 2.2) on page 182).

Your assessment criteria:

3.1 Identify the transitions experienced by most children and young people

3.2 Identify transitions that only some children and young people may experience, e.g. bereavement

3.3 Describe, with examples, how transitions may affect the development and behaviour of children and young people

Key terms

Selective mutism: choosing not to speak in certain situations or with certain people

Over to you!

Think about some of the major transitions in your own life. Create a timeline to show when the transitions happened. Can you remember how the different transitions affected you? What helped you to cope?

Knowledge Assessment Task   3.1   3.2   3.3

You have been asked to write an article for a parenting website about different transitions experienced by children and young people.

In your article you should describe and give examples of:

▶ transitions experienced by most children and young people
▶ transitions experienced only by some children and young people
▶ how transitions can affect the development of children and young people.

Keep your article as evidence towards you assessment.

Are you ready for assessment?

AC	What do you know now?	Assessment task	✓
1.1	The expected pattern of development in children and young people from birth to 19 years, including physical, communication, intellectual, social, emotional and behavioural development	Page 127	
1.2	How different aspects of development can affect one another	Page 127	
2.1	The factors that can influence the development of children and young people, including background, health and environment	Page 129	
2.2	The importance of recognising and responding to concerns about the development of children and young people	Page 129	
3.1	Identify the transitions experienced by most children and young people	Page 131	
3.2	Identify transitions that only some children and young people may experience, e.g. bereavement	Page 131	
3.3	How transitions may affect the development and behaviour of children and young people	Page 131	

There is no practical assessment for this unit, but your tutor or assessor may question you about some of the following points:

What can you do now?	✓
Can you apply your knowledge about the development of children and young people to your practice in the real work environment?	
Can you recognise different milestones of development? Could you recognise and respond to concerns about the development of children and young people in your setting?	
Can you apply your knowledge about the effects of transitions on the development of children and young people in the real work environment? Do you have any specific examples as evidence of this?	

6 | Safeguarding the welfare of children and young people (TDA 2.2)

Assessment of this unit

This unit is about safeguarding the welfare of children and young people. It covers the important legislation, policies and procedures for keeping children and young people safe. It also includes how to recognise different types of child abuse and the actions that should be taken if there are any concerns that a child or young person has been abused or harmed. The unit also considers some common childhood illnesses and the importance of knowing what to do if children or young people are ill or injured.

In order to successfully complete this unit, you will need to produce evidence of your knowledge, as shown in the chart below. Your tutor or assessor will help you to prepare for your assessment, and the tasks suggested in this chapter will help you to create the evidence you need.

AC	What you need to do
1.1	The legislation, guidelines, policies and procedures for safeguarding the welfare of children and young people including e-safety
1.2	The roles of different agencies involved in safeguarding the welfare of children and young people
2.1	The signs and symptoms of common childhood illnesses
2.2	The actions to take when children or young people are ill or injured
2.3	The circumstances when children and young people might require urgent medical attention
2.4	The actions to take in response to emergency situations including: fires; security incidents missing children or young people
3.1	The characteristics of different types of child abuse
3.2	The risks and possible consequences for children and young people using the internet, mobile phones and other technologies
3.3	The actions to take in response to evidence or concerns that a child or young person has been abused, harmed (including self harm) or bullied, or maybe at risk of harm, abuse or bullying
3.4	The actions to take in response to evidence or concerns that a colleague may be failing to comply with safeguarding procedures or harming a child or young person
3.5	The principles and boundaries of confidentiality and when to share information

The assessment of this unit is all knowledge based (things that you need to know about), but it is also very important to be able to apply your knowledge practically in the real work environment. Although there is no practical assessment for this unit, but your tutor or assessor may question you about some of the following points.

What you need to do

Apply your knowledge about safeguarding policies and procedures in the real work environment

Be clear about your own responsibilities in the case of any evidence or concerns about child abuse in the work environment

Apply your knowledge about illness, injuries and emergency situations with children and young people in the real work environment

This is an extremely important unit of study and it links with some of the other mandatory units:

SCH 21	Introduction to communication in health, social care or children and young people's settings
MU 2.4	Contribute to children and young people's health and safety
MU 2.8	Contribute to the support of the positive environments for children and young people
MU 2.9	Understand partnership working in services for children and young people
MPII 002	Managing paediatric illness and injury

Some of your learning will be repeated in these units and will give you the chance to review your knowledge and understanding.

Why do we need to safeguard the welfare of children and young people?

Safeguarding the welfare of children and young people is extremely important. It involves more than just protecting children from abuse – it also includes promoting their interests, keeping them safe and protecting their rights.

Young children are extremely **vulnerable** and rely on adults to meet all their basic needs. This includes providing food, warmth and shelter, as well as protecting their security and keeping them safe from neglect or harm. Children and young people also need to be supported to develop a strong sense of self-esteem. This helps them to become more **resilient** in making positive decisions to protect themselves. Children who are more self-confident are less likely to be vulnerable to abuse. Adults can help children by giving them lots of praise and encouragement, supporting them to do things for themselves and teaching them how to be **assertive**.

Key terms

Assertive: the quality of being self-assured and confident

Resilient: able to recover from setbacks and cope with stress

Vulnerable: more prone to risk and harm

The internet is a very useful tool, but can be used as a vehicle for child pornography. Children and young people can also be exploited through social networking sites and need to be aware of e-safety measures. Professionals have a duty to protect children by making them aware of the dangers and supporting them to deal with situations they are not comfortable with. Parents and carers may also need advice about how to supervise children's internet use or how to control access to certain material.

Text messaging, emailing and social networking sites can also be potential avenues for **cyber-bullying**. This can be an extremely destructive process and adults need to be aware of procedures to support children and young people who may be at risk.

It is very important for anyone who works with children or young people to be aware of safeguarding procedures and to know how to respond to any evidence or concerns about children's welfare and safety.

All children and young people have a right to grow up in safety, and adults have a duty to protect them from being harmed or abused in any way.

Key terms

Cyber-bullying: bullying which uses e-technology as a means of victimising others

Legislation and guidelines

Some of the main legislation around safeguarding children began with the Children Act (1989). This was updated with the Children Act (2004) which, among other things, included the principle of **integrated children's services** and incorporated the five main principles of **Every Child Matters** (2003), which clearly states that every child is entitled to:

1. be healthy
2. stay safe
3. enjoy and achieve
4. make a positive contribution
5. achieve economic wellbeing.

In 2010, another key document was updated and published by the government. Called 'Working Together to Safeguard Children', it outlines the key responsibilities for professionals in protecting children from harm and keeping them safe.

A very important organisation involved in safeguarding the welfare of children and young people is the **Independent Safeguarding Authority** (ISA). This organisation is responsible for helping to

Your assessment criteria:

1.1 Identify the current legislation, guidelines, policies and procedures for safeguarding the welfare of children and young people including e-safety

Key terms

Every Child Matters: a UK government initiative launched in 2003 to improve outcomes for children and young people

Integrated children's services: different services working together to support children, young people and their families

Working Together to Safeguard Children

A guide to inter-agency working to safeguard and promote the welfare of children

prevent unsuitable people from working with children or young people. One of the ways it does this is to carry out **Criminal Records Bureau** (CRB) checks on anyone who works with or applies to work with children or young people.

In settings caring for children aged 0–5 years, the regulatory requirements for safeguarding children's welfare are included in the Statutory Framework for the **Early Years Foundation Stage** (EYFS). The welfare requirements of the EYFS are **statutory** and include important regulations about safeguarding and promoting children's welfare, suitable people and suitable premises, environment and equipment (see Chapter 10 (MU 2.8) on page 190).

see Chapter 10 (MU 2.8) on page 190

Key terms

Criminal Records Bureau: an agency of the Home Office providing access to criminal record information (equivalent national organisations are Disclosure Scotland and Access Northern Ireland)

Early Years Foundation Stage: A framework for the care and education of children from birth to 5 years introduced in England in 2008. (The Early Years Framework in Scotland covers children from birth to 8 years, the Curriculum Guidance for Pre-school Education operates in Northern Ireland and the Foundation Phase for Children's Learning for 3–7 year olds in Wales)

Independent Safeguarding Authority: a public body created by the government in 2007 to improve procedures for checking the suitability of those who wish to work with children or young people

Statutory: relating to the law (statute)

Over to you!

Think about your own CRB check for working or being in placement with children or young people.

▶ *How long did it take for the process to be completed?*

▶ *When will you be required to undertake another CRB check?*

▶ *Why do you think CRB checks are important for anyone who works with children or young people?*

Policies and procedures

It is very important for all workplace settings to have clear policies and procedures for safeguarding children and young people. Some of the key issues that should be included are:

▶ a key member of staff being the 'named person' as the main contact for all safeguarding issues

▶ clear procedures for managing the personal care of children (e.g. helping them with toileting or changing nappies)

▶ clear procedures about appropriate physical contact with children and young people (e.g. cuddling children or restraining young people)

▶ clear policies about taking photographs or filming children, including the use of mobile phones in the work setting

▶ security measures for protecting children, for example CCTV, **biometric** access devices (e.g. fingerprint recognition) or the use of webcams

▶ clear procedures for risk assessment (e.g. regular checking of equipment for damage and to make sure it is safe)

▶ clear arrangements for confirming parents or carers who are collecting children and for checking the identity of any visitors to the setting

▶ clear policies about sharing information and **confidentiality**

▶ activities to empower and educate children and young people (e.g. about confidence in their own bodies or being assertive when making decisions)

▶ the importance of observation and listening to children and young people

▶ the importance of all staff knowing their own role and responsibilities

▶ the importance of regular staff training and updating on safeguarding issues.

Your assessment criteria:

1.1 Identify the current legislation, guidelines, policies and procedures for safeguarding the welfare of children and young people including e-safety

3.5 Describe the principles and boundaries of confidentiality and when to share information

Key terms

Biometrics: using physical characteristics for the purpose of personal identification

Confidentiality: treating information as private

Parents and carers will find it reassuring to know that there are clear policies and procedures for safeguarding children.

Knowledge Assessment Task · 1.1 · 3.5

Investigate the safeguarding policy in your placement or work setting and write a report which outlines the following:

1. What are the procedures for parents, carers or visitors to gain access to your setting?

2. What is the policy about taking photographs of children or young people in your setting?

3. What is the policy about confidentiality and information sharing?

4. How does the safeguarding policy in your placement or work setting meet the requirements of government guidelines and relevant legislation, including e-safety?

Keep your notes as evidence towards your assessment.

Agencies involved in safeguarding the welfare of children and young people

Safeguarding the welfare of children and young people is a complex process, which relies on effective partnership working between different agencies. There may be several different services involved with the family, including health, education, social services and voluntary agencies, each with their own area of responsibility (see Chapter 11 (MU 2.9) on page 228). For example, concerns about the welfare of a 4 year old in nursery might involve the child's key person, the family health visitor, the GP, the social worker and the family support worker. Concerns about cyber-bullying among teenagers in a secondary school might involve their teachers, mentors, parent support advisor or voluntary worker from an organisation like **Kidscape.**

Professionals within different agencies and organisations will all have specific responsibilities regarding safeguarding children and young people. See Figure 6.1.

Key terms

Kidscape: an anti-bullying charity supporting children, young people and their families

Health services

▶ *Health visitors* have a responsibility for the health and development of children under the age of 5. They usually have contact with families both in the clinic or health centre and on home visits. Health visitors may often be the first people to identify concerns about a child's safety, health or welfare.

▶ *General practitioners (GPs)* have a responsibility for the general health of registered patients in their local community. They usually have contact with children and families in the surgery or health centre, and may identify safeguarding concerns as a result of a routine visit or general health check-up.

▶ *Hospital staff* may be involved in safeguarding issues if a child or young person attends the accident and emergency department as the result of a non-accidental injury.

Social services

▶ *Social workers* have a responsibility to provide services for vulnerable children and their families. This might be because parents are struggling to care for their children or when families are trying to cope with challenging situations like imprisonment or alcohol and other drug use. Social workers will always be involved in situations of abuse or harm with children or young people.

Figure 6.1 The different agencies involved in safeguarding the welfare of children and young people

▶ *Residential care workers* have a responsibility for children who are living in residential care homes and not with their own families (often called 'looked-after' children). Children and young people in care are particularly vulnerable, and residential care workers have a specific duty to safeguard their health and welfare.

▶ *Family support workers* have a responsibility to provide support for vulnerable children and their families. They will usually have contact with families, both at the local children's centre and on home visits, and are often called upon to monitor families when there are concerns about safety, health or welfare.

Education services

▶ *Teachers* have a responsibility for the education and welfare of children and young people. Their work involves close observation of pupils in the classroom, and this can frequently trigger concerns about health or welfare.

▶ *Children's service workers* may work in schools, pre-schools, nurseries or out-of-school clubs. They have a responsibility for the safety and welfare of children and young people and may often be the first people to identify safeguarding concerns.

Legal and criminal services

▶ *Police* have a responsibility for the safety and protection of the general public. They will be involved in any criminal proceedings that may result from safeguarding situations.

▶ *Probation officers* have a responsibility to support the rehabilitation of some offenders in the community. This will involve monitoring people convicted of offences against children to ensure that they do not continue to pose a threat.

Voluntary services

A wide range of voluntary organisations and groups may be involved in safeguarding the welfare of children and young people. Some of these include:

▶ NSPCC

▶ Childline

▶ Kidscape

▶ Scout/Cub and Guide/Brownie leaders

▶ sports coaches.

It is extremely important that all these people work together and share information in order to co-ordinate support for the child or young person and their family. It is also vitally important that professionals apply strict codes of confidentiality when sharing information (see Chapter 11 (MU 2.9) on page 228).

Know how to respond to evidence or concerns that a child or young person has been abused, harmed or bullied

What are the different types of child abuse?

Abuse, harm or bullying of children and young people can take many different forms. Often, more than one type of abuse is experienced at the same time, for example, a child may be both physically abused and neglected.

The four main types of child abuse are shown in Figure 6.2.

Your assessment criteria:

3.1 Identify the characteristics of different types of child abuse

Figure 6.2 Characteristics of different types of child abuse

Type of abuse	Characteristics	Signs and symptoms
1. Physical	Hitting, shaking, throwing, burning or scalding, beating with objects or otherwise causing physical harm or injury. It can result in pain, bruising, broken bones and sometimes disability or even death.	Unexplained injuries, bruising or burns; reluctance or refusal to undress (e.g. for PE, games or a medical exam); wearing layers of clothing or heavy clothes to cover injuries; aggressive behaviour; fear of physical contact.
2. Emotional	Shouting, swearing and negative criticism; withholding love and affection; bullying, including cyber-bullying; causing children to feel worthless and useless. It can result in low self-esteem and extreme fearfulness.	Lack of confidence, particularly in new situations; becoming very withdrawn; delayed development; nervous behaviour (e.g. fidgeting or rocking back and forth).
3. Sexual	Forcing or enticing into sexual activities; viewing pornographic material, including on the internet; encouraging inappropriate physical touching; sexual harassment.	Disturbed behaviour, including self-harm, personality changes, regression, inappropriate sexual behaviour; medical problems such as repeated urinary infections; insecurity and lack of trust.
4. Neglect	Not providing food, clothing, warmth, shelter, basic hygiene, care or protection. It can result in **failure to thrive** and developmental delay.	Constant hunger; tiredness (always falling asleep); poor personal hygiene; inadequate or inappropriate clothing; poor interpersonal and social skills.

Which of the following would you identify as forms of abuse towards children or young people? *

▶ leaving a child alone for long periods

▶ smacking

▶ not giving a child enough food

▶ shouting at a young person a lot

▶ not changing a baby's nappy frequently

▶ not keeping a child clean

▶ criticising a young person a lot

Compare your responses with others in the group. Where did you agree/disagree? Give reasons for your answers.

Knowledge Assessment Task   3.1

Write a brief report to identify the possible types of child abuse in the following situations:

1. Ryan, aged 4 years, comes to nursery every day dressed in inappropriate clothing, smelling of urine and is constantly hungry.

2. Vicky, aged 14 years, has been forced by her stepfather to view internet pornography. He shouts and swears at her and threatens to lock her in her room if she does not comply with his demands.

3. Evie, aged 8 months, has been shaken violently by her teenage mother, Stacey, because she would not stop crying. Stacey frequently leaves Evie to cry alone in her cot for long periods of time.

Keep your notes as evidence towards your assessment.

Key terms

Failure to thrive: not growing or gaining weight at the expected rate

*The NSPCC defines all of them as forms of abuse.

Responding to evidence or safeguarding concerns

It is extremely important for anyone who works with children or young people to fully understand their own responsibilities in relation to safeguarding issues. One of the most important things to remember is that if you ever have concerns about the welfare of a child or young person, you should always make those concerns known to an appropriate person. In most work situations, that will be your manager or supervisor. **Local Safeguarding Children Boards** are statutory organisations, which operate within each local area to ensure that services co-operate to promote the welfare of children and young people.

Many children living in abusive or harmful situations are in a constant state of anxiety and fear. It can therefore be very difficult for them to talk to anyone else about it. The act of a child or young person telling you or suggesting that he or she has been abused, harmed or bullied is called **disclosure**. The details can be distressing to hear, and knowing how to respond to a disclosure is an important part of professional practice. Some of your key actions should include:

▶ Listen carefully, without showing shock or disbelief.

▶ Do not ask leading questions (like 'Where did he hurt you?').

▶ Accept what the child or young person says and do not rush them.

▶ Reassure them and emphasise that they have done the right thing by telling someone.

▶ Never promise that you will keep what they have said a secret.

▶ Follow the procedure for your work setting (which will usually involve telling your supervisor in the first instance, and you may be required to write a report).

Your assessment criteria:

1.2 Describe the roles of different agencies involved in safeguarding the welfare of children and young people

3.3 Describe actions to take in response to evidence or concerns that a child or young person has been abused, harmed (including self harm) or bullied, or maybe at risk of harm, abuse or bullying

Key terms

Disclosure: revealing sensitive information

Local Safeguarding Children Boards: statutory organisations established in 2006 in each Children's Service authority in England to oversee service provision for promoting the welfare of children and young people

Knowledge Assessment Task   1.2   3.3

Jamie is 4 years old, and has been attending Rosebuds Nursery for 15 months.

His key person, Jo, has recently noticed a change in his behaviour. Jamie had always been a boisterous boy who loved outdoor play and physical activity. Recently, however, Jamie has appeared sullen and gloomy; he has to be coaxed to go outside, and even then he tends to wander around on his own and does not play with other children. Jo has also noticed that Jamie often appears to be dirty and smelly, frequently wearing the same clothes day after day. These days he very rarely speaks, but just shakes his head in response to her questions.

Jo has spoken to Jamie's mum, Sheila, and has discovered that she and Jamie's dad have split up. Sheila is concerned that Jamie has started wetting the bed at night, and she is worried about what happens to Jamie now that he spends every other weekend with his dad and his dad's new girlfriend.

One day, Jamie arrives at nursery with a very bruised cheek. Jo comments on this, saying, 'Ooh, that looks really sore Jamie.' Jamie runs off into the toilets.

1. Explain why Jo should be concerned about Jamie's welfare.

2. Describe the action Jo should take in response to her concerns about Jamie.

3. Describe the roles of different agencies that might be involved in this situation.

Keep your notes as evidence towards your assessment.

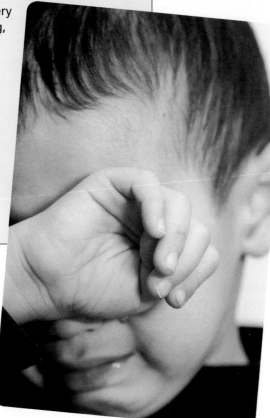

E-safety

Children and young people are particularly at risk from some forms of technology, which can present a threat to their safety and welfare. The internet is a powerful tool, but it can also expose children and young people to unsuitable sites and potentially harmful material. Young people need to be aware of the possible dangers from using the internet, including social networking sites.

Many children and young people have access to the use of a mobile phone, and the benefits of being able to communicate may be a great reassurance to parents. However, mobile phones may also be an instrument for cyber-bullying, which can cause a great deal of distress for many young people and their parents.

Your assessment criteria:

3.2 Describe the risks and possible consequences for children and young people using the internet, mobile phones and other technologies

Over to you!

Think about your own internet use.

▶ *What precautions do you take to ensure your own safety when using social networking and other internet sites?*

▶ *What e-safety measures are taken in your placement or work setting to protect children and young people?*

Compare your experiences with others in the group.

Knowledge Assessment Task 3.2

Ali is 12 years old and enjoys using her computer and mobile phone to communicate with her friends. She has a computer in her bedroom and often uses it to investigate different internet sites. One of her friends from school has sent a text message to Ali with a link to a pornographic website and a message saying, 'We dare you to look at this when your mum and dad are not around.' Ali is worried that if she doesn't look at this website she will be excluded from her friendship group at school.

1. Describe the risks that Ali might be taking by viewing this website.

2. Explain what Ali should do about this text message.

3. Describe some of the possible consequences for children and young people using the internet, mobile phones and other technologies.

Keep your notes as evidence towards your assessment.

Professional responsibility

It is extremely important that everyone who works with children and young people can be completely trusted to comply with safeguarding procedures. Most people would take this for granted as a vital part of the job, but there have been situations where professionals fail to follow procedures or, in some cases, actually inflict harm or abuse on children or young people. Working with children and young people is a position of great responsibility, and professionals must always follow procedures to keep children safe.

Your assessment criteria:

3.4 Describe the actions to take in response to concerns that a colleague may be: failing to comply with safeguarding procedures; harming, abusing or bullying a child or young person

Knowledge Assessment Task 3.4

Think about how you might respond to the following situations:

1. You are working in a nursery and an unfamiliar adult comes to collect a child at the end of the day. He says that he is the child's uncle and that the mother has asked him to collect the child. One of your colleagues says that will be OK.

2. You are working at an out-of-school club and you observe a colleague viewing an inappropriate website on the computer with a group of 8 year olds.

Describe how you would respond in each case and the action you would take.

Keep your notes as evidence towards your assessment.

Know what to do when children or young people are ill or injured, including emergency procedures

How do you recognise childhood illness?

Most children and young people will experience some episodes of illness in their life. Common illnesses, like coughs and colds, are not usually serious. However, illnesses such as **meningitis** are more serious and will need specialist medical care. Illnesses such as chicken pox are infectious (easily spread) and others, like **asthma**, are not infectious at all. It is important for anyone who works with children and young people to be able to recognise the signs of illness and know what action to take.

The main signs of illness in a child or young person are:

▶ poor appetite

▶ no energy

▶ change in behaviour (unusually quiet, not sleeping well, crying more than usual)

▶ constipation or diarrhoea

▶ vomiting

▶ skin rash

▶ raised body temperature

▶ a cough, headache, stomach ache, earache or runny nose.

Signs and symptoms

Young children find it difficult to describe how they feel. They may say that they have 'tummy ache' when they actually feel upset, afraid or worried. Children's **symptoms** can worsen very quickly and should always be taken seriously and not ignored.

Key terms

Asthma: a non-infectious condition that can be triggered by allergic reactions and causes breathing difficulties

Meningitis: a serious infectious disease affecting the meninges around the brain and spinal cord

Symptoms: changes in the body caused by an illness

Over to you!

In pairs or small groups, make a list of all the childhood illnesses you can think of. Include serious and non-serious conditions, infections and other illnesses.

Compare your notes with others in the group.

Infectious illnesses

Infectious illnesses are caused by bacteria or viruses and are easily spread, particularly in settings among groups of children or young people. Most infectious diseases start with symptoms like a bad cold, with a slight rise in body temperature, a sore throat and generally feeling unwell. Some infectious diseases, such as measles and chicken pox, also produce a rash.

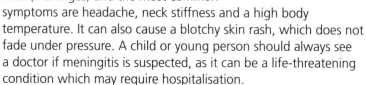

Children will recover completely from most of the common infectious diseases within a few weeks. Others, like meningitis, are more serious. Meningitis affects the protective covering around the brain and spinal cord (meninges) and the most common symptoms are headache, neck stiffness and a high body temperature. It can also cause a blotchy skin rash, which does not fade under pressure. A child or young person should always see a doctor if meningitis is suspected, as it can be a life-threatening condition which may require hospitalisation.

Non-infectious illnesses

Some illnesses are not infectious but can still cause health problems for children and young people. Conditions such as earache, stomach upsets and diarrhoea are often experienced by children, particularly once they start mixing with other children. These are not usually serious unless they continue without improvement, in which case a doctor should always be consulted.

Asthma is a non-infectious condition that causes breathing difficulties for children. It can be triggered by allergic reactions to materials like pollen or animal fur. Asthma can be very successfully managed and treated with specific medicine, which is usually taken by the child using a special inhaler.

Knowledge Assessment Task — 2.1

Investigate these common childhood illnesses:

- measles
- common cold
- asthma
- chicken pox.

Create an information leaflet or web page for parents, highlighting the main symptoms of these illnesses and how each should be treated.

Keep your notes as evidence towards your assessment.

Dealing with illness and injuries

Being ill or injured can be a frightening experience for both children and young people. It is important to take appropriate action and always respond in a calm and reassuring manner. (See also Chapter 13 (MPII 002) on page 274.)

Dealing with illness

There will be times when children or young people become ill in your setting, and it is important to know what to do. Make sure you are familiar with the setting's policy about illness and what your responsibilities are. Sick children need to be comfortable and may need to rest in a quiet part of the setting. Young children may find it comforting to listen to a familiar story or watch a DVD. You must always contact their parents or carers, who should come and take the child home or to the doctor if necessary. You may need to stay with the sick child to observe and make notes on their condition.

Most children recover very quickly from illness, but it is important to know when emergency medical help may be needed. You should always seek urgent medical attention or call an ambulance if a child or young person has any of these symptoms:

▶ a very high temperature (39°C or above)

▶ breathing difficulties

▶ a **convulsion** or fit

▶ become unconscious

▶ very severe or constant diarrhoea and/or vomiting

▶ a purple/red rash that doesn't fade under pressure (sign of meningitis).

Dealing with injuries

Even with the most reliable policies and procedures in a setting, children will occasionally have accidents and experience injuries. It is very important to know what action to take in these situations as it can save a life.

One of the most important things to remember when dealing with emergency situations is to remain calm and appear confident (even if you don't feel it!). Children and young people often panic when they are injured, and they will look to you for reassurance and support. Every setting must have a first aid policy and at least one qualified first aider on the staff team, who is responsible for first aid treatment.

Many injuries in the work setting will be relatively minor, involving cut fingers and grazed knees, but some injuries will be more serious and may need more involved treatment. (See also Chapter 12 (PEFAP 001) on page 246 Chapter 13 (MPII 002) on page 274.)

Your assessment criteria:

2.2 Describe the actions to take when children or young people are ill or injured

2.3 Identify circumstances when children and young people might require urgent medical attention

2.4 Describe the actions to take in response to emergency situations including: fires; security incidents missing children or young people

Over to you!

▶ *Can you remember being sick as a child? What was it like for you?*

▶ *Share your memories with others in your group and compare your experiences.*

Key terms

Convulsion: uncontrollable contraction of muscles in the body, causing jerky movements

Over to you!

▶ *Make a list of all the possible injuries you can think of that might happen to children or young people in your placement or work setting.*

▶ *Compare your list with others in your group.*

Knowledge Assessment Task   2.2   2.3

1. In your placement or work setting, investigate the procedures for dealing with illness and injuries.

2. Give examples of some of the circumstances when children or young people might need urgent medical attention.

3. Describe the action you would take in the following situations:

   a) Salim, aged 7 years, who suffers from asthma and uses an inhaler regularly, has a severe asthma attack.

   b) Jack, aged 10 months, develops a temperature of 40 °C and has a convulsion.

   c) Suzie, aged 3 years, falls off the climbing frame in the outdoor play area and hits her head on one of the metal bars.

Keep your notes as evidence towards your assessment.

Over to you!

- Have you been involved in a fire drill or evacuation exercise in your placement or work setting?
- Do you know where the emergency exits are?
- What would your own role be in an emergency situation, such as an evacuation procedure?
- Compare your ideas with others in the group.

Emergency situations

An important part of safeguarding the welfare of children and young people is knowing how to respond in emergency situations. This can include incidents involving fire, evacuation procedures or security issues. The Health and Safety at Work Act (1974), sets out the regulations for safety policies to deal with emergency situations. There can be many different kinds of emergencies when working with children and young people and it is important to know what to do, particularly for fires, security incidents or if a child goes missing (see Chapter 4 (MU 2.4) on page 86).

Emergency procedures should be visibly displayed, with clear instructions about the location of emergency exits and assembly points. Regular drills should be carried out to make sure that all staff understand their responsibilities and that children know what to do.

In the case of a child or young person going missing, the parents should always be informed immediately, as well as the local police.

Knowledge Assessment Task   2.4

Investigate the emergency policies and procedures at your placement or work setting. Describe the action you would take in response to the following situations:

1. a fire in the setting

2. a security incident involving evacuation of the premises

3. a child or young person goes missing from the setting.

Keep your notes as evidence towards your assessment.

Are you ready for assessment?

AC	What you need to do	Assessment task	✓
1.1	The legislation, guidelines, policies and procedures for safeguarding the welfare of children and young people including e-safety	Page 141	
1.2	The roles of different agencies involved in safeguarding the welfare of children and young people	Page 147	
2.1	The signs and symptoms of common childhood illnesses	Page 151	
2.2	The actions to take when children or young people are ill or injured	Page 153	
2.3	The circumstances when children and young people might require urgent medical attention	Page 153	
2.4	The actions to take in response to emergency situations including: fires; security incidents missing children or young people	Page 153	
3.1	The characteristics of different types of child abuse	Page 145	
3.2	The risks and possible consequences for children and young people using the internet, mobile phones and other technologies	Page 148	
3.3	The actions to take in response to evidence or concerns that a child or young person has been abused, harmed (including self harm) or bullied, or maybe at risk of harm, abuse or bullying	Page 147	
3.4	The actions to take in response to evidence or concerns that a colleague may be failing to comply with safeguarding procedures or harming a child or young person	Page 149	
3.5	The principles and boundaries of confidentiality and when to share information	Page 141	

There is no practical assessment for this unit, but your tutor or assessor may question you about some of the following points.

What can you do now?   ✓

Can you apply you knowledge about safeguarding policies and procedures in the real work environment? Do you have any examples as evidence of this?

Are you clear about your own responsibilities in the case of any evidence or concerns about child abuse in the work environment? Could you tell your assessor about this?

Can you apply your knowledge about illness, injuries and emergency situations with children and young people in the real work environment? Do you have any examples as evidence of this?

7 | Maintain and support relationships with children and young people (TDA 2.7)

Assessment of this unit

This unit is all about developing relationships with children and young people. It covers the skills required to communicate effectively and the importance of trust and respect. It also explores ways of helping children and young people to get along with others and to understand diversity and individual differences.

The assessment of this unit is all competence based (things that you need to be able to do), but it is also very important to understand the reasons behind your actions and why you need to work in specific ways in the real work environment.

In order to successfully complete this unit, you will need to produce evidence of your competence, as shown in the following charts. Your tutor or assessor will help you to prepare for your assessment and the tasks suggested in this chapter will help you to create the evidence that you need.

All of the assessment for this unit must be completed in the workplace, but your tutor or assessor may question you about some of the following points:

What you need to know

The importance of appropriate communication and active listening with children and young people

The importance of trust and respect in developing and maintaining relationships with children and young people

How to respond to children's and young people's questions, ideas and concerns and provide reasons for actions

How to encourage children and young people to make choices for themselves

The importance of helping children and young people to understand diversity, individual differences and other people's feelings

AC	What you need to do
1.1	Communicate appropriately with children and young people using conventional language and body language
1.2	Actively listen to children and young people and value what they say, experience and feel
1.3	Check that children and young people understand what is communicated
2.1 2.2	Demonstrate how to establish respectful relationships with children and young people and give them individual attention
2.3	Demonstrate realistic responses to their questions, ideas, suggestions and concerns
2.4 2.5	Provide children and young people with reasons for actions and encourage them to make choices for themselves
3.1 3.4	Support children and young people to communicate effectively with others and to develop group agreements about the way they interact with others
3.2 3.3	Encourage children and young people to understand other people's diversity and differences and to respect other people's feelings and points of view
3.5	Demonstrate ways of encouraging children and young people to deal with conflict for themselves

This unit also links to some of the other mandatory units:

SHC 21	Introduction to communication in health, social care or children's and young people's settings
SCH 23	Introduction to equality and inclusion in health, social care or children's and young people settings
MU 2.8	Contribute to the support of the positive environments for children and young people
TDA 2.9	Support children and young people's positive behaviour

Some of your learning will be repeated in these units and give you the chance to review your knowledge and understanding.

Be able to communicate with children and young people

Your assessment criteria:

1.1 Communicate with children and young people in a way that is appropriate to the individual, using both conventional language and body language

1.2 Actively listen to children and young people and value what they say, experience and feel

1.3 Check that children and young people understand what is communicated

Why is it important to communicate effectively?

Communication is one of the most important features of developing a relationship with children and young people. Effective communication is an essential tool for developing trust and gaining respect, as it forms the basis of how people get along with each other. We communicate in a wide variety of different ways, using both **verbal** and **non-verbal communication** methods (see also Chapter 1 (SHC 21)).

Verbal communication

Verbal communication is used to engage with children and young people in developing relationships. It is used to ask questions, give instructions and information, express feelings or discuss ideas.

Verbal communication with children and young people needs to take account of their age, stage of development and level of understanding. It involves not only the words spoken, but also factors like verbal expression and tone of voice. It is important to speak clearly and to use language that is easily understood. This is particularly important for children or young people whose first language is not English. Verbal expression and tone of voice can suggest a range of different meanings, for example, a harsh tone can suggest anger or frustration, whereas a warmer tone of voice can suggest affection or friendship. Speaking in a quiet voice or a whisper can sometimes help young children to calm down, but a loud voice can sometimes be more effective for reading stories or giving important instructions outdoors. Babies are more responsive to a 'sing-song' tone of voice ('**parentese**'), whereas some older children may react more positively to a humorous tone.

A very specific form of communication is sign language. This is often used with children and young people who have a hearing

Key terms

Non-verbal communication: the exchange of information without using words (for example body language)

Parentese: a non-standard form of speech used by adults in communicating with babies

Verbal communication: the exchange of information using sounds and words (including written communication)

Over to you!

▶ *Make a list of all the different ways that you communicate with your friends and family, both verbally and non-verbally.*

▶ *Compare your list with others in the group.*

impairment or other special needs. There are many different ways of using signs to communicate, but one of the most frequently used methods is **Makaton**. This system uses simple gestures to communicate words and phrases and is often used as part of everyday communication with all the children in some work settings.

Children and young people also use written communication in different ways, for example, by using text messaging, email or social networking sites (see also Chapter 1 (SHC 21)).

Non-verbal communication

Non-verbal communication is often more important than verbal communication in developing relationships with children and young people. It includes all the different ways of communicating that do not involve actual words, such as body language, facial expressions, gestures and physical touch. Children and young people are very sensitive to non-verbal communication. It can be a very powerful way to express meaning and can change the way that communication is understood. For example, babies are very responsive to positive facial expressions such as smiling and eye contact. The use of gestures, like waving 'bye-bye', can help a toddler to understand the meaning of some words and many young children will be comforted and reassured with a cuddle. Some non-verbal communication can suggest negative messages, for example, pointing a finger at someone can be interpreted as being aggressive, and crossed arms, yawning or staring into space can be a sign of boredom in some young people.

Non-verbal communication can be very important for children and young people who use English as an additional language. Facial expressions, gestures and body language take on a special meaning when it is difficult to understand the words being spoken. It is important for anyone working with **bilingual** children or young people to be aware of non-verbal communication and to use it effectively.

Key terms

Bilingual: the ability to speak two languages

Makaton: a system of communication that uses manual signs, symbols and speech

Over to you!

▶ Think about the different ways you use verbal communication with children or young people in your placement or work setting.

▶ In small groups, share some examples of how you use your tone of voice and verbal expression in different situations with children and young people, for example:
 – individually or in groups
 – at story time
 – when children are upset
 – when you want children to calm down.

▶ How do you change your communication style when children are behaving inappropriately?

Case study

Josh is 3 years old and it is his first day at nursery. He arrives with his mother and seems very anxious about leaving her. Although he is not crying, he looks very upset and clings to his mother's hand as they enter the main room of the nursery.

Describe how you would use different communication skills to:

▶ reassure Josh and make him feel welcome in the nursery

▶ help him to understand what is going to happen during his morning at nursery

▶ help him to separate from his mother.

Think about both your verbal and non-verbal communication skills, including your tone of voice and verbal expression.

Listening skills

Listening is an extremely important part of communication with children and young people. **Active listening** is a way of showing that you are really paying attention and that you value what children and young people have to say. It is sometimes too easy to 'pretend' to listen, when you are really busy doing or thinking about something else.

One of the most important ways to show that you are listening to children or young people is to look at them. With young children, this may involve crouching down to their eye level and giving them plenty of time. Children and young people can become very frustrated when adults are constantly too busy to listen to what they have to say.

Another way to demonstrate active listening when dealing with children and young people is to repeat or summarise what has been said. For example, in a conversation with a young person, you might respond with, *'So, what you seem to be telling me is….'* With a younger child you might adapt your response to repeat what the child has said, for example, *'Oh, so you went to the seaside at the weekend, how exciting!'*

This kind of response demonstrates that you are interested, paying attention and really value what the child or young person has to say.

Communicating through play

Young children will often use play as a means of communicating their thoughts and feelings. It is very important to observe children's play and to be aware of the different ways that children express themselves. For example, very shy children might be reluctant to speak to an adult, but they may communicate with a puppet. Children who are feeling upset might express themselves by painting or drawing a picture and children who are angry or frustrated might communicate their feelings by pounding clay or play dough.

Books and stories can be a very effective way to communicate with children, particularly stories that relate to real events in their own lives. For example, stories about having a new baby in the family or going to the dentist can help children to understand these challenging experiences.

Key terms

Active listening: the process of listening carefully to what someone is saying

Over to you!

▶ *How do you know when someone is really listening to you?*

▶ *How do you feel when you know that someone is not really listening to you?*

▶ *How do you show that you are really listening to someone?*

▶ *Make a list of your top five tips for active listening and share your list with others in the group.*

Play can be a very useful way to connect with children on their own terms and an effective method in the process of developing a positive relationship.

Understanding communication

Another important factor in effective communication is making sure that children and young people actually understand what is being said. It is sometimes easy to assume that you have been understood, when in reality, the meaning has been completely misunderstood.

Young children tend to interpret things in a very **literal** way and young people can often misinterpret what has been said. It is very important to speak clearly, avoid using jargon and always check that children and young people understand what you are communicating to them. When dealing with young children it is particularly important not to give too much information all at once because this can be too complicated to understand completely.

For children who speak English as an additional language and for some children with special needs, using visual prompts like pictures can help their understanding. For example, by using pictures of different events that happen during the day, like snack time, story time or home time, we can help children to understand the routine of the day. Observing children's reactions to communication is another way to check their understanding. With older children, questioning can be a useful way to check if communication has been fully understood.

Key terms

Literal: following the basic meaning word of a word

Practical Assessment Task	1.1	1.2	1.3

Think about how you communicate effectively with children or young people in your placement or work setting. Make notes on specific examples that demonstrate how you use verbal and non-verbal communication, and active listening.

Think about how you check that children and young people understand what you communicate to them. Make notes on specific examples from your placement or work setting as evidence of your competence.

Keep your notes as evidence towards your assessment. Your evidence for this task must be based on your practice in a real work environment and must be presented in a format acceptable to your assessor.

Over to you!

▶ *Think about examples from your own experience where you have misunderstood information or 'got the wrong end of the stick'.*

▶ *What helps you to understand instructions or other information that is communicated to you?*

▶ *How do you make sure that other people have understood you?*

Share your ideas with others in your group.

Be able to develop and maintain relationships with children and young people

Your assessment criteria:

2.1 Demonstrate how to establish rapport and respectful, trusting relationships with children and young people

2.2 Give attention to individual children and young people in a way that is fair to them and the group as a whole

Why are trusting relationships important?

When developing relationships with children and young people it is extremely important to build up trust and respect. Children need to feel confident and secure in relationships as this helps them to develop independence and a positive outlook. There are many different factors involved in developing respectful, trusting relationships with children and young people, including:

▶ consistency – always responding in a reliable, dependable way

▶ fairness – avoiding discrimination or favouritism

▶ honesty – being truthful and sincere

▶ appropriate communication – using verbal, non-verbal and active listening skills

▶ valuing individuality – acknowledging and appreciating individual differences.

In most early years settings providing care for children aged 0 to 5 years, children are allocated a **key person**. The role of a key person is to develop a close relationship with the child and to take on a greater responsibility for the child's welfare in the setting. It is a requirement of the Early Years Foundation Stage (EYFS) that all children in registered settings have a key person.

Key terms

Key person: the main adult carer for a child in an early years setting

162

'Positive relationships' is one of the four main themes of the EYFS (see Chapter 10 (MU 2.8) on page 206). This theme states that children need positive relationships with their parents or carers and other significant people in their lives. Positive relationships help children to feel safe, secure and loved.

Over to you!

Think about some of the factors which help you in developing relationships with others.

▶ *What helps you to trust other people?*

▶ *What makes you a reliable and trustworthy person, and how do other people recognise this?*

▶ *What do you think other people most respect about you?*

Make a list of the characteristics that you respect in other people, and share your list with others in the group.

Practical Assessment Task   2.1   2.2

Think about how you develop respectful relationships with children or young people in your placement or work setting. Make notes on specific examples that demonstrate your competence in the following areas:

1. How do you make sure you are consistent in responding to children?

2. How do you value every child's individuality?

3. How do you avoid showing favouritism towards some children?

Keep your notes as evidence towards your assessment. Your evidence for this task must be based on your practice in a real work environment and must be presented in a format acceptable to your assessor.

Responding to children

An important part of developing respectful relationships with children and young people is to respond appropriately to their questions, ideas and concerns. Children need to know that they are being taken seriously and that their opinions are valued. Disregarding children's ideas makes them feel worthless or stupid and can be very damaging to their self-esteem.

Developing a trusting relationship is a two-way process and it is very important for anyone who works with children or young people to respect different views and consider alternative ideas. Children need realistic explanations and supportive responses to help them develop positive relationships.

Your assessment criteria:

2.3 Demonstrate supportive and realistic responses to children and young people's questions, ideas, suggestions and concerns

2.4 Provide children and young people with reasons for actions when appropriate

2.5 Encourage children and young people to make choices for themselves

Case study

Describe how you would provide supportive and realistic responses to these children's concerns, ideas and questions in the following situations:

1. You are working in a nursery and preparing to read a story about bears to a group of children. Tommy, aged 4, says he is frightened of bears and does not want to sit and listen to the story.

2. You are working in an out-of-school club and Parveen, aged 9, loves dancing. She wants the whole group to work on a dance routine and give a performance for parents. Some of the other children are not keen on this idea and don't really want to take part.

3. You are supporting a teacher in a Year 1 class and Chloe, aged 6, says to you: *'I want to go outside to play. Why can't I play outside instead of staying in here doing writing?'*

Encouraging choices

Another important aspect of developing relationships with children and young people is encouraging them to think for themselves and make choices. In order to do this, children need clear information, support and guidance.

This process can start at a very early age when toddlers are encouraged to choose from limited options. For example, what they would like to play with (bricks or playdough), or what they would like for breakfast (cereal or toast). In this way, young children are supported to make decisions. As children get older, they will learn more about the **consequences** of the choices they make, for example, *'If you choose to play outside without your coat on, then you will soon get cold'*. Older children can be encouraged to make decisions based on wider choice options, for example, *'What would you like to do today?'*

Key terms

Consequence: the outcome of an event

Practical Assessment Task   2.3   2.4   2.5

Think about the different ways that you respond to children or young people in your placement or work setting. Make notes with specific examples to discuss with your assessor about how you:

▶ provide realistic responses to children's questions, ideas, suggestions and concerns

▶ provide explanations and reasons for children or young people

▶ encourage children or young people to make choices for themselves.

Keep your notes as evidence towards your assessment. Your evidence for this task must be based on your practice in a real work environment and must be presented in a format acceptable to your assessor.

Children and young people need to learn to get along with each other.

How can positive relationships be encouraged between children, young people and others?

It is important for children and young people to learn to get along with each other. This can be a challenging process involving effective communication, positive social interaction and an understanding of individual differences. Adults who work with children and young people can help to encourage this process in different ways, including:

▶ being a good role model through their own communication and behaviour

▶ supporting effective, respectful communication between children, young people and others

▶ promoting the importance of listening to each other

▶ encouraging and appreciating individual differences and diversity

▶ providing consistent rules and boundaries about social interaction and behaviour.

Effective communication and interaction

The importance of effective communication has been discussed in Unit SHC 21 on page xx. Children and young people need support to develop their communication skills with each other. Young children need to learn how to take turns in a conversation and to listen to each other. As they get older, children will learn how to discuss different ideas and how to negotiate and compromise in a group situation.

Over to you!

Think about the ways that you develop agreements with your friends and family.

▶ *How do you resolve issues when people want or expect different things?*

▶ *What skills do you use to reach a solution that everyone is happy with?*

▶ *Think about your group agreement as students.*

Make a list of some of the rules about your behaviour and interactions with each other that everyone is expected to follow.

Adults can help children with this process from an early age. For example, through nursery activities like **circle time** young children can be supported to take turns when speaking and encouraged to listen to each other. Using a 'talking stick' or a simple timer can be a useful way to reinforce children's individual involvement in a group conversation.

Even young children can be involved in discussing how they should interact with others and get along together. Many pre-schools and nurseries will include children in developing simple rules about the importance of respecting each other, being kind and not hurting people's feelings.

Key terms

Circle time: group time when children come together for a shared activity

Case study

St Wilfred's after-school club provides care for children aged 5–10 years between 3pm and 6pm from Monday to Friday. Most of the children come from the local primary school and stay at the club for a couple of hours each day. The club offers drinks and snacks as well as a variety of activities including art and crafts, computer games and an outdoor play area.

It is the start of a new term and the children are working on their 'club rules' with the playworker who is in charge. The children have decided that the rules should be a group agreement and include things like how they get along with each other and their behaviour at the club.

1. How could the playworker support these children to develop their group agreement?
2. Why is it important to include children in developing their own agreements?
3. What skills will the children be using in developing their group agreement?

Practical Assessment Task   **3.1**   **3.4**

Think about the different ways that you support relationships between children or young people in your placement or work setting.

Make notes on specific examples to discuss with your assessor about how you:

▶ support children and young people to communicate effectively with each other
▶ support children and young people to develop group agreements about the way they interact with others.

Keep your notes as evidence towards your assessment. Your evidence for this task must be based on your practice in a real work environment and must be presented in a format acceptable to your assessor.

Children and young people need to develop an understanding of individuality and diversity.

Understanding diversity

Individual difference, equality and diversity have been discussed in Chapter 2 (SHC 23). It is extremely important for anyone who works with children or young people to be aware of their own attitudes towards diversity and to challenge discrimination in any situation.

In supporting relationships between children and young people it is also important to encourage an appreciation of individual differences. Children and young people need to develop an understanding of individuality and diversity.

Developing empathy

The ability to be sensitive to the feelings or beliefs of others requires the skill of **empathy**. This is particularly difficult for young children because their thinking is very **egocentric**. It can therefore be very challenging for them to understand and respect other people's feelings and points of view. Children need the support of sensitive adults to help them develop empathy and consideration for others.

Your assessment criteria:

3.2 Encourage children and young people to understand other people's individuality, diversity and differences

3.3 Help children and young people to understand and respect other people's feelings and points of view

3.5 Demonstrate ways of encouraging and supporting children and young people to deal with conflict for themselves

Over to you!

► *Think about the children or young people in your placement or work setting. Make a list of all the ways they are different (for example, gender, race, height, etc.).*

► *Compare your list with others in the group.*

► *Think about the ways in which you appreciate and celebrate individual differences with the children or young people in your placement or work setting.*

Share your ideas with others in the group.

Key terms

Egocentric: centred on the self with little regard for others

Empathy: the ability to understand the feelings of others

Play can be a very important way to help young children develop an understanding of diversity. For example, in a nursery setting, children will have access to a variety of play resources representing diverse cultures, customs and beliefs. Dressing-up clothes, role-play equipment, small world play and books can all provide a rich background to support children's understanding of difference. **Persona dolls** or puppets can be very useful resources to help young children develop empathy and respect for diversity. Older children can be encouraged to celebrate different faiths and festivals and to share ideas about individual differences through discussions and debates.

Persona dolls: special dolls representing different genders, ethnicities and abilities, which are designed to teach children about diversity and inclusion

Case study

A group of 4-year-old boys are playing together in the garden at Happy Days nursery. They have constructed a den and are busily organising large cardboard boxes to make a 'defence wall' around their play space.

Liam, also aged 4 years, uses a wheelchair. He approaches the boys and watches their play with interest from a distance. The four boys ignore Liam in his wheelchair and carry on playing.

Emma, Liam's support worker, quietly asks Liam if he would like to play with the four boys and he says that he would.

1. How could Emma encourage the four boys to include Liam in their play?
2. Why is it important for Emma to help the four boys to respect Liam's feelings?
3. How could Emma encourage all the children at Happy Days nursery to understand and appreciate individual differences?

Children and young people often need support to help them deal with conflict.

Dealing with conflict

An important part of helping children and young people to get along with each other is to support them in dealing with conflict. This can be a challenging process as children learn how to handle disagreements between themselves. In very young children, this can often be achieved by using distraction, for example, by offering one child a different toy to play with. However, as children get older, this can become more complex and requires more sensitive handling by offering reasons and explanations.

Two essential elements in helping children and young people to deal with conflict are consistency and fairness. Adults who work with children and young people need to make sure that their own behaviour is consistent and that their actions are always seen to be fair. Some of the ways that adults can help children and young people to deal with conflict are shown in Figure 7.1.

Your assessment criteria:

3.2 Encourage children and young people to understand other people's individuality, diversity and differences

3.3 Help children and young people to understand and respect other people's feelings and points of view

3.5 Demonstrate ways of encouraging and supporting children and young people to deal with conflict for themselves

Over to you!

What strategies do you use for dealing with conflict when you have disagreements or arguments with your friends or family?

Think of a recent example of a disagreement you have been involved in and share the experience with a partner.

▶ *What happened and what did you do?*

▶ *Is there anything you could have done better or differently?*

▶ *What would your partner have done in the same situation?*

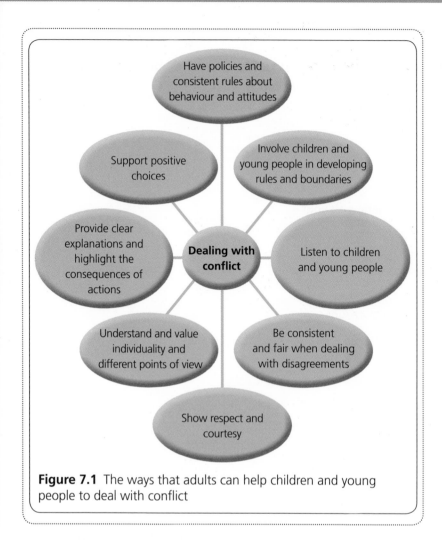

Figure 7.1 The ways that adults can help children and young people to deal with conflict

---

Practical Assessment Task   3.2   3.3   3.5

In your placement or work setting think about the ways that you encourage children or young people to understand diversity and different points of view. Make notes on specific examples to discuss with your assessor about how you help children and young people to:

▶ understand other people's individuality
▶ understand and respect other people's feelings
▶ deal with conflict for themselves.

Keep your notes as evidence towards your assessment. Your evidence for this task must be based on your practice in a real work environment and must be presented in a format acceptable to your assessor.

Are you ready for assessment?

There are no specific knowledge assessment tasks for this unit, but your tutor or assessor may ask you questions about the following:

What do you know now?	✓
The importance of appropriate communication and active listening with children and young people	
Do you have any practical examples to share with your tutor or assessor?	
The importance of trust and respect in developing and maintaining relationships with children and young people	
How to respond to children's and young people's questions, ideas and concerns and provide reasons for actions	
Do you have any practical examples of how you have done this, to share with your tutor or assessor?	
How to encourage children and young people to make choices for themselves	
The importance of helping children and young people to understand diversity, individual differences and other people's feelings	
Can you give some examples from your placement or work setting?	

Your tutor or assessor may need to observe your competence in your placement or work setting.

AC	What can you do now?	Assessment task	✓
1.1	Communicate appropriately with children and young people using conventional language and body language	Page 161	
1.2	Actively listen to children and young people and value what they say, experience and feel	Page 161	
1.3	Check that children and young people understand what is being communicated	Page 161	
2.1 2.2	Demonstrate how to establish respectful relationships with children and young people and give them individual attention	Page 163	
2.3	Demonstrate realistic responses to their questions, ideas, suggestions and concerns	Page 165	
2.4 2.5	Provide children and young people with reasons for actions and encourage them to make choices for themselves Do you have any specific examples to share with your assessor?	Page 165	
3.1 3.4	Support children and young people to communicate effectively with others and to develop group agreements about the way they interact with others	Page 167	
3.2 3.3	Encourage children and young people to understand other people's diversity and differences and to respect other people's feelings and points of view. Could you discuss this with your assessor?	Page 171	
3.5	Demonstrate ways of encouraging children and young people to deal with conflict for themselves. Do you have any specific examples to share with your assessor?	Page 171	

8 | Support children and young people's positive behaviour (TDA 2.9)

Assessment of this unit

This unit is all about supporting and encouraging positive behaviour in children and young people. It includes the knowledge and skills required to promote positive behaviour and strategies for dealing with inappropriate behaviour. It is important both to understand the policies and procedures for supporting behaviour and to be able to apply these in practice.

The assessment of this unit includes some things that you need to know about (knowledge) and some things that you need to be able to do in the real work environment or in your placement (competence).

In order to complete this unit, you will need to produce evidence of both your knowledge and your competence, as shown in the charts. Your tutor or assessor will help you to prepare for your assessment and the tasks suggested in this chapter will help you to create the evidence that you need.

CHAPTER 8

AC   What you need to know

1.1	The policies and procedures of the setting relevant to promoting children and young people's positive behaviour
1.2	The importance of all staff consistently and fairly applying boundaries and rules for children and young people's behaviour in accordance with the policies and procedures of the setting

AC   What you need to do

2.1	Describe the benefits of encouraging and rewarding positive behaviour
2.2	Apply skills and techniques for supporting and encouraging children and young people's positive behaviour
2.3	Demonstrate realistic, consistent and supportive responses to children and young people's behaviour
2.4	Provide an effective role model for the standards of behaviour expected of children, young people and adults within the setting
3.1	Select and apply agreed strategies for dealing with inappropriate behaviour
3.2	Describe the sorts of behaviour problems that should be referred to others and to whom these should be referred

This unit also links to some of the other mandatory units:

SCH 23	Introduction to equality and inclusion in health, social care or children's and young people's settings
MU 2.8	Contribute to the support of the positive environments for children and young people
TDA 2.7	Maintain and support relationships with children and young people
CCLDMU 2.2	Contribute to the support of child and young person development

Some of your learning will be repeated in these units and will give you the chance to review your knowledge and understanding.

Know the policies and procedures of the setting for promoting children and young people's positive behaviour

What are the policies and procedures for promoting positive behaviour?

Children and young people need consistent support as they learn how to behave appropriately. Policies and procedures provide the framework that sets the standards for behaviour, so everyone knows the rules and is treated fairly. Behaviour policies should include clear guidance about what is expected of children and young people and should be consistent, not just with the accepted values and beliefs of the setting, but with those of society as a whole. Procedures should also support staff in encouraging children and young people to behave appropriately.

One of the most successful ways of developing policies and procedures about behaviour is to include children and young people when creating the rules. Even quite young children can be encouraged to think about how they should behave and how they would like others to behave towards them, for example, *we are kind and we don't hurt each other'*. This helps children to feel ownership of the system and to take responsibility for maintaining positive behaviour standards.

Your assessment criteria:

1.1 Describe the policies and procedures of the setting relevant to promoting children and young people's positive behaviour

Over to you!

Think about your own behaviour and how you expect other people to behave towards you. Discuss your ideas with a colleague and create your 'Top 5 Golden Rules for Acceptable Behaviour'.

Most policies and procedures for promoting positive behaviour in settings include:

▶ a code of conduct relating to acceptable and appropriate behaviour in the setting

▶ strategies for encouraging positive behaviour, for example by using rewards and **positive reinforcement**

▶ strategies for dealing with inappropriate behaviour, such as using sanctions

▶ guidance on inclusion, for example, an anti-discrimination policy

▶ strategies for dealing with bullying

▶ guidance on attendance.

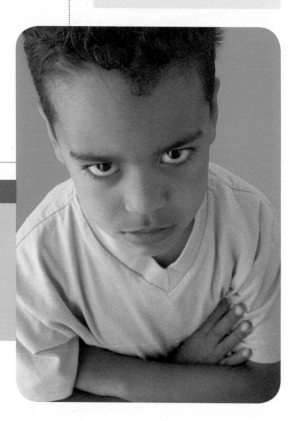

Key terms

Positive reinforcement: giving encouragement to a particular behaviour, with the result that it is more likely to be repeated (see also page 181)

Over to you!

Investigate the organisation Kidscape (www.kidscape.org.uk) and the work it does to protect children and prevent bullying.

Examine the advice page for professionals on how to deal with bullying and bullies.

Look at the anti-bullying policy provided as an example and make notes on some of the key points.

The importance of consistency

As children and young people learn about the rules of appropriate behaviour they need to be supported with consistency and fairness. This helps them to understand what is acceptable and reinforces positive messages about behaviour. For example, if children are expected to wash their hands after using the toilet, this should be applied consistently by every member of staff every time a child uses the toilet. If expectations suddenly change or if children are given different rules, they will become confused and anxious.

Consistency is also important for children's safety. For example, some rules about play behaviour are required in order to minimise the risk of accidents and injuries. Rules and boundaries help children to know what is expected of them and to feel secure.

Your assessment criteria:

1.1 Describe the policies and procedures of the setting relevant to promoting children and young people's positive behaviour

1.2 Describe, with examples, the importance of all staff consistently and fairly applying boundaries and rules for children and young people's behaviour in accordance with the policies and procedures of the setting

Case study

The children at Little Acorns nursery school have been involved in creating their group rules with the teacher. They have agreed that they should be kind to each other, not hurt each other and always be good friends. The behaviour policy at the nursery school includes the following rules:

► Children should not bring their own toys from home because the toys may become lost or broken, or may cause conflict.

► Only four children can play on the bikes outside at any one time in order to minimise accidents and arguments.

► At snack time, children are expected to wash their hands, sit at the snack table and use polite table manners.

Describe how you would respond to the following situations involving children at the Little Acorns nursery school:

1. Ryan, aged 4 years, has a new super hero toy and brings it to school to show his friends.

2. Jamilla, aged 4 years, wants to play on a bike outside. Four boys are already playing on the bikes.

3. Gemma, aged 3 years, has been playing outside. She comes in for snack, goes straight to the table and grabs a biscuit.

Over to you!

Think about situations from your own experience where you think you have not been treated fairly.

► *What happened to you? How were you treated?*

► *How did it make you feel?*

► *How did you respond?*

Share your experiences with others in the group.

Knowledge Assessment Task   1.1   1.2

Investigate the policies and procedures for behaviour in your placement or work setting.

▶ Write a brief account to describe how the policies promote positive behaviour in children or young people.

▶ Think about the importance of being consistent in encouraging positive behaviour and describe two examples of situations where you have experienced staff being consistent and fair with children or young people.

Keep your written work and notes as evidence towards your assessment.

What is positive behaviour?

Positive behaviour is helpful and constructive. It is appropriate and conforms to the accepted values and beliefs of the setting and society as a whole. Positive behaviour can be demonstrated through actions, speech and non-verbal communication; for example, holding a door open, being polite, writing a thank-you note or smiling as a welcoming greeting.

Over to you!

Think about the example you set through your own behaviour in your placement or work setting:

▶ *Are you always polite?*

▶ *Do you always use appropriate language?*

▶ *Do you show children through your own behaviour how to be patient, take turns and be considerate of others?*

▶ *How do you model appropriate behaviour for the children or young people in your setting?*

Encouraging and rewarding positive behaviour

Figure 8.1 outlines some of the ways to encourage positive behaviour in children and young people.

Figure 8.1 Ways to encourage positive behaviour

Be a good role model	Anyone who works with children or young people should set a good example through their own behaviour. Children learn by watching the people around them and adults should make sure that their own behaviour is always appropriate.
Give positive attention	Children and young people respond well to praise and encouragement from adults. When children are rewarded for their behaviour, they usually behave in that way again. This is called **positive reinforcement**. The most important reward is adult attention, with lots of smiles and praise, but reward can also be stickers, special badges or treats.
Be consistent	Children need to know what is expected of them regarding their behaviour. This helps them to feel secure and is sometimes important for their safety. For example, children should know that they must always keep away from a hot oven. Young people also need to know what is expected of them and adults should always give the same messages about behaviour and provide consistent boundaries.
Give choices	Children and young people like to feel in control of what happens to them, as it boosts their confidence and self-esteem. Giving children choices helps them to feel in control and can encourage positive behaviour. For example, if an adult wants a child to put on a coat before going out to play, instead of saying *'Put your coat on now'*, if the adult says *'Would you like to put your coat on by yourself or would you like me to help you?'* the child has a choice, but the desired behaviour is achieved (the coat is put on).
Provide stimulating activities	Some children or young people behave inappropriately because they are bored. Keeping children engaged and challenged with a variety of interesting activities will reduce the likelihood of their behaviour becoming a problem.

Key terms

Positive reinforcement: giving encouragement to a particular behaviour with the result that it is more likely to be repeated

Encouraging and rewarding positive behaviour *continued*

As shown in Figure 8.1, some of the most important ways to encourage positive behaviour are through being a good role model, giving positive attention, providing children with boundaries and realistic choices, and being consistent in your approach.

Praise is extremely important for encouraging positive behaviour. When children or young people feel that they have been rewarded for their behaviour, it encourages them to behave in that way again. This is called positive reinforcement.

Rewarding positive behaviour supports children who are learning about what is acceptable and appropriate, helping them to feel valued and building their self-esteem. The most important reward of all is positive attention from caring adults; most children respond extremely well to smiles, encouraging words, and to warm and appropriate physical contact, such as a pat on the back. There are many other ways to reward positive behaviour, including stickers, star charts and special badges.

Your assessment criteria:

2.1 Describe the benefits of encouraging and rewarding positive behaviour

2.2 Apply skills and techniques for supporting and encouraging children and young people's positive behaviour

2.3 Demonstrate realistic, consistent and supportive responses to children and young people's behaviour

2.4 Provide an effective role model for the standards of behaviour expected of children, young people and adults within the setting

Over to you!

In your placement or work setting, what kinds of rewards have you seen being used to promote children's positive behaviour?

Share your experiences with others in the group and compare the similarities and differences.

Focus on the positive

It can be easy to pay attention to children who are behaving inappropriately, for example, scolding a child for pushing, snatching or being rude (in effect, reinforcing unacceptable behaviour); it is more challenging to remember to make the effort to praise a child who is sitting quietly, showing consideration to others or responding in a thoughtful way.

Rewards for positive behaviour need to be given immediately, particularly to young children who have very little concept of time. If children are rewarded immediately, they are more likely to link the reward with their behaviour. If rewards are saved until the end of the day, it is likely that the behaviour will be forgotten.

In using praise and rewards with children and young people, it is always more effective to be specific and detailed rather than generic. For example, *'you were so patient to wait for your turn on the bike David – I think that deserves a special sticker'* would be more effective than a simple 'well done'. Explaining why you are pleased helps children to understand the link between their behaviour and the reward, and they are more likely to do it again.

One of the most effective ways to support acceptable behaviour with children and young people is to focus on the positive rather than the negative. Using positive statements helps children to develop appropriate behaviour patterns, for example, say 'remember to walk down the corridor Jamie' rather than 'don't run in the corridor Jamie'.

For children with some special needs, visual prompts can help to reinforce the rules and boundaries for behaviour. For example, using pictures or special charts can help to promote positive behaviour and guide children towards acceptable behaviour patterns.

Over to you!

Describe how you could support positive behaviour in the following situations:

1. *In a nursery setting, how could you encourage the children to tidy up and put away their toys when they have finished playing?*

2. *In a school setting, how could you make sure that the children listen carefully to instructions from the teacher?*

3. *In an out-of-school club setting, how could you support the children to share and take turns when playing with the computer games?*

Practical Assessment Task | 2.1 | 2.2 | 2.3 | 2.4

In your placement or work setting, think about the strategies that are used to support and encourage positive behaviour in children or young people. (You can cross-reference this work to your evidence for Unit MU2.2, AC 4.1 and 4.2.) Make notes to discuss with your assessor about:

▶ the benefits of encouraging and rewarding positive behaviour
▶ skills and techniques that are used to support positive behaviour
▶ the importance of realistic, consistent responses to children and young people's behaviour
▶ the importance of being an effective role model for the standards of behaviour expected in the setting.

Keep your notes as evidence towards your assessment. Your evidence for this task must be based on your practice in a real work environment and must be presented in a format acceptable to your assessor.

Be able to respond to inappropriate behaviour

Your assessment criteria:

3.1 Select and apply agreed strategies for dealing with inappropriate behaviour

What is inappropriate behaviour?

Inappropriate behaviour conflicts with the accepted values and beliefs of the setting and society as a whole. It can be demonstrated through actions, speech or non-verbal behaviour, for example, pushing into a queue, using offensive language or disrespectful gestures. Inappropriate behaviour includes all types of bullying, discrimination of any kind, and physical aggression or abuse.

Strategies for dealing with inappropriate behaviour

In order to deal with inappropriate behaviour, it is important to understand how and why children respond in different situations. Children often act impulsively, have difficulty expressing themselves and can find it hard to control their feelings. As a result, children can struggle to manage their own behaviour. Adults need to support children and young people by acting as positive role models, providing consistent boundaries and using lots of praise and encouragement.

Observation

Observation can be a very useful tool for dealing with inappropriate behaviour. Observing children and young people can help practitioners to develop a complete picture of what is happening, leading to a better understanding of a particular behaviour pattern. For example, observation can help practitioners find out what happened before the inappropriate behaviour occurred and what happened as a result. It may be possible to identify the **trigger** for the behaviour and then to implement an appropriate strategy to deal with the situation.

> **Over to you!**
>
> *In your placement or work setting, think about examples of inappropriate behaviour that you may have witnessed among the children or young people. How did the staff at the setting handle the inappropriate behaviour in each case?*
>
> *Share your experiences with others in the group and compare your responses.*

> **Key terms**
>
> **Trigger:** a stimulus to make something happen

Positive reinforcement

The strategy of positive reinforcement works by giving lots of praise and encouragement when children behave in the way we want them to, but ignoring their inappropriate behaviour. Most children crave attention from adults and so, when we deny them this attention, we are giving out a strong message that their behaviour is not acceptable. When using this strategy, it is important to be clear with the child that you are ignoring their *behaviour* and not ignoring *them*.

One strategy that uses this principle is often referred to as 'time out'. Children are removed from the presence of the adult for a short period in order to have some time to calm down. This creates a non-rewarding environment for unacceptable behaviour, and both time and space for the child to settle down.

Sanctions

Specific **sanctions** can also be an effective strategy to reinforce this principle. This can be achieved by denying children or young people access to something they really want or like for a period of time, for example, not allowing children to play their favourite game or to have time on the computer.

Any strategy for dealing with inappropriate behaviour must be applied consistently and fairly by all the adults involved. If children are exposed to different expectations and inconsistent boundaries, they can easily become confused and anxious. Behaviour strategies should be constant and reliable if children and young people are to understand what is expected of them.

Over to you!

Think about situations where you have observed parents dealing with their children's inappropriate behaviour in public places (for example, in the supermarket).

What kind of responses have you seen from parents?

Think about how you might deal with a child having a temper tantrum in a public place.

Key terms

Sanction: a penalty imposed for breaking the rules

Case study

Sophie is 3 years old and attends Little Ducklings pre-school every morning. She has outbursts of temper whenever she doesn't get her own way, involving screaming, lashing out and kicking whoever happens to be around.

Emily is Sophie's key person in the nursery and she has spoken with Sophie's mum. Sophie's mother says that she can't deal with these tantrums, so she always ends up letting Sophie have her own way.

A particular incident occurs at circle time in the nursery when Sophie refuses to come and sit down for a story. Emily tries to encourage Sophie to come and join the group, but Sophie just screams and kicks Emily's legs.

1. Describe an appropriate strategy that Emily could use to deal with Sophie's unacceptable behaviour.

2. Explain why it is important for Emily to be consistent in her approach when dealing with Sophie's behaviour.

3. What advice could Emily give to Sophie's mum to support her in dealing with Sophie's inappropriate behaviour?

Your assessment criteria:

3.1 Select and apply agreed strategies for dealing with inappropriate behaviour

3.2 Describe the sorts of behaviour problems that should be referred to others and to whom these should be referred

Referring problem behaviour

In most cases of inappropriate behaviour, strategies can be implemented to support children and young people. However, in some cases, individuals with behaviour problems need additional support; it is important for practitioners to know when to refer children and young people for more specialised help with their behaviour.

Some examples of behaviour problems that should be referred to other practitioners are highlighted in Figure 8.2.

Figure 8.2 Sources of help with different behavioural problems

Type of behaviour	Characteristics	Refer to
Attention Deficit Hyperactivity Disorder (ADHD)	• Extremely hyperactive, disruptive behaviour • Inability to sit still or concentrate	• Behaviour support team • Educational psychologist
Autistic spectrum disorder (ASD)	• Difficulty in interacting with others • Rigid, inflexible behaviour patterns • Communication difficulties	• Autism team • Special Educational Needs Co-ordinator (SENCO) • Educational psychologist
Self-harming behaviour	• Inflicting harm on self, for example, cutting, head banging, extreme rubbing or picking at skin to cause bleeding	• GP • Child and Adolescent Mental Health Service (CAMS) team • Educational psychologist
Selective mutism	• Refusal to speak in certain situations or with specific people	• Speech and language therapist
Extremely violent or unco-operative	• Extreme physical aggression • inflicting harm on others • bullying	• Behaviour support team • Educational psychologist
Explicit sexualised behaviour	• Frequent, obvious masturbation • Imitation of sexual intercourse with toys, play materials or other children	• Child and Adolescent Mental Health Service (CAMS) team • Educational psychologist

Practical Assessment Task   3.1   3.2

Investigate the strategies that are used to deal with inappropriate behaviour in your placement or work setting.

▶ Make notes about situations in which you have experienced inappropriate behaviour. Describe how each situation was tackled.

▶ Describe examples of behaviour problems that would be referred to other practitioners and find out which specialists might be involved.

Keep your notes as evidence towards your assessment. Your evidence for this task must be based on your practice in a real work environment and must be presented in a format acceptable to your assessor.

Are you ready for assessment?

AC	What do you know now?	Assessment task	✓
1.1	The policies and procedures of the setting relevant to promoting children and young people's positive behaviour	Page 179	
1.2	The importance of all staff consistently and fairly applying boundaries and rules for children and young people's behaviour in accordance with the policies and procedures of the setting	Page 179	

Your tutor or assessor may want to observe you actually doing this in your placement or work setting.

AC	What can you do now?	Assessment task	✓
2.1	Describe the benefits of encouraging and rewarding positive behaviour	Page 183	
2.2	Apply skills and techniques for supporting and encouraging children and young people's positive behaviour	Page 183	
2.3	Demonstrate realistic, consistent and supportive responses to children and young people's behaviour Do you have specific examples of this to discuss with your assessor?	Page 183	
2.4	Provide an effective role model for the standards of behaviour expected of children, young people and adults within the setting	Page 183	
3.1	Select and apply agreed strategies for dealing with inappropriate behaviour Do you have specific examples of this to discuss with your assessor?	Page 187	
3.2	Describe the sorts of behaviour problems that should be referred to others and to whom these should be referred	Page 187	

9 | Contribute to the support of child and young person development (CCLDMU 2.2)

Assessment of this unit

This unit is all about supporting the development of children and young people. It covers the observation of children's development and the assessment of their developmental needs in the work setting. The unit also explores the importance of promoting positive behaviour and supporting children and young people who are experiencing transitions.

The assessment of this unit is partly knowledge based (things that you need to know about) and partly competence based (things that you need to be able to do in the real work environment or in your placement). In order to successfully complete this unit, you will need to produce evidence of both your knowledge and your competence, as shown in the following charts. Your tutor or assessor will help you to prepare for your assessment, and the tasks suggested in this chapter will help you to create the evidence you need.

AC	What you need to know
3.1	How to describe the different transitions children and young people may experience
3.2	How to explain how to give support children and young people who are experiencing transitions

CHAPTER 9

AC   What you need to do

1.1	Observe and record aspects of the development of children or young people
1.2	Identify different observation methods and knowing why they are used
1.3	Support assessments of the development needs of children and young people
1.4	Suggest how these needs can be met in the work setting
2.1	Carry out activities with a child or young person to support their holistic development
2.2	Record observations of children or young people participating in activities
2.3	Contribute to the evaluation of activities to meet the development needs of children and young people
4.1 **4.2**	Explain how a work setting can encourage children and young people's positive behaviour and demonstrate how children and young people are encouraged to engage in positive behaviour
4.3	Reflect on your own role in promoting positive behaviour in children or young people
5.1 **5.2**	Review the effectiveness of your own role in assessing developmental needs and supporting the development of children and young people
5.3	Identify any changes you could make to your own practice in supporting children and young people's development

This unit also links to some of the other mandatory units:

TDA 2.1	Child and young person development
TDA 2.9	Support children and young people's positive behaviour
MU 2.8	Contribute to the support of the positive environments for children and young people

Some of your learning will be repeated in these units and will give you the chance to review your knowledge and understanding.

Why is observation and assessment important?

Observation is a highly skilled task and an important part of the job for anyone who works with children or young people. It is the main way to find out what children can do, what young people are interested in and what they might find difficult or need help with. The information from observations can be used for monitoring progress, planning activities and sharing with parents or carers. It is very important that observations are carried out carefully and that the information is recorded accurately.

In any situation involving information about children and young people, **confidentiality** is extremely important. Adults wishing to observe children or young people should always gain permission, either from parents or from young people themselves. Children's own wishes should also be taken into consideration and you should never disclose information about children or young people outside of the work setting. Children and young people will behave differently depending on what they are doing, the time of day and sometimes how they are feeling, so a variety of different observations should be carried out in order to get a balanced picture of the child or young person.

Observing development and behaviour

When observing children and young people it is important to:

▶ watch – how they behave, what they do and how they do it

▶ listen – to what they say, the questions they ask and the responses they give

Key terms

Confidentiality: treating information as private

- find out – information from parents, carers or other professionals involved with the child (e.g. psychologist or speech therapist)

- be discreet – try to be unobtrusive and remain 'on the sidelines' when observing

- be objective – try not to allow personal views or bias to influence the observation (e.g. because you have an attachment to a particular child).

Observations of children and young people may focus on many different areas of development or behaviour, including:

- *individual interests* – for example, observing what children like to play with, their friendship groups and their enthusiasms (e.g. for dinosaurs, Spiderman, football, dance or gaming)

- *individual needs* – for example, observing if children are right- or left-handed, bilingual or need to wear glasses for reading

- *physical skills* – for example, how children control their bodies and co-ordinate their movements to ride a bicycle, or how a child uses **hand–eye co-ordination** and manipulative skills to operate a computer keyboard

- *intellectual (cognitive) skills* – for example, how a toddler uses problem-solving skills to operate a pop-up toy, or how a child uses their memory and concentration to play Picture Lotto and later learns to read, write and count

- *communication skills* – for example, how toddlers learn to use language to communicate their needs, how a child starts to learn the rules of grammar (and says things like 'feets' and 'sheeps'), or the communication skills a young person uses to negotiate with parents or persuade their friends to do something

- *social, emotional and behavioural skills* – for example, how toddlers start to do things for themselves and develop independence, how children learn to share, play together and take turns, or how young people learn to express and manage their feelings.

Key terms

Hand–eye co-ordination: the ability to make the hands work together with what the eyes can see

Over to you!

Think about some of the things you are interested in, for example, music, films, gaming or sports. Make a list of your interests and share them with a member of your group.

Think about some of the skills you have, for example, using technology, playing a musical instrument or a team sport.

Make a list of your skills and share them with a member of your group.

Holistic development

In most situations, observations of children and young people will include several aspects of development or behaviour. For example, when observing a 6-year-old girl using a computer with a friend, you might notice:

▶ her fine motor skills on the keyboard, her manipulation of the mouse and her hand–eye co-ordination

▶ her level of concentration or how easily she is distracted

▶ her understanding of the computer programme and how she follows the instructions to work out what she needs to do

▶ how she communicates with her friend and the language she uses

▶ how willing she is to share the task with her friend and take turns

▶ how she expresses her feelings and whether she seems to be enjoying the activity or becomes frustrated when she cannot do something.

Your assessment criteria:

1.1 Observe and record aspects of the development of a child or young person

1.3 Support assessments of the development needs of a child or young person

---

Practical Assessment Task   1.1   1.3

In your placement or work setting, observe a child or young person engaged in play or a specific activity for about five minutes. Complete an observation record sheet to assess and record the following aspects of their development:

▶ physical skills (e.g. gross and fine motor skills)

▶ evidence of learning (e.g. working things out, problem-solving, creativity, concentration)

▶ how they communicate (e.g. body language, gestures and spoken words)

▶ emotional wellbeing and social interaction (e.g. evidence of feelings expressed, confidence, sharing or co-operating with others).

Keep your observation record as evidence towards your assessment. Your evidence for this task must be based on your practice in a real work environment and must be presented in a format acceptable to your assessor.

Key terms

Holistic: emphasising the importance of the whole child

Recording observations

Observations should always be recorded accurately. They should also be dated as this helps you to monitor and keep track of children's progress. Sometimes observations can be used as evidence in meetings about children or young people, and having the date on your recording can be very important.

When you are observing children and young people, it is important to record what you actually see, and not what you think or assume. Always try to be as accurate as you can when recording information from observations.

There are many different ways to record observations and assessments of children and young people. Some examples are listed in the chart below:

Recording method	Description and use
Written record (also called narrative or free description)	A full written report on the behaviour or development of a child or young person for a short period of time. This is a useful method for observing several areas of development together.
Time sample	Observing a child or young person at regular intervals (say every 15 minutes) for a certain period of time (e.g. the whole morning). This can be a useful method for observing behaviour (e.g. a child who is having difficulty settling into nursery).
Event sample	Used for focusing on a specific aspect of development or behaviour (e.g. biting). A recording is made every time the child engages in that behaviour and the observations can be used to explore possible reasons or behaviour patterns.
Checklists	Used for structured assessments of children's development and for monitoring progress against expected milestones. Checklists can be quite limiting as a recording method, but are useful for routine check-ups.
Photographs/Video	Visual evidence of children's development or behaviour can be extremely useful, but it is very important to obtain all the necessary permissions before doing this. Photographs can be an excellent way of sharing observations with parents or carers, but visual images of children or young people should never be disclosed outside of the work setting.
Audio recording	Digital recording devices can be used to record children's language and communication. Playing the recording back can be a useful way to assess a child's language development at different stages.

Practical Assessment Task 1.2

In your placement or workplace, carry out *two* observations on different children or young people using *two different* recording methods. Explain why you have used the different recording methods for each observation.

Remember to include the dates of your observations and the ages of the children or young people.

Keep your observations as evidence towards your assessment. Your evidence for this task must be based on your practice in a real work environment and must be presented in a format acceptable to your assessor.

Be able to support the development of children and young people

Your assessment criteria:

1.4 Suggest ways the identified development needs of a child or young person can be met in the work setting

2.1 Carry out activities with a child or young person to support their holistic development

2.2 Record observations of the child or young person's participation in the activities

2.3 Contribute to the evaluation of the activities meeting the child or young person's identified development needs

How can we use the information from observations and assessments?

Observation is a very useful tool and can provide a lot of information about children and young people. This can be used for:

- ▶ monitoring and assessing progress
- ▶ finding out about individual needs and additional support that may be required
- ▶ planning experiences and activities that will interest children and young people and encourage their developmental progress
- ▶ sharing with parents, carers and others.

In a work setting, observations are frequently used to identify the development needs of children and young people. This information can then be used to plan individual support and activities to encourage developmental progress.

Over to you!

Think about how observations are used in your placement or work setting.

- ▶ *How is the information used to plan activities for children or young people?*
- ▶ *How are observations shared with parents or carers?*

Compare your experiences with others in your group.

196

Case study

Ryan is 3 years old and attends a local nursery every morning. His key person at the nursery is Sam and she carries out observations of Ryan on a regular basis. She uses the information from these observations to plan interesting activities for Ryan and to support his individual learning and development. Sam has observed that Ryan enjoys painting. He uses a chunky paintbrush, which he holds in the fist of his right hand. His paintings are usually circular patterns and dominated by the colour red. Ryan does not like to get messy or use his fingers in the paint. Sam has also observed that Ryan likes to play outside with his friend Hassan. They love to run around pretending to be super heroes and enjoy making up different adventures. Sam has observed that Ryan is usually very quiet and withdrawn with other children in the nursery and he doesn't usually talk or contribute in group activities or circle time.

1. From Sam's observations of Ryan, what might you identify as his individual interests?

2. What does this information tell you about Ryan's developmental needs?

3. Suggest three different activities that might support Ryan's development in the nursery.

Practical Assessment Task   1.4   2.1   2.2   2.3

In your placement or workplace, observe a child or young person engaged in an activity (for example, playing in the sand, playing a computer game or playing an imaginative game outside with others).

1. Complete an observation record sheet and remember to include the date of your observation and the age of the child or young person.

2. Write an evaluation that summarises the child or young person's developmental needs (for example, they may need support and encouragement with language, social interaction or using scissors).

3. Explain how that activity would meet the individual needs of the child or young person you have observed (for example, it might encourage new vocabulary, creativity or fine motor skills).

4. Suggest another activity that would meet the individual needs of the child or young person you have observed.

Keep your observations and notes as evidence towards your assessment.

Know how to support children and young people experiencing transitions

Your assessment criteria:

3.1 Describe the different transitions children and young people may experience

3.2 Explain how to give adult support for each of these transitions

What are the different transitions children and young people may experience?

Look back at the information about **transitions** in Unit TDA 2.1 on page XX. Look at Figure 5.7 which shows the transitions that affect most children and young people and Figure 5.8 which shows the transitions that affect only some children and young people.

Key terms

Transitions: changes from one place, state or stage to another

Knowledge Assessment Task   3.1

Using ICT, create a timeline to show some of the major transitions that affect most children and young people from birth to the age of 19 years. Choose two of the major transitions from your timeline and describe the effects these might have on the lives of children or young people.

Keep your notes as evidence towards your assessment. You can cross-reference your evidence with Unit TDA 2.1 AC 3.1 and 3.2.

Supporting transitions

When children and young people are experiencing changes in their lives they need consistent support. Adults need to make sure that as far as possible children have some degree of stability to help them cope.

Some of the ways that children and young people can be supported with transitions include:

▶ *Providing information*: explaining what is going to happen and what that might mean for the child. With young children, it is important to use simple language and not provide too

Over to you!

In your placement or work setting, think about the different transitions that children or young people experience.

▶ *How are children supported when they first start at the setting?*

▶ *How do they know what to do and where to put their things?*

▶ *What happens when children or young people leave the setting and move on?*

▶ *How are they supported to cope with their new experiences?*

198

much information at once. It might also include using picture books, photographs and different play activities to help them understand. For example, playing at doctors and nurses in preparation for going into hospital or sharing a book about babies when a new baby is expected in the family. With young people, this might include information from websites or additional information from specific organisations such as information about drugs, contraception or sexually transmitted infections for young people who are transitioning into adulthood.

▶ *Listening*: allowing time for information to be taken in and for children to respond. Some children will need more time than others to process information and it is important not to rush this. Adults should never dismiss children's concerns as 'being silly', but should treat them seriously and always pay attention to what children and young people have to say.

▶ *Being honest*: being truthful with children and young people is very important, especially when answering their questions, which may be difficult. When children and young people are experiencing transitions, they need to trust the adults in their lives. This helps them to feel more secure with the changes that are happening.

▶ *Acknowledging feelings*: it is normal for children and young people to express a variety of feelings when they are dealing with transitions. Often, these are negative feelings like frustration or anger. Adults will sometimes dismiss children's feelings and say things like 'don't cry'. It is important to acknowledge the feelings of children and young people and to give them the opportunity to express themselves

Knowledge Assessment Task 3.2

Describe how you might provide support for each of the following children and young people experiencing transitions:

1. Vikram is 4 years old and his mother is expecting a new baby in two months' time.
2. Gemma is 7 years old and her parents are currently going through a divorce.
3. Chris is 11 years old and will be moving up from primary to secondary school next month.

Keep your notes as evidence towards your assessment. You can cross-reference your evidence with Unit TDA 2.1 AC 3.3.

Your assessment criteria:

4.1 Explain how a work setting can encourage children and young people's positive behaviour

4.2 Demonstrate how children and young people are encouraged to engage in positive behaviour

How can we support positive behaviour?

Learning how to behave appropriately can be quite challenging for some children and young people. Behaviour is part of development, just like learning to walk or talk, and children still need support, encouragement and lots of practice! One of the difficulties for young children when learning about behaviour is that the rules often change. What is considered to be acceptable behaviour in one situation may be very different in another. For example, the expectations on a child's behaviour in school may be very different from those at home and it can be difficult for children to adapt.

Another difficulty with behaviour is that adults are very good at telling children what *not* to do, rather than what they want children to do. For example, a parent might say *'Don't throw sand'* or *'Don't hit your sister'*. One of the main principles of supporting positive behaviour in children is to actively promote 'good' (acceptable) behaviour rather than focusing on the negative.

Some of the ways to encourage positive behaviour are outlined below:

Be a good role model	Anyone who works with children or young people should set a good example through their own behaviour. Children learn by watching the people around them and adults should make sure that their own behaviour is always appropriate.
Give positive attention	Children and young people respond well to praise and encouragement from adults. When children are rewarded for their behaviour, they usually behave in that way again. This is called **positive reinforcement**. The most important reward is adult attention, with lots of smiles and praise, but reward can also be stickers, special badges or treats.
Be consistent	Children need to know what is expected of them regarding their behaviour. This helps them to feel secure and is sometimes important for their safety. For example, children should know that they must always keep away from a hot oven. Young people also need to know what is expected of them and adults should always give the same messages about behaviour and provide consistent boundaries.
Give choices	Children and young people like to feel in control of what happens to them, it boosts their confidence and self-esteem. Giving children choices helps them to feel in control and can encourage positive behaviour. For example, if an adult wants a child to put on a coat before going out to play, instead of saying *'Put your coat on now'*, if the adult says *'Would you like to put your coat on by yourself or would you like me to help you?'* the child has a choice, but the desired behaviour is achieved (the coat is put on).
Provide stimulating activities	Some children or young people behave inappropriately because they are bored. Keeping children engaged and challenged with a variety of interesting activities will reduce the likelihood of their behaviour becoming a problem.

Practical Assessment Task   4.1   4.2

Think about the different ways that positive behaviour is promoted when dealing with children or young people in your placement or work setting. You can cross-reference your evidence with Unit TDA 2.9 AC 2.1, 2.2, 2.3 and 2.4. Write a reflective account which:

▶ explains how positive behaviour is encouraged in your placement or work setting

▶ describes a specific incident where you have promoted positive behaviour, or you have observed positive behaviour being promoted in your placement or work setting.

Keep your notes as evidence towards your assessment. Your evidence for this task must be based on your practice in a real work environment and must be presented in a format acceptable to your assessor

Key terms

Positive reinforcement: giving encouragement to a particular behaviour with the result that it is more likely to be repeated

Your assessment criteria:

4.3 Reflect on own role in promoting positive behaviour in children or young people

5.1 Review effectiveness of own contribution to the assessment of the developmental needs of a child or young person

5.2 Review effectiveness of own role in supporting the child or young person's development

5.3 Identify changes that can be made to own practice in supporting child and young person development

What is reflective practice?

It is important for anyone who works with children or young people to think about how effectively they are doing their job and if there are any ways they could do it better. This is called reflective practice and it is an important skill to develop. You can start the process of reflection by thinking about how effective you are with children or young people in your placement or work setting. The next part of the reflective process is to identify the changes you could make in order to improve your practice. You can do some reflection on your own, but it is also helpful to have support and guidance from a supervisor, mentor or tutor.

Case study

Karin is a newly qualified early years worker and has just started her job at Little Wonders nursery. She is working in the pre-school room, with children aged 3–4 years. Karin has just had to deal with a dispute between Harry and Sarah, both aged 3, who were squabbling over whose turn it was on the ride-in-car when they were playing outside. Harry had pushed Sarah away so that he could get into the car and Sarah had fallen over and grazed her knee.

Karin shouted at Harry that he was 'naughty' and ordered him to go inside, then she went over to Sarah and attended to her grazed knee. While she was doing this, Karin was then called to help with the children's lunches and the dispute was forgotten.

1. How effectively did Karin deal with the children's behaviour?
2. How could Karin have improved how she dealt with the situation?
3. Why is it important for Karin to reflect on her professional practice?

Reflecting on your own professional practice

One way of using reflective practice is to keep notes about your own role in your placement or work setting. This can help you to get into the habit of regular reflection and the more you do, the easier it gets!

Practical Assessment Task   4.3   5.1   5.2   5.3

Use the table below as a model to create your own record of reflective practice. Use your chart to record examples of your own effectiveness in supporting children and young people's development and behaviour. Identify changes you could make to your own practice and make a note of the help you need from others.

Reflection on practice	Evidence	How I could improve (5.3)	Things I need help with
Contribute to the assessment of the development needs of a child or young person (5.1) Do you observe what children or young people are interested in and what they can do? How well can you record observations of children or young people? Do you take note of any difficulties children/young people have?			
Support the development of children or young people (5.2) Can you provide activities for children or young people to support and encourage their development at different stages? Can you contribute to the evaluation of activities to review how effective they have been?			
Promote positive behaviour with children or young people (4.3) Are you a good role model through your own behaviour? Do you listen to children and give them lots of positive attention? Are you consistent in your approach to children's and young people's behaviour?			

Your evidence for this task must be based on your practice in a real work environment and must be presented in a format acceptable to your assessor.

Are you ready for assessment?

AC	What do you know now?	Assessment task	✓
3.1	How to describe the different transitions children and young people may experience	Page 198	
3.2	How to explain how to give support children and young people who are experiencing transitions	Page 199	

Your tutor or assessor may want to observe you actually doing this in your placement or work setting.

AC	What can you do now?	Assessment task	✓
1.1	Observe and record aspects of the development of children or young people	Page 194	
1.2	Identify different observation methods and knowing why they are used Do you have evidence of observations you have made on children and young people using different recording methods?	Page 195	
1.3	Support assessments of the development needs of children and young people	Page 194	
1.4	Suggest how these needs can be met in the work setting	Page 197	
2.1	Carry out activities with a child or young person to support their holistic development	Page 197	
2.2	Record observations of children or young people participating in activities Do you have evidence of observations you have made on children and young people participating in activities?	Page 197	
2.3	Contribute to the evaluation of activities to meet the development needs of children and young people	Page 197	
4.1 4.2	Explain how a work setting can encourage children and young people's positive behaviour and demonstrate how children and young people are encouraged to engage in positive behaviour	Page 201	
4.3	Reflect on your own role in promoting positive behaviour in children or young people Do you have any specific examples to share with your assessor?	Page 203	
5.1 5.2	Review the effectiveness of your own role in assessing developmental needs and supporting the development of children and young people	Page 203	
5.3	Identify any changes you could make to your own practice in supporting children and young people's development Do you have any specific examples to share with your assessor?	Page 203	

10 | Contribute to the support of the positive environments for children and young people (MU 2.8)

Assessment of this unit

This unit is all about the importance of positive environments for children and young people, both indoors and outdoors. It examines how to provide stimulating surroundings and create an encouraging atmosphere to meet the individual needs of children and young people. It includes the support of children's personal care needs and dietary requirements.

The assessment of this unit is partly knowledge based (things that you need to know about) and partly competence based (things that you need to be able to do in the real work environment or in your placement). In order to successfully complete this unit you will need to produce evidence of both your knowledge and your competence as shown in the charts.

Your tutor or assessor will help you to prepare for your assessment, and the tasks suggested in this chapter will help you to create the evidence that you need.

AC	What you need to know
1.1	What is meant by a positive environment for children and young people
1.2	The regulatory requirements that underpin a positive environment
4.1 4.2	The basic nutritional requirements of children and young people to ensure a balanced diet and meet government guidance
4.3	Basic food safety when providing food and drinks for children and young people

AC	What you need to do
2.1	Meet and greet children and young people in a way that welcomes them into the work setting
2.2 2.3	Provide opportunities and resources for children and young people to engage in activities of choice to meet their individual needs
2.4	Support the engagement of children or young people in activities that promote use of their senses
2.5	Give praise and encouragement to children and young people for individual achievements
3.1	Explain how to effectively care for children or young people's skin, hair and teeth
3.2	Support personal care routines that meet the individual needs of children or young people and promote their independence
3.3	Explain how a positive environment and routine meet the emotional needs of children and their families
3.4	Describe the importance for physical and mental wellbeing of balancing periods of physical activity with rest and quiet time

This unit also links to some of the other mandatory units:

MU 2.2	Contribute to the support of child and young person development
TDA 2.7	Maintain and support relationships with children and young people
TDA 2.2	Safeguarding the welfare of children and young people

Some of your learning will be repeated in these units and will give you the chance to review your knowledge and understanding.

What are the requirements for a positive environment?

Children and young people thrive in positive surroundings. They need to feel welcome, safe and stimulated in an environment that supports their learning and development.

A positive environment should be a place where children and young people feel:

▶ welcome

▶ safe and secure

▶ valued

▶ interested and challenged.

There are specific government regulations that support the maintenance of a positive environment for children and young people. One of the most important frameworks in England is known as Every Child Matters (ECM). This framework outlines five main outcomes for the wellbeing of children and young people up to the age of 19 years. (ECM is explained fully in Chapter 6 (TDA 2.2) on page 138.)

Regulatory requirements

In settings caring for children aged 0–5 years in England, the regulatory requirements for supporting a positive environment are included in the Statutory Framework for the Early Years Foundation Stage (EYFS). This is covered by the Early Years Framework in Scotland, the Curriculum Guidance for Pre-school Education in Northern Ireland and the Foundation Phase for Children's Learning in Wales.

The EYFS is based on four main 'themes' and 'principles', including 'enabling environments', as shown in Figure 10.1. The welfare requirements of the EYFS are statutory, and include important regulations about 'suitable premises, environment and equipment', as shown in Figure 10.2.

In England, these regulations are monitored by the government organisation **Ofsted**, (the Education and Training Inspectorate in Northern Ireland, Estyn in Wales and **HMIE** in Scotland). These organisations are also responsible for inspecting schools and other registered settings to make sure that the regulatory requirements for a positive environment are being met for all children and young people.

Key terms

HMIE: Her Majesty's Inspectorate of Education (in Scotland)

Ofsted: abbreviation for the Office for Standards in Education

Statutory: relating to the law (statute)

Figure 10.1 Themes and principles of the EYFS

Theme	Principle	Role of the practitioner
1. A unique child	All children are individuals with the ability to learn.	To value children as unique individuals and to understand that all children have different needs
2. Positive relationships	Children need positive relationships with their parents/carers and other significant people in their lives.	To develop positive relationships with children and their parents/carers
3. Enabling environments	The environment (both indoors and outdoors) is very important for children's learning and development.	To provide a safe, stimulating indoor and outdoor environment with a variety of opportunities and experiences
4. Learning and development	Children learn and develop at different rates and in different ways. All areas of learning and development are interlinked.	To observe children's learning and development and plan appropriate activities to meet their needs

Figure 10.2 Welfare requirements of the EYFS

Statutory welfare requirements of the EYFS	Role of the practitioner
1. Safeguarding and promoting children's welfare	To keep children safe, promote good health and manage children's behaviour appropriately
2. Suitable people	To have relevant qualifications, skills and knowledge and be a suitable person to look after children
3. Suitable premises, environment and equipment	To make sure that indoor and outdoor spaces are safe and that furniture, equipment and toys are safe and suitable for children in the setting
4. Organisation	To plan and organise the setting to make sure that individual children's needs are met
5. Documentation	To keep accurate records that meet the needs of the children

---

Knowledge Assessment Task `1.1` `1.2`

1. Think about how a positive environment is created for the children or young people in your placement or work setting. Create a poster or display to highlight the factors that make the surroundings safe, stimulating and supportive.

2. Investigate the regulatory requirements that influence the provision of a positive environment in your placement or work setting. Summarise the key guidance and create a webpage that could be used to inform a new member of staff.

Take photographs of your display and keep your work as evidence towards your assessment.

Why is it important to support a positive environment?

Children and young people need to develop a sense of belonging in any setting. It can be a very daunting experience for children entering a new or unfamiliar environment, for example, starting school or nursery. First impressions can be very important in determining how a child will settle in a new place and how they will react to that experience. A positive environment is very important in helping children and young people to feel secure and stimulated.

Providing a positive environment

It is important that children and young people feel welcome in the work setting. Greeting them personally by name with a friendly smile will help them to feel at ease. Children will feel more secure if they are shown where to put their belongings, told what is going to happen during the day and introduced to the routine of the setting.

Your assessment criteria:

2.1 Meet and greet children and young people in a way that welcomes them into the work setting

Over to you!

► *How did you feel on your first day in your placement or work setting?*

► *Did anyone welcome you or show you around? What might have made the experience better for you?*

► *Share your experiences with others in the group.*

It is a useful to try to think about the environment from the child's point of view. What does a child see, hear and smell? Imagine some of the concerns that a child may have:

▶ Will I be safe here?

▶ Who will look after me?

▶ What happens here and what can I do?

▶ Where do I put my things, eat my lunch and go to the toilet?

Young people can be equally worried by new situations and may be concerned about what they can do and what the routine will be. These concerns can be even more troubling for children or young people with special needs. They may be anxious about being able to move around safely, use equipment correctly or understand instructions, and it is important to ensure that the environment is **inclusive** for all the children.

Key terms

inclusive: non-discriminatory

Practical Assessment Task   2.1

Think about how you meet and greet children or young people in your placement or work setting. How do you help children to feel welcome when they arrive? Think of some specific examples to share with your assessor.

Supporting a positive environment

Some of the factors to consider when supporting a positive environment for children and young people are listed in the table below:

Factor	What to consider
Design and layout of the environment, indoors and outdoors	Safety and access with space to move around Providing different areas for children to have both physical activity and quiet time (both indoors and outdoors)
Appearance of the environment	Attractive, welcoming surroundings, with inclusive images and displays of children's work Welcoming signs and labels in different languages
Provision of activities and resources	A wide variety of resources that are visible, interesting and inviting for children Activities that are inclusive, age/stage appropriate and safe A range of activities for children to make their own choices
Atmosphere	A balance of calm/reassuring and stimulating/challenging An organised routine
Staff approach	Professional and positive Caring and respectful, providing praise and encouragement for all children's efforts and achievements

Activities and resources

An important part of supporting a positive environment for children and young people includes the provision of activities and resources that will stimulate their interest and meet their individual needs.

Children need a variety of different resources that they can use in activities of their own choosing, both indoors and outdoors. For example, by providing a selection of cardboard boxes and fabric children may choose to create a spaceship, a magic den or a dragon's cave.

Resources should be visible and accessible for children, as well as inviting, exciting and safe to use.

Resources and activities also need to be age/stage appropriate and inclusive in order to meet the individual needs of children and young people, for example, providing left-handed as well as right-handed scissors and other tools, using pictures and symbols as well as words to label resources, and providing a range of activities outdoors as well as inside.

When providing activities and resources for children and young people it is important to:

▶ ensure resources are age/stage appropriate

▶ provide a wide variety for children to make their own choices

▶ ensure that activities are inclusive and meet their individual needs and interests

▶ keep resources visible and easily accessible

▶ ensure that all resources and activities are safe

▶ make resources and activities inviting and challenging

▶ provide a range of resources and activities both indoors and outdoors.

Case study

Olga is 4 years old. She was born in Poland but has lived in this country for the past 3 years. She lives with her mum and dad and her baby sister who is 9 months old. Olga likes to help her mum look after the baby and she enjoys playing with her baby sister in the bath. Olga's mum has bought her a doll and a play pushchair so that Olga can look after her own 'baby'.

Olga's dad speaks English but her mother speaks only Polish. Olga can speak some English, although Polish is the main language spoken at home.

Olga has been offered a nursery place at the local children's centre and Alice will be Olga's key person. Alice met Olga and her mother when they visited the nursery last week, so she does have some information about the family. Alice is now preparing to welcome Olga into the setting on her first day.

1. How could Alice help Olga to feel welcome on her first day at the nursery?

2. What resources and activities might Alice make available for Olga to play with?

3. How can a positive environment support children in unfamiliar situations?

Sensory activities

Research has shown that sensory activities are very important for children's early learning. Babies will investigate their surroundings with their sight, hearing and touch, often using their mouth as well as their hands to explore objects. **Treasure baskets** containing a variety of safe objects are often used to encourage babies to explore using all their **senses**.

As young children develop their own learning style, they need a variety of different sensory activities, for example, visual stimulation from pictures, auditory stimulation from music and sounds and **tactile** stimulation from practical, hands-on activities.

Your assessment criteria:

2.2 Provide opportunities for children and young people to engage in activities of choice

2.3 Provide activities and resources to meet the individual needs of children and young people

2.4 Support the engagement of children or young people in activities that promote use of their senses

2.5 Demonstrate how to give praise and encouragement to children or young people for individual achievements

Case study

Describe how the following activities are promoting children to use their different senses:

1. Jessica, aged 10 months, enjoys splashing and kicking her legs in the bath. Her mother uses scented bubble bath to make lots of bubbles. Jessica enjoys sucking on the face cloth and playing with a squeaky, plastic duck in the water.

2. Rashid, aged five years, enjoys baking buns with his mum. He helps to sift the flour and mix the butter and sugar into the mixture. Together they spoon the mixture into bun cases and put them in the oven. Rashid and his mum wash up all the utensils and enjoy the smell of the buns cooking. The best part is eating them once they have cooled!

3. Thomas, aged 9 years, enjoys playing in the woods with his friends. They make up adventures as they run around and chase each other through the trees. Thomas and his friends make a den in the woods using fallen branches and an old blanket that Thomas's mum gives them. Thomas likes to run through the piles of leaves on the ground and roll down the grassy bank into the field. Thomas and his friends have made up special whistling sounds that they use to call to each other in the woods when they play hide and seek.

Key terms

Senses: the five main methods of perception: vision, hearing, smell, taste and touch

Tactile: relating to the sense of touch

Treasure baskets: a basket containing a selection of safe, everyday objects, designed to stimulate all of the baby's senses

The importance of praise and encouragement

Another important aspect of providing a positive environment for children and young people is the supportive attitude of adults. Encouraging children and praising their efforts and achievements is extremely important for developing self-esteem.

It is far more effective to use specific praise when dealing with young children rather than a more generalised approach, for example:

'I really like the way you have used all those colours in your painting. Well done, Jessica', is much more effective than 'That's lovely, Jessica'.

Some of the ways that adults can praise and encourage children and young people include:

▶ giving verbal praise, for example: 'You have tried really hard with that, well done'

▶ giving non-verbal praise, for example, smiles and hugs

▶ showing genuine interest in children's efforts and achievements

▶ giving positive feedback

▶ displaying their work, for example, putting paintings on the wall or exhibiting models they have made

▶ giving rewards or special stickers

▶ spending special time together.

Over to you!

Think about the different ways that children's work is displayed in your placement or work setting.

Why do you think it is important for children's work to be displayed?

Make a list of the different places where children's work can be seen around your setting.

Compare your list with others in the group.

Practical Assessment Task   2.2   2.3   2.4   2.5

1. Write a reflective account giving specific examples of how you provide opportunities for children or young people to engage in activities at your placement or work setting.

2. Think about and make notes on:

   ▶ how you provide activities for children to make their own choices

   ▶ how you provide resources to meet the individual needs of children or young people

   ▶ how you support children or young people in activities to use their senses

   ▶ how you give praise and encouragement to children and young people for their individual achievements.

Your evidence for this task must be based on your practice in a real work environment and must be presented in a format acceptable to your assessor.

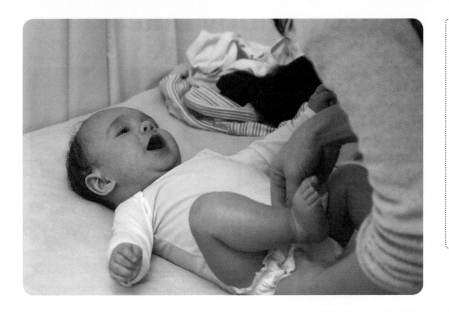

Why is it important to support the personal care needs of children and young people?

Personal care is very important for the basic needs of all children and young people. Good general hygiene, keeping clean and taking care of our skin, hair and teeth are all part of personal care routines. Young children will develop independence through learning how to wash themselves, go to the toilet and brush their own teeth. These regular routines will help them to establish good hygiene habits for life. Young people also need to take responsibility for their own personal care and may need support as they develop their own routine and individual appearance.

Care of skin, hair and teeth

Good basic hygiene is very important for the care of skin, hair and teeth. Babies depend on adults to keep them clean through washing, bathing and changing their nappies. Young children must learn the importance of hand washing to prevent the spread of infection, and need support as they develop independence in going to the toilet by themselves. Older children learn how to brush their own teeth and may need help with washing and styling their own hair. Young people may need support and advice about individual personal hygiene or healthy eating to promote good dental health.

Personal care routines vary and it is important to respect the individual needs of children and young people. For example, children with some special needs may require more help and support in going to the toilet. Some children may need specific skin care because of an allergy or medical condition and others may need different personal care because of their individual skin or hair type.

Supporting children and young people with their personal care routines is important for developing life-long habits and in preventing conditions such as:

▶ body odour, spots or skin infections

▶ dandruff, scalp irritation or head lice

▶ bad breath, gum disease or tooth decay.

Factors to consider in supporting children and young people's individual personal care routines include:

▶ religion or culture

▶ skin or hair type

▶ age or stage of development

▶ allergy or medical condition

▶ physical disability

▶ learning difficulty.

Practical Assessment Task 3.1 3.2

In your placement or work setting, think about how you care for children or young people's skin, hair and teeth and support their personal care routines. Make notes with examples of the following:

▶ How do you encourage children and young people to be independent with their individual personal care routines?

▶ How do you support children or young people to wash their hands effectively?

▶ How do you promote hair care and the prevention of head lice?

▶ How do you encourage children or young people to take care of their teeth?

If there are babies in your setting, you could also make notes on the nappy changing procedure and the care of babies' skin.

If you work with children with special needs, think about how you meet their specific personal care routines.

Keep your notes and your account to help you with your assessment. Your evidence for this task must be based on your practice in a real work environment and must be presented in a format acceptable to your assessor.

The importance of routines

A positive environment is very important for children and young people's emotional needs.

Children need to feel secure in their surroundings and to have a sense of what will happen to them. Having a consistent routine and being cared for by familiar adults helps children feel safe and protected. When children and young people know what to expect, they can feel more confident and self-assured.

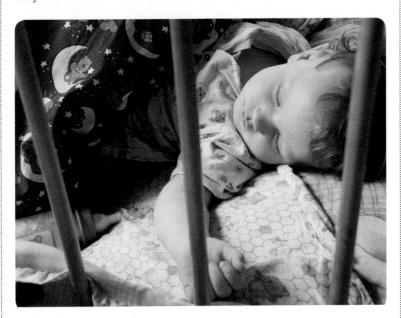

In settings providing care for babies and very young children, routines should try to reflect what usually happens at the child's home and take account of their individual needs, for example, the way a baby's nappy is changed or a child who always has a particular soft toy to cuddle at nap time. This is reassuring for both the child and their family, who can be confident that the routine in the setting will be familiar.

Parents and carers must know about the routine of the setting, for example, what time to bring their child and pick them up at the end of the day. Parents must also be informed about changes to the routine, for example, if a special visit has been planned or if particular clothing or equipment is needed for the day.

Routines should be flexible and include a variety of physical activity and quiet time. This provides a balance to the day and is important for children's physical and mental wellbeing.

Your assessment criteria:

3.3 Explain how a positive environment and routine meet the emotional needs of children and their families

3.4 Describe the importance for physical and mental wellbeing of balancing periods of physical activity with rest and quiet time

Over to you!

▶ *Think about your own daily routine. Create a timeline to show the different events that happen and things you do every day.*

▶ *How do you feel if things don't work out as they usually do or if your routine has to be changed for any reason?*

A variety of routines, including physical activity and quiet time, provide balance to the day.

Practical Assessment Task   `3.3` `3.4`

1. Think about a specific child or young person in your work setting or placement and create a timeline of their daily routine.

2. Write a reflective account about that child or young person that outlines:

   ▶ how a positive environment and daily routine meet the emotional needs of the child and their family

   ▶ how you balance periods of physical activity with rest and quiet time during the day, and why this is important for the child's physical and mental wellbeing.

Keep your timeline and account to help you with your assessment. Your evidence for this task must be based on your practice in a real work environment and must be presented in a format acceptable to your assessor.

Understand how to support the nutritional and dietary needs of children and young people

Why is healthy eating important?

Children and young people should always be encouraged to eat healthy food and establish sensible eating patterns. Healthy eating habits can be developed from a young age and are very important in preventing **obesity** and other related health problems such as **diabetes**. See Figure 10.3.

Key terms

Diabetes: a disease that causes high levels of sugar in the blood

Obesity: the condition of being extremely overweight; more than 20% above the ideal body weight

Over to you!

Investigate the advice on healthy eating for children at Change 4 Life, www.nhs.uk/change4life.

Make a list of healthy snacks for children and young people.

Nutritional requirements

Food contains **nutrients** that are essential for good health. A healthy diet contains a balance of these important nutrients, which all perform a different function in the body.

Figure 10.3 What goes into a healthy diet?

Nutrient	Function in the body	Example foods
Protein	Growth and repair of body tissue	Meat, fish, milk, cheese, eggs, soya, beans, pulses
Carbohydrate (starches and sugars)	Provides energy	Starch: bread, potatoes, pasta, rice Sugar: sugar, sweets, chocolate
Fat	Provides warmth and energy	Butter, cream, cheese, eggs, olive oil, nuts
Fibre	Helps digestion and prevents constipation	Fruit, vegetables, wholegrain cereals and bread
Vitamins		
A	Healthy skin and eyes	Oily fish, green vegetables
B group	Healthy nervous system	Wholegrain cereals and bread
C	Protects against infection	Citrus fruits, green vegetables
D	Helps the body to use calcium	Oily fish, eggs, natural sunlight on the skin
Minerals		
Iron	Healthy red blood cells	Red meat, green vegetables
Calcium	Strong bones and teeth	Milk, cheese, yogurt, green vegetables, nuts

Over to you!

Find out more about diabetes in childhood at www.diabetes.co.uk.

Make a list of the risk factors for type 2 diabetes and the main signs and symptoms.

Healthy eating

Most foods contain several nutrients, for example milk contains protein, fat, vitamin B and calcium. When planning meals, it is important to include foods that contain a balance of all the essential nutrients. This is vital for young children who are growing quickly and have high energy levels. Freshly prepared food with plenty of fruit and vegetables, wholegrain cereals and starchy food like pasta will provide children with the essential nutrients they need for good health. Processed foods like hot dogs and ready prepared meals can be very high in fat, sugar and salt and should be avoided. Children should be encouraged to drink water, milk or unsweetened juice rather than fizzy, sugary drinks.

The government provides a variety of guidance about healthy eating. The Food Standards Agency has developed the 'eatwell plate', which shows the different types of foods that make up a healthy diet. The government also recommends that children and young people (and adults too) should eat five portions of fruit or vegetables every day ('5 A DAY').

Your assessment criteria:

4.1 Define the basic nutritional requirements of children and young people to ensure a balanced diet and meet government guidance

4.2 Explain how to establish the different dietary requirements of children and young people

Over to you!

▶ *Make a list of everything you have eaten over the past two days. How does it compare to the government guidance?*

▶ *What improvements could you make to your own diet?*

▶ *Discuss your ideas with others in the group.*

The eatwell plate

Use the eatwell plate to help you get the balance right. It shows how much of what you eat should come from each food group.

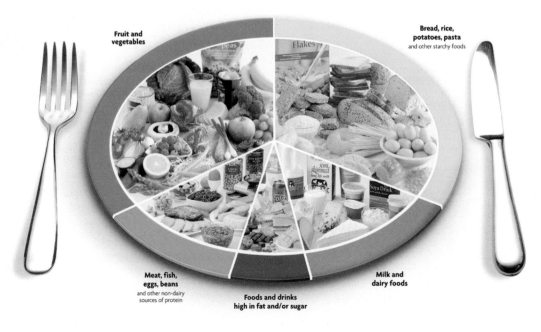

Figure 10.4 The eatwell plate

Different dietary requirements

Vegetarian and vegan

Some parents choose to be vegetarian or **vegan** and may want their children to follow similar eating patterns. Vegetarians do not eat any meat or fish and vegans do not eat any animal products, including eggs and cows' milk. Soya and other sources of plant protein are therefore very important. If children follow a vegetarian or vegan diet, then special care will need to be taken to make sure all the essential nutrients are included in their diet.

Religion and culture

Some religions and cultures have strict guidance about what kinds of food should be eaten and even how animals should be killed. For example, Jews do not eat any meat from a pig (pork, bacon, ham) and many Hindus do not eat any meat at all. Islamic (Muslim) law requires meat to be **halal** and in some settings, any meat provided for Muslim children may have to be obtained from a special halal butcher.

Allergies and health

Some children may have special dietary requirements because of allergies or health conditions. For example, some children are allergic to nuts or eggs and it is very important to make sure that these foods are avoided. This can mean checking the ingredients of some food products very carefully, as even small amounts can cause problems for allergic children.

Some medical conditions can be influenced by a child's diet. For example, food additives can affect the behaviour of some children with Attention Deficit Hyperactivity Disorder (ADHD).

> ### Key terms
>
> **Vegan:** a strict vegetarian who eats no animal or dairy products at all
>
> **Halal:** Muslim dietary law that forbids the eating of pigs and requires meat to be killed and prepared in a religious way

Knowledge Assessment Task   `4.1`   `4.2`

1. Using the 'eatwell plate' to help you, define the basic nutritional requirements of children and young people to ensure a balanced diet which meets government guidance.

2. Write a short report explaining the factors you would need to consider to meet the different dietary requirements of children and young people.

Keep your report as evidence towards your assessment.

The importance of food safety

Food safety is very important when preparing and providing food and drinks for children and young people. Basic food hygiene procedures and safety when using utensils and other equipment are essential in order to maintain good health in children and young people.

Infection can spread easily if strict hygiene procedures are not followed. Babies and young children have very little resistance to infection and are vulnerable to conditions such as **gastroenteritis**.

Personal hygiene

Personal hygiene is crucial in preventing the spread of infection when preparing and providing food and drinks for children and young people. The advice below should always be followed:

▶ Wash your hands before touching food, after using the toilet or handling anything dirty.

▶ Cover any cuts on your hands with waterproof plasters.

▶ Do not cough or sneeze over food.

Children should be taught good hygiene habits from an early age. They should be encouraged in routine hand washing before meals or snacks, after using the toilet and following any messy or outdoor play.

Your assessment criteria:

4.3 Describe basic food safety when providing food and drink to children and young people

Key terms

Gastroenteritis: a stomach infection caused by bacteria, with symptoms of extreme vomiting and diarrhoea

Over to you!

In your placement or work setting, think about your own personal hygiene when you are preparing and providing food and drinks for children.

▶ *Do you set a good example with your own behaviour?*

▶ *How do you help children to develop good hygiene habits around food?*

Food hygiene is also very important when storing, preparing and cooking food for children. Extra care should be taken when preparing formula feeds for babies, making snacks with children or in cooking activities.

Fresh drinking water should be available for children at all times. When providing drinks in the work setting, children should always be encouraged to use their own cups and all utensils should be thoroughly washed or properly disposed of.

It is essential to follow the food hygiene advice below:

▶ Always keep food covered.

▶ Keep the fridge at a temperature between 0 and 5°C.

▶ Always cook food thoroughly and never reheat food more than once.

▶ Follow strict hygiene procedures when making up formula feeds for babies.

▶ Keep all food preparation surfaces clean and always use clean utensils.

▶ Empty kitchen rubbish bins regularly.

▶ Always check 'use by' dates on food products.

Safety is another important consideration when preparing and providing food and drinks for children and young people. Young children are often involved in making their own snacks or cooking and baking activities. Extra care should be taken when using knives and other sharp utensils, and children should be taught about the dangers of hot ovens and other cooking equipment. Microwave ovens should not be used for reheating bottle feeds for babies. This can cause 'hot spots' to develop in the milk which could scald the baby's mouth.

Over to you!

Find out more about hygiene procedures for making up formula feeds for babies at:

www.healthystart.nhs.uk/en/pdfs/ bottle_feeding.pdf.

Knowledge Assessment Task　　　4.3

Describe the food safety and hygiene measures you would need to consider in the following situations:

1. Making jam sandwiches to have as a snack with a small group of four year olds.
2. Preparing a variety of fruit for a tasting activity with a group of eight year olds.
3. Baking buns with a small group of six year olds.

Keep your written work as evidence towards your assessment.

Are you ready for assessment?

AC	What do you know now?	Assessment task	✓
1.1	What is meant by a positive environment for children and young people	Page 209	
1.2	The regulatory requirements that underpin a positive environment	Page 209	
4.1 4.2	The basic nutritional requirements of children and young people to ensure a balanced diet and meet government guidelines	Page 223	
4.3	Basic food safety when providing food and drinks for children and young people	Page 225	

Your tutor or assessor may want to observe you actually doing this in your placement or work setting.

AC	What can you do now?	Assessment task	✓
2.1	Meet and greet children and young people in a way that welcomes them into the workplace setting	Page 211	
2.2 2.3	Provide opportunities and resources for children and young people to engage in activities of choice to meet their individual needs	Page 215	
2.4	Support the engagement of children or young people in activities that promote use of their senses	Page 215	
2.5	Give praise and encouragement to children and young people for individual achievements	Page 215	
3.1	Explain how to effectively care for children or young people's skin, hair and teeth Could you discuss this with your assessor?	Page 217	
3.2	Support personal care routines that meet the individual needs of children or young people and promote their independence	Page 217	
3.3	Explain how a positive environment and routine meet the emotional needs of children and their families Could you discuss this with your assessor?	Page 219	
3.4	Describe the importance for physical and mental wellbeing of balancing periods of physical activity with rest and quiet time Do you have specific examples to share with your assessor?	Page 219	

11 | Understand partnership working in services for children and young people (MU 2.9)

> ## Assessment of this unit
>
> This unit is all about working together in services for children and young people. It covers the importance of effective communication, some of the difficulties that can occur with information sharing and the importance of working in partnership with parents and carers.
>
> The assessment of this unit is all knowledge based (things that you need to know about), but it is also very important to be able to apply your knowledge practically in the real work environment or in your placement. In order to successfully complete this unit, you will need to produce evidence of your knowledge, as shown in the chart below. Your tutor or assessor will help you to prepare for your assessment and the tasks suggested in this chapter will help you to create the evidence that you need.

AC	What you need to know
1.1	Why working in partnership with others is important for children and young people
1.2	Who relevant partners would be in own work setting
1.3	The characteristics of effective partnership working
1.4	Barriers to partnership working
2.1	Why clear and effective communication between partners is required
2.2	Policies and procedures in the work setting for information sharing
2.3	Where there may be conflicts or dilemmas in relation to sharing information with partners and maintaining confidentiality
2.4	Why it is important to record information clearly, accurately, legibly and concisely meeting legal requirements
2.5	How communications and records are recorded and securely stored meeting data protection requirements
2.6	Why and how referrals are made to different agencies
3.1	The reasons for partnerships with carers
3.2	How partnerships with carers are developed and sustained in own work setting
3.3	Circumstances where partnerships with carers may be difficult to develop and sustain

There is no practical assessment for this unit, but your tutor or assessor may question you about some of the following points:

What you need to do

Apply your knowledge about partnership working in the real work environment

Use your knowledge about effective communication, sharing information and confidentiality in the real work environment

Record information clearly and accurately, meeting legal requirements

This unit also links to some of the other mandatory units:

SHC 21   Introduction to communication in health, social care or children's and young people's settings

TDA 2.2   Safeguarding the welfare of children and young people

CCLDMU 2.2 Contribute to the support of child and young person development

Some of your learning will be repeated in these units, to give you the chance to review your knowledge and understanding.

Understand partnership working within the context of services for children and young people

Your assessment criteria:

1.1 Explain why working in partnership with others is important for children and young people

Why is working in partnership important?

The provision of services for children and young people can involve many different agencies, each with their own roles and responsibilities. Different professionals may work with children in a range of situations and will therefore gain different information about them. In order to create a **holistic** view of the child or young person, it is extremely important that this information is shared, both between the professionals themselves and with the child's parents or main carers. **Multi-agency** and **integrated working** are terms that are used to describe different services working together to meet the needs of children, young people and their parents or carers.

Working in partnership is important in order to:

▶ identify the needs of children, young people and their families

▶ plan and provide services to meet the different needs of children, young people and their families

▶ share information between different service providers

▶ avoid duplication of services

▶ reduce confusion for children, young people and their families.

Key terms

Holistic: emphasising the importance of the whole child

Integrated working: everyone who is supporting children, young people and families working together to meet their needs

Multi-agency: involving several different organisations that work together for a shared aim

Case study

Nine-month-old Jamie is looked after by a childminder for 3 days every week. He attends a nursery on 2 mornings every week and is cared for by his mother during the rest of the week. His mother takes him to the baby clinic on a regular basis, where he is seen by the health visitor, and when he is poorly he is seen by the family doctor (GP) at the health centre. All these professionals experience Jamie in different ways and gather different information about him and his family. The childminder will mostly see Jamie in his regular daily routine: eating, sleeping, having his nappy changed and going out and about in his pushchair. Jamie's key person at the nursery will see Jamie in a different environment, away from his mother, interacting with other young children or playing on his own. The health visitor may observe different aspects of Jamie's development and the doctor may see Jamie when he is undressed, upset or in pain.

1. Give two examples of information that the childminder might have about Jamie.

2. Give two examples of information that Jamie's key person at the nursery might have about him.

3. Explain why it is important for the childminder, key person and Jamie's mother to work in partnership.

Effective partnership working

Several agencies may be involved in the provision of services for children and young people. Different professionals may offer a range of support services to meet the different needs of children and their families. For example, a 4-year-old girl with **Down's syndrome** may need support for her health, development, language and education, in addition to information, advice and guidance for her family. This might involve services from the family doctor (GP), the health visitor, a speech and language therapist, an early years worker or special needs teacher and a social worker.

A 14-year-old boy with **Attention Deficit Hyperactivity Disorder (ADHD)** may need support with his education, behaviour and medication. This might involve input from his teacher, an educational psychologist, the family GP and a youth worker.

Professional involvement with children and their families usually happens through the process of **referral**. This means that the various professionals involved need to communicate with each other and with the family in order to share information about how they could best provide support. Referrals can be made verbally, for example, in person or by telephone, or in writing, for example, by letter or email. The referral process can be started either by a professional, a parent or main carer, or in some cases by the child or young person themselves. For example, a health visitor may have concerns about a child's speech following a routine visit at the health centre. The health visitor would then discuss this with the parents and make a referral to the speech and language therapist. Another example might be a young person who makes their own referral to a family planning clinic for advice about contraception or sexually transmitted infections.

Figure 11.1 shows some of the relevant partners who may be working together to meet the needs of children, young people and their families. It also shows some of the reasons why referrals might be made to their services.

Your assessment criteria:

1.1 Explain why working in partnership with others is important for children and young people

1.2 Identify who relevant partners would be in own work setting

2.6 Explain why and how referrals are made to different agencies

Key terms

Attention Deficit Hyperactivity Disorder (ADHD): a condition characterised by behavioural and learning difficulties

Down's syndrome: a condition caused by an extra chromosome in the body's cells, resulting in learning difficulties

Referral: a recommendation for an individual to receive specialist care or services

Figure 11.1 Partners who may be working together

Professional	Main area of responsibility	Possible reasons for referral (area where support is given)
Health visitor	Monitoring the health and development of all children from 0 to 5 years	Health or development (eg developmental delay)
Social worker	Supporting vulnerable children and their families, including children with special needs	Concerns about welfare or safety (e.g. neglect or abuse)
Speech and language therapist	Supporting children and young people with speech, language or communication difficulties (SLCD)	Communication (e.g. a child or young person with **Autistic Spectrum Disorder: ASD**)
Educational Psychologist	Supporting children and young people with special educational needs, including behavioural difficulties	Behaviour or ability to engage in mainstream education (e.g. children with learning difficulties)
Family doctor (GP)	The health of children, young people and their families	Health issues, medication or treatment (e.g. routine immunisations, childhood **asthma**)
Family support worker	Providing assistance for families and advice about support groups and local services	Information about local services (e.g. parent and child play groups, parenting support and training)
Teacher	Educating and supporting children aged 4 to 16 years	Educational progress (e.g. monitoring educational achievement)
Early years worker	Providing care and early education for children aged 0 to 5 years	Care, early learning or development (e.g. monitoring young children's developmental progress)
Youth worker	Supporting and mentoring young people	Welfare (e.g. anti-social behaviour)

Knowledge Assessment Task   1.1   1.2   2.6

1. In your placement or work setting, identify and make a list of the relevant partners who might be involved in providing services for the children or young people who attend.
2. Write a report to explain:
   ▶ why working in partnership with others is important for children and young people
   ▶ how and why you would make referrals to different agencies for children or young people from your placement or work setting.

Keep your written work as evidence towards your assessment.

Key terms

Asthma: a non-infectious condition that can be triggered by allergic reactions and cause breathing difficulties

Autistic Spectrum Disorder (ASD): a condition characterised by problems with social interaction and communication

Characteristics of effective partnership working

Effective partnership working has many advantages for children, young people and their families as well as all the professionals involved. It is an efficient way of providing a holistic service that meets all the needs of children and their families.

Some of the key characteristics of effective partnership working include:

▶ effective communication between all partners and the family

▶ sharing of information

▶ accurate record keeping

▶ well-defined roles and areas of responsibility for all partners involved

▶ clear policies and procedures

▶ shared goals

▶ efficient co-ordination of service provision

▶ regular evaluation and review.

Your assessment criteria:

1.3 Define the characteristics of effective partnership working

1.4 Identify barriers to partnership working

Barriers to effective partnership working

There can sometimes be problems with partnership working, particularly when roles are not clearly defined, information is not shared or communication between partners is poor. Different professionals provide a wide range of services for children, young people and their families. If the approach is not co-ordinated, then it can result in duplication of services and confusion for everyone involved.

Some of the barriers to effective partnership working include:

▶ poor communication between partners

▶ lack of information sharing between partners

▶ lack of co-ordination between different service providers

▶ inaccurate or inconsistent record keeping

▶ ineffective policies and procedures

▶ lack of understanding about the roles or involvement of different partners

▶ lack of evaluation and no review process of service provision.

Knowledge Assessment Task   1.3   1.4

Kevin is 4 years old and attends the Shining Stars nursery every morning. Amy is Kevin's key person at the nursery and she carries out regular observations to monitor his development and individual needs. Amy has noticed that Kevin has some speech difficulties and the other children often struggle to understand him. Amy has mentioned this to Kevin's mum, who said that she hadn't been paying much attention to Kevin's speech recently, because she has just had a new baby and has been feeling a bit depressed. Amy discussed the situation with her manager who suggested that a referral might be made to Kevin's health visitor and the speech and language service. She also suggested that Kevin's mum may benefit from seeing the family GP to discuss her depression and that a family support worker may also be able to help the family. Amy discusses this with Kevin's mum who is very thankful for the help. Together they work out a plan to contact the health visitor for advice and arrange for Kevin's mum to visit the GP. Amy records this information and plans to talk to Kevin's mum again in 2 weeks' time.

1. What are the characteristics of effective partnership working in this situation?

2. Identify the possible barriers to effective partnership working in this situation.

Keep your notes as evidence towards your assessment.

Why is effective communication important?

In order for professionals to work in the best interests of children, young people and their families, it is extremely important that information is shared and effectively communicated. The co-ordination of services relies on everyone working together and this requires all communication to be clear and accurately recorded. This may involve all forms of written and verbal communication, including telephone messages, emails and other electronic communication systems. Some of the most tragic situations, often involving the death of children or young people, have highlighted failings in partnership working and a lack of effective communication between professionals.

Policies and procedures

Settings that provide services for children and young people need to have clear policies and procedures for sharing information. This usually includes guidelines for sharing information with parents or carers as well as between colleagues and other professionals. It should also include a clear policy about the confidentiality of information about children, young people and their families. Private information is often disclosed in work settings, and families need to be sure that practitioners can be trusted to respect confidentiality. Professionals who work with children and young people should never gossip about families and should always be mindful of the regulations about confidentiality and information sharing.

Policies and procedures about sharing information and confidentiality should cover the following:

▶ how, why and where information should be recorded

▶ how information should be securely stored for both paper-based and electronic records

▶ who can have access to information and how it is monitored

▶ obtaining permission to share information or take photographs of children and young people

▶ the importance of privacy when discussing private information with families

▶ strict policies on confidentiality and the importance of not discussing confidential information outside of the work setting.

Conflicts with confidentiality

There will be some situations where the procedures for sharing information are not straightforward. It is important to understand some of the difficult issues of confidentiality and to know what to do. For example, if you ever have any concerns about the welfare of a child or young person, particularly relating to an abusive situation or a safeguarding issue, then it is extremely important that you pass on the information to an appropriate person, according to the procedures of the setting. In some situations, maintaining confidentiality can present difficult challenges, for example, when responding to informal requests for information or dealing with telephone calls.

Knowledge Assessment Task   2.1   2.2   2.3

In your placement or work setting, investigate the policies and procedures for information sharing and confidentiality.

Create a leaflet or fact sheet for students or new members of staff, which includes the following information:

▶ a list of 'dos and don'ts' for sharing information and maintaining confidentiality

▶ how to deal with conflicts in relation to sharing information and confidentiality

▶ why clear and effective communication between partners is important.

Keep your leaflet as evidence towards your assessment.

Record keeping

In all settings providing care for children and young people, information is recorded for many different reasons and in many different forms, including:

▶ personal details of children, young people and their families – for example, dates of birth, emergency contact information and details about the language spoken at home

▶ individual needs – for example health conditions, allergies or special dietary requirements

▶ child development records – for example, monitoring children's progress in education and development

▶ observations – for example, information about children's interests or individual needs

▶ planning documents – for example, ideas for different activities to meet the individual needs of children or young people

▶ information for parents and carers – for example, progress reports, newsletters or notice boards

▶ reports for other professionals – for example, highlighting concerns about children or young people's developmental progress or welfare

▶ safety checks and risk assessments – for example, reporting faulty equipment, accident or incident reports

▶ daily records – for example, information about babies' feeding or sleeping patterns

▶ staff records – for example, qualifications, information about training needs and appraisal records.

In many settings, information is recorded electronically rather than as handwritten notes, but whatever method is used, it is extremely important that information is recorded clearly and accurately and that it meets legal requirements.

Storage of information

The Data Protection Act (1998) regulates the recording and storage of personal information to make sure that settings work within the law. It is extremely important that any personal or confidential information relating to children, young people or their families is stored securely in the work setting.

Your assessment criteria:

2.4 Describe why it is important to record information clearly, accurately, legibly and concisely, meeting legal requirements

2.2 Identify how communications and records are recorded and securely stored meeting data protection requirements

This relates to both paper-based and electronic records. When storing information the following points are important:

- ▶ secure, locked storage for paper based records
- ▶ not leaving any paper-based records lying around in the setting
- ▶ secure, password protected systems for electronic records
- ▶ always logging off the computer after accessing electronic records
- ▶ only recording information that is strictly relevant for the care and welfare of the child or young person
- ▶ keeping backups of electronic records
- ▶ policies about keeping photographs of children.

Over to you!

- ▶ *How is information about children and young people recorded in your placement or work setting?*
- ▶ *What security measures are in place to ensure confidentiality of the information?*

Compare your responses with others in your group.

Case studies

Describe what could happen as a result of the following situations involving the recording of information:

1. Polly, a nursery worker, has written down the wrong contact telephone number for one of the children in her group.

2. Stuart has sent out a letter to parents about the out-of-school trip next week, but he has forgotten to include information about picking up children at the end of the day.

3. Guan-yin Chung and Chyou Chang are both 14 months old and attend Little Lambs nursery every morning. Guan-yin Chung is allergic to cows' milk and this is recorded in her notes. Lisa, who works at the nursery, has written out a notice for the nursery kitchen as follows: 'Chan-yin Chang is allergic to cows' milk'.

4. Emily works at a primary school and has been outside with the children at playtime. Two children had an accident in the playground and bumped heads with each other. Emily completes an accident report and writes: 'George and Wayne bumped into each other in the playground. They both seemed all right'.

Knowledge Assessment Task   2.4   2.5

Investigate and summarise the policies and procedures for recording and storing information in your placement or work setting. Prepare a presentation that could be used as part of the induction training for new staff and includes:

- ▶ the importance of recording information clearly and accurately when working with children and young people
- ▶ some of the main points to consider about the storage of information relating to children, young people and their families.

You can illustrate your presentation using PowerPoint slides or other visual aids.

Keep your presentation and notes as evidence towards your assessment.

Understand the importance of partnerships with carers

Your assessment criteria:

3.1 Identify the reasons for partnerships with parents or carers

Over to you!

Think about your relationship with your own parents or main carers. How do they support you? What do you rely on them for?

Why are partnerships with carers important?

Parents and carers are extremely important in the lives of all children and young people. The influence of parents is probably the most significant factor in shaping children's wellbeing, achievements and life chances. For most children, parents provide security, support and guidance through being good role models and encouraging success. Being a parent is a very challenging job and individual people will carry out the role in different ways. However, the majority of parents and carers want the best for their children and work hard to provide opportunities for them to do well.

In order for practitioners to meet the individual needs of children and young people, it is vital to form meaningful partnerships with parents and carers. This involves not only effective communication, but also respect for the expertise of parents and carers as specialists in the care of their own children.

Developing partnerships

Partnerships with parents and carers can be developed in many different ways and it is important to remember that for any partnership to be effective, there needs to be **mutual respect**. It is particularly important to be aware of the needs of parents who may have special needs, for example physical disabilities or those parents whose first language is not English. Some of the main methods involved in developing effective partnerships are outlined in Figure 11.2.

Key terms

Mutual respect: consideration for each other

Figure 11.2 Effective partnerships with parents and carers

Method	Developing effective partnerships
Communicate effectively	Make time to talk with parents and listen to their questions and concerns. Be open, friendly and approachable. Be aware of parents whose first language is not English and make alternative arrangements for communication. Provide privacy for discussing personal issues. Provide opportunities for parents to give their own feedback about their child or the setting (child observations or ideas from home, suggestions box, comment slips, etc.).
Provide information	Keep parents informed about their children (daily routines, progress and achievements). Display current or important information clearly on notice boards. Send out newsletters with information about the setting and upcoming events. Use text messaging or email for parents who prefer this, and have an up-to-date website for the setting. Organise coffee mornings or special parent days or evenings to provide updates on children's progress.
Encourage involvement	Have an 'open door' policy so that parents are welcome in the setting at any time. Provide a parents' room where parents and carers can meet and chat together. Encourage parents to help out on a regular basis, for example helping with activities, playing sports or listening to children read. Encourage parents to help with special events, fund raising or planning trips out. Arrange special days, for example, just for dads, family cooking sessions or a gardening event in the vegetable plot.
Make use of parental expertise	Find out about specific skills that parents may have, for example, in music, art or cookery and organise special sessions for the children to gain new experiences such as Indian dancing, Chinese cookery or an art or sculpture project. Use parents' experiences, for example, invite a mother who has recently had a new baby to come into the setting and spend time with the children and her new baby.
Plan activities	Plan activities that involve the family and home life of children and young people, for example, make 'All about Me' books, or organise activities about different religions, cultures and languages.

Difficulties with partnerships

There may be some circumstances where partnerships with parents or carers may be difficult to develop and sustain, for example if:

▶ a parent's first language is not English, then communication may be more challenging

▶ a parent has a physical disability, then it may be more difficult for them to be involved with the setting

▶ parents have different working patterns, then they may have very limited time available

▶ a family is dealing with a crisis or a difficult situation, for example a bereavement or a parent is in hospital, then they may be more difficult to engage with

▶ a family has a **transient lifestyle**, for example Roma or traveller families, then they may not stay in an area for any length of time.

Key terms

transient lifestyle: living in a place for only a brief time and then moving on

Over to you!

Think about the relationships with parents and carers in your placement or work setting.

▶ *How are parents and carers made to feel welcome in the setting?*

▶ *How are parents and carers kept informed about what is happening at the setting?*

Make a list of the different ways that parents and carers are involved in activities or events at the setting

Compare your ideas with those of others in your group.

Case study

Danny is 6 years old and attends Beacon House primary school. His sister Rosie is 3 years old and she goes to a nursery at the children's centre every morning. Danny's dad works long hours, he leaves very early in the morning and is often not home until after Danny has gone to bed. Danny's mum has just had a new baby boy, who is still in the hospital because he was born 3 weeks early. Danny's mum takes Danny to school every morning, then she drops Rosie off at the nursery before going to the hospital to visit the new baby. Beacon house primary school has sent out a letter inviting Danny's mum and dad to a parents' evening at the school next week. Danny's dad knows he will not be able to attend because he will be working. Danny's mum keeps the letter from school and makes a note of the date, but then she forgets all about it and doesn't attend the evening.

1. Explain why it may be difficult for the staff at Beacon House primary school to develop a partnership with Danny's parents.

2. Give two examples of how the school staff could improve this situation.

3. Why is it important for the staff at Beacon House primary school to develop a partnership with Danny's parents?

Knowledge Assessment Task   3.1   3.2   3.3

In your own placement or work setting, investigate how partnerships with parents and carers are developed and sustained.

Create a display that highlights:

▶ the importance of developing partnerships with parents and carers

▶ how partnerships with parents and carers can be developed and sustained

▶ circumstances where partnerships with parents or carers may be difficult to develop or sustain.

You may choose to use actual work products as part of your display and you could take photographs of your display as evidence towards your assessment.

Are you ready for assessment?

AC	What you need to know	Assessment task	✓
1.1	Why working in partnership with others is important for children and young people	Page 233	
1.2	Who relevant partners would be in own work setting	Page 233	
1.3	The characteristics of effective partnership working	Page 235	
1.4	Barriers to partnership working	Page 235	
2.1	Why clear and effective communication between partners is required	Page 237	
2.2	Policies and procedures in the work setting for information sharing	Page 237	
2.3	Where there may be conflicts or dilemmas in relation to sharing information with partners and maintaining confidentiality	Page 237	
2.4	Why it is important to record information clearly, accurately, legibly and concisely meeting legal requirements	Page 239	
2.5	How communications and records are recorded and securely stored meeting data protection requirements	Page 233	
2.6	Why and how referrals are made to different agencies	Page 233	
3.1	The reasons for partnerships with carers	Page 243	
3.2	How partnerships with carers are developed and sustained in own work setting	Page 243	
3.3	Circumstances where partnerships with carers may be difficult to develop and sustain	Page 243	

There is no practical assessment for this unit, but your tutor or assessor may question you about some of the following points:

What can you do now?	✓
Can you apply your knowledge about partnership working in the real work environment? Could you tell your tutor or assessor about this?	
Can you use your knowledge about effective communication, sharing information and confidentiality in the real work environment? Do you have any specific examples of this?	
Can you record information clearly and accurately, meeting legal requirements? Do you have any examples to show your tutor or assessor?	

12 | Paediatric emergency first aid (PEFAP 001)

Assessment of this unit

This unit is about dealing with a range of paediatric emergency first aid situations. It includes conditions such as choking, shock and severe bleeding as well as life-saving measures such as cardiopulmonary resuscitation (CPR).

The assessment of this unit is partly knowledge based (things that you need to know about) and partly competence based (things that you need to be able to do in the real work environment or in your placement). Some of the practical assessment in this unit may be carried out in realistic, simulated first aid situations. It is important to remember that being able to give competent first aid treatment can save a child's life and so the assessment of this unit should be taken very seriously.

In order to successfully complete this unit, you will need to produce evidence of both your knowledge and your competence, as shown in the following charts. Your tutor or assessor will help you to prepare for your assessment, and the tasks suggested in this chapter will help you to create the evidence that you need.

AC	What you need to know
1.1	The responsibilities of a paediatric first aider
1.2	How to minimise the risk of infection to self and others
1.3	A description of suitable first aid equipment, including personal protection, and how it is used appropriately
1.4	The information that needs to be included in an accident/incident record and how to record it
1.5	The definition of an infant and a child for the purposes of first aid treatment

AC	What you need to do
2.1 **2.2**	Demonstrate how to conduct a scene survey and a primary survey on an infant and a child
2.3	Identify when and how to call for help
3.1	Demonstrate how to place an infant and a child into the appropriate recovery position
3.2	Describe how to continually assess and monitor an infant and a child while in your care
4.1 **4.2**	Identify when to administer CPR to an unresponsive infant and a child who is not breathing normally and demonstrate how to administer CPR using an infant and child manikin
4.3	Describe how to deal with an infant and a child who is experiencing a seizure
5.1	Differentiate between a mild and a severe airway obstruction
5.2 **5.3**	Demonstrate how to treat an infant and a child who is choking and describe the procedure to be followed after administering treatment
6.1	Describe common types of wounds
6.2	Describe the types and severity of bleeding and the effect it has on an infant and a child
6.3	Demonstrate the safe and effective management for the control of minor and major external bleeding
6.4	Describe how to administer first aid for minor injuries
7.1 **7.2**	Describe how to recognise and manage an infant and a child who is suffering from shock or from anaphylactic shock

This unit also links to some of the other mandatory units:	
MPII 002	Managing paediatric illness and injury
MU 2.4	Contribute to children and young people's health and safety
Some of your learning will be repeated in these units and will give you the chance to review your knowledge and understanding.	

Understand the role of the paediatric first aider

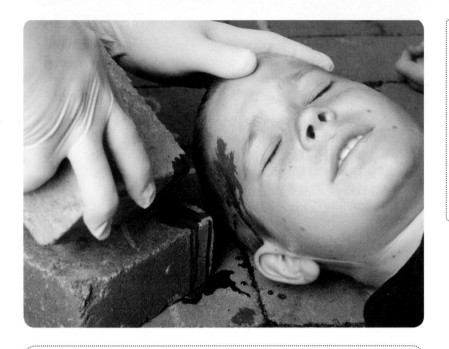

Your assessment criteria:

1.1 Identify the responsibilities of a paediatric first aider

1.2 Describe how to minimise the risk of infection to self and others

1.5 Define an infant and a child for the purposes of first aid treatment

What is first aid?

First aid is the first assistance or treatment given to an ill or injured person (**casualty**) before the arrival of an ambulance or qualified medical help.

The aims of first aid treatment are to:

▶ preserve life

▶ prevent the condition worsening

▶ promote recovery.

For first aid purposes, an infant is usually defined as under the age of one year and a child from one year to approximately 12 years old. However, some first aid treatment will vary depending on the size and weight of the casualty and techniques should always be adapted accordingly.

In this chapter, the ill or injured person is referred to as the casualty.

Key terms

Casualty: a person who is the victim of an accident, injury or trauma

The responsibilities of a paediatric first aider

The role of a first aider is extremely important and should always be taken seriously (see Figure 12.1). One of the most important responsibilities of a paediatric first aider is to appear calm and reassuring. Accident and emergency situations are very frightening for children and the first aider needs to be confident and comforting.

Over to you!

▶ Have you ever been involved in a first aid or emergency situation or witnessed an accident?

▶ Did anyone need first aid treatment?

▶ How did you feel at the time?

Share your experiences with others in the group.

Figure 12.1 The main responsibilities of a paediatric first aider

Responsibility	Description
Remain calm at all times	Appear confident and reassuring
Conduct a scene survey	Assess the situation without endangering your own life
Conduct a primary survey	Identify and assess the extent of the illness, injury or condition of the casualty
Attend to the needs of other children or bystanders	Ensure their safety and manage behaviour
Send for medical help	Ambulance, police or emergency rescue services (as a first aider, you should always stay with the casualty and send someone else to call for help if possible)
Give immediate, appropriate treatment	To preserve life, prevent the condition worsening and promote recovery
Take appropriate precautions to minimise infection	Protect yourself and the casualty by using appropriate techniques and equipment
Arrange for further, qualified medical attention	Transporting the casualty to hospital or arranging for a medical examination
Reporting and recording	Verbal and written records, completing accident and incident reports
Maintaining first aid equipment, including first aid kits	Ensure equipment is up-to-date and first aid kits are well stocked
Keeping up-to-date with first aid procedures	Take part in regular updating and training

Minimising the risk of infection

In many first aid situations, particularly those involving blood or body fluids, there is always a risk of infection, both to the casualty and to the first aider. If the casualty's skin is damaged, there is a chance that **bacteria** could enter their bloodstream and cause infection to spread. Equally, if the casualty already has an infection such as **hepatitis** or **human immunodeficiency virus (HIV)**, this could be transmitted to the first aider if appropriate precautions are not taken.

These are some of the most important things that a first aider can do to minimise the risk of infection:

▶ Always wash your hands before and after giving first aid treatment.

▶ Always wear disposable gloves for dealing with any first aid situations involving blood or other body fluids (e.g. vomit).

▶ Cover the casualty's open wounds with appropriate sterile dressings.

▶ Make sure your own cuts or sores are adequately covered by plasters.

▶ Use appropriate protective equipment where your own safety may be put at risk, e.g. face shields.

▶ Dispose of any soiled dressings (e.g. blood soaked), or other first aid materials, in appropriate clinical waste disposal bags.

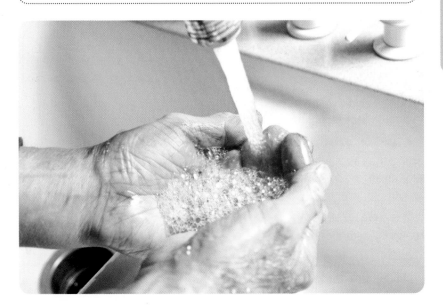

Key terms

Bacteria: microscopic organisms which can cause disease

Hepatitis: an infectious disease which is caused by a virus and transmitted in the blood, resulting in liver damage

Human immunodeficiency virus (HIV): a virus which is transmitted in the blood and can cause acquired immunodeficiency syndrome (AIDS)

Over to you!

Find out more about HIV and Hepatitis at:

www.nhs.uk/Conditions/HIV/Pages/Introduction.aspx

www.nhs.uk/Conditions/Hepatitis/Pages/Introduction.aspx

Make a list of the causes of these conditions and the different ways they can be spread.

Case studies

Using the chart in Figure 12.1, identify the responsibilities of the paediatric first aider in each of the following situations:

1. Ewan, aged 5 years, falls in the playground and grazes his knee. Dirt and grit have got into the wound, which is bleeding slightly.

2. Ellen, aged 6 years, falls from the climbing frame outside and bangs her head. She appears to be fully conscious, but says that her head hurts.

3. Rashid, aged 8 years, collapses during a tackle in a game of football. He seems to be in pain and is rolling around clutching his leg. A crowd of team mates has gathered around him on the pitch.

Knowledge Assessment Task   1.1   1.2   1.5

In your placement or work setting, talk to one of the first aiders about their duties.

Write a reflective report that summarises:

▶ the responsibilities of a paediatric first aider

▶ how a first aider can minimise the risk of infection to themselves and others

▶ the definition of an infant and a child, for the purposes of first aid treatment.

Keep your notes as evidence towards your assessment.

First aid equipment

First aid equipment usually consists of a collection of supplies for administering first aid, minimising the risk of infection and personal protective equipment (PPE). A first aid kit must be easily identifiable and clearly labelled, usually with a white cross on a green background. It is important that first aid equipment is easily accessible and not locked away, and the location of the first aid kit should always be clearly signed. It is a first aider's responsibility to check and stock up first aid kits regularly and to make sure that nothing is damaged.

The contents of a first aid kit will vary slightly depending on the policies and procedures of the setting. Some settings do not use plasters or cleansing wipes because of allergy risks for children. General first aid kits should never contain medicines of any kind, even basic painkillers. First aiders are not qualified to give medicines to children as they do not know the medical history or any allergies the child may have. A standard first aid kit will usually contain the following:

▶ sterile dressings of different sizes (e.g. sterile gauze pads, eye pads)

▶ bandages of different types and sizes (e.g. triangular, roller, finger bandages)

▶ adhesive tape (non-allergenic)

▶ disposable gloves

▶ scissors

▶ tweezers

▶ safety pins

▶ disposable face shields

▶ disposable thermometers.

Accident and incident reports

It is very important that any accident, illness or injury with infants or children is accurately recorded. Settings have a legal duty to report any incidents and specific forms must be completed for this purpose.

The main reasons for completing an accident or incident report are:

▶ It is a legal requirement.

▶ It provides a record in the event of complications (e.g. following a head injury).

▶ It informs parents and carers.

Your assessment criteria:

1.3 Describe suitable first aid equipment, including personal protection, and how it is used appropriately

1.4 Identify what information needs to be included in an accident report/incident record, and how to record it

▶ It can help to monitor potential hazards in the setting.

▶ It may be required as evidence in suspected cases of abuse or non-accidental injuries.

Information should always be recorded clearly and accurately and should be signed and dated by the first aider. Some accident report forms use body diagrams to help in the description of specific injuries, for example, showing exactly where bruising appeared or the particular area where a child feels pain.

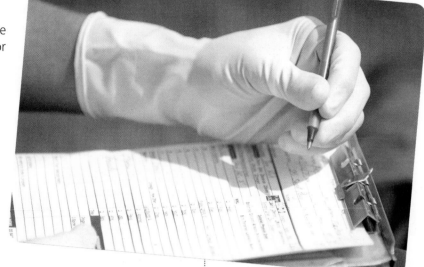

The main information recorded should include:

▶ details of the injured or sick child (name, date of birth, main contact details)

▶ details of the accident or incident (date, time, where it happened)

▶ details of action or treatment given (what happened, extent of any injuries, treatment given)

▶ advice or further treatment recommended (e.g. hospital treatment)

▶ informing parents and carers (when and how parents have been contacted)

▶ signature of the first aider, the date and time.

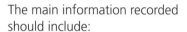

Knowledge Assessment Task — 1.3 1.4

1. In your placement or work setting, investigate the location and contents of the first aid kit. Make a list of the contents. Talk to one of the first aiders and ask them about how they deal with accident and emergency situations. Make notes about the correct use of first aid equipment, including personal protection.

2. Investigate the type of accident and incident report forms used in your placement or work setting. Make a note of the key information that should be included on an accident or incident report form and how it should be recorded (take a photocopy if you can).

Keep your notes as evidence towards your assessment.

Be able to assess an emergency situation and act safely and effectively

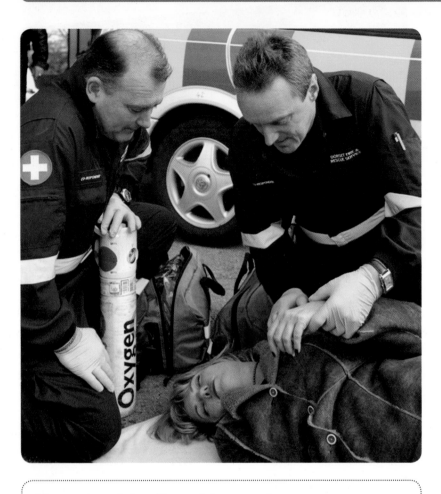

Your assessment criteria:

2.1 Demonstrate how to conduct a scene survey

2.2 Demonstrate how to conduct a primary survey on an infant and a child

How should a first aider act in an emergency situation?

It is the responsibility of a first aider to act quickly and calmly. A common sense approach will help you to focus your actions and prioritise your treatment. It is very important that first aiders do not put themselves at risk in emergency situations (for example, jumping into water to save a drowning child when they can't swim!)

Conducting a scene survey

A scene survey involves your initial assessment of the emergency situation and deciding on the priorities of your action. Use your senses to assess what might have happened:

► Look for clues (e.g. an empty medicine bottle beside an unconscious child).

► Listen to information from others (e.g. other children telling you what happened).

► Smell anything unusual (e.g. gas or other fumes).

When conducting a scene survey, you must consider:

▶ whether you or the casualty are in any danger (e.g. if the building is on fire)

▶ if the casualty has any life-threatening conditions (e.g. not breathing)

▶ if any bystanders can help you (e.g. other children or colleagues)

▶ whether you need to call for further assistance (e.g. ambulance, police or rescue services).

Conducting a scene survey helps the first aider to assess the seriousness of the situation and decide on the priorities for action. It also assists in deciding what further help, if any, is required. If there is more than one casualty, then the first aider needs to prioritise treatment, deal with the most serious first and remember that the quietest casualty often needs the most help.

In calling for help, the first aider must decide what help is required and how to send for help. Some situations may involve sending for emergency services such as ambulance, police or fire and rescue. Other situations may need the assistance of another adult, a colleague, manager or supervisor.

Conducting a primary survey

Once you have conducted a scene survey and decided on your priorities, then a primary survey will provide a more detailed assessment of the casualty. To do this you must consider **DRABC**:

Danger – If you have not already done so, make sure the casualty is safe.

Response – Ask the casualty 'Can you hear me?' or 'What happened?' If they respond, then you know that they are conscious and breathing and you should remain calm, reassure the casualty and continue with your examination. If there is no response, then you should send for help and proceed as follows:

Airway – Open the airway by gently tilting the head back and lifting the chin. This will prevent the casualty's tongue from blocking their airway.

Breathing – Look to see if the chest is rising and falling, listen for breathing sounds and place your cheek close to the casualty's nose and mouth to feel for breath. If the casualty is breathing normally, place them in the recovery position, unless you suspect a spinal injury (see page 258), and continue with your examination. If the casualty is not breathing, then give five rescue breaths and prepare to begin **CPR** (see page 261).

Circulation – Check the casualty's pulse by feeling the major artery in the neck, (carotid artery) just below the jaw line.

(see page 258), (see page 261).

Key terms

CPR (cardiopulmonary resuscitation): an emergency procedure consisting of external heart massage and artificial respiration

Calling for help

A trained first aider should always stay with the casualty and send someone else to call for help. This allows the first aider to monitor the condition of the casualty and perform any treatment if required, for example carrying out CPR if the casualty stops breathing. Never leave an infant or child casualty unattended.

If any of the emergency services are required, this should be done by telephoning 999. It is essential to communicate the following information accurately:

▶ which emergency service is required (ambulance, police and/or fire and rescue service)

▶ a contact telephone number (usually the number the call is made from)

▶ the exact location of the incident (local landmarks provide a useful guide)

▶ the type and seriousness of the incident (e.g. road traffic accident, school bus collided with two other vehicles, blocking a major road junction)

▶ the number and approximate age of casualties involved (e.g. five children and one adult injured, two children in a serious condition).

Having dealt with the priorities, you should now conduct a more detailed examination of the casualty. This will include any information from the casualty and the **signs** and **symptoms** (see Figure 12.2). If the child is old enough, ask them what happened,

Your assessment criteria:

2.1 Demonstrate how to conduct a scene survey

2.2 Demonstrate how to conduct a primary survey on an infant and a child

2.3 Identify when and how to call for help

Key terms

Signs: details discovered by using the senses of sight, touch, hearing and smell, for example evidence of bleeding or swelling

Symptoms: sensations described by the casualty, for example pain or nausea how they feel and where they hurt. Other children or bystanders may also be able to give you information too. You should always deal with life-threatening signs and symptoms first, for example, obvious and severe bleeding (see page 266) or shock (see page 270).

A general examination should begin at the casualty's head and work down the body. Remember to move the casualty as little as possible and use your senses to look, feel, listen and smell. Use both hands to compare any differences between the two sides of the body. Reassure infants and young children with soothing words and a gentle touch.

Over to you!

If there was an emergency first aid situation in your placement or work setting, would you know the exact location to inform the emergency services?

▶ What is the exact address and postcode of your setting?

▶ Are there any local landmarks to help with directions?

▶ What is the telephone number of your setting?

Figure 12.2 Signs to look for on examination of a casualty

Area to examine	What to look for
Head	Any bleeding, bruising or swelling (could indicate a fractured skull)
Face	Colour of the skin, e.g. pale, blueness (could indicate shock)
	Flushed, sweating, clammy
Eyes	Unequal pupil size, bloodshot eyes
Mouth	Any bleeding, vomit, blueness of the lips (could indicate poisoning)
Ears and nose	Any bleeding (could indicate a fractured skull)
Whole body, neck, arms and legs	Any bleeding, swelling, bruising or deformity (could indicate a fracture)

Practical Assessment Task 2.1 2.2 2.3

Emily works in a primary school and is supervising children playing outside at lunchtime. Robin, aged 6 years, comes running over and says that Jaafar (also aged 6 years) has fallen from the top of the climbing frame and is lying on the ground, not moving. As a trained first aider, Emily is responsible for dealing with this incident.

1. Describe how Emily should conduct a scene survey.

2. Describe how Emily should conduct a primary survey on Jaafar.

3. Identify when and how Emily should call for help.

Keep your notes to help you with your assessment. Your assessor will need to assess your competence in a realistic, simulated environment, but your notes will help you to prepare.

Key terms

Simulated: made to imitate a real situation

Be able to provide first aid for an infant and a child who is unresponsive and breathing normally

What is meant by the term 'unresponsive'?

An unresponsive casualty is not fully aware of his or her surroundings and is described as being **unconscious**.

Unconsciousness is the result of an interruption in the normal activity of the brain. There are many different causes, including head injuries, seizures and poisoning. An unconscious casualty may be breathing normally, but this can change suddenly, particularly in young children. Unconsciousness can be life-threatening and an ambulance should always be called.

The recovery position

The recovery position is very important in first aid. It places the casualty in a stable position and ensures that an open airway is maintained. The main advantages of the recovery position are:

▶ It prevents the tongue from falling back into the throat and blocking the airway and so maintains an open airway.

▶ Vomit or other fluid can drain easily from the casualty's mouth, preventing choking.

▶ It keeps the casualty in a safe and comfortable position.

Recovery position for infants and children

For an infant less than a year old, a modified recovery position must be adopted:

▶ Cradle the infant in your arms, with their head tilted downwards to prevent choking on the tongue or inhaling vomit.

▶ Monitor the infant's breathing and pulse continuously.

For a child over the age of one year, follow these instructions:

▶ Turn the child onto their side.

▶ Lift the chin forward into the open airway position and adjust the child's hand under the cheek as necessary.

▶ Check that the child cannot roll forwards or backwards.

▶ Monitor the child's breathing and pulse continuously.

If you suspect spinal injury, use the jaw thrust technique. Place your hands on either side of the child's face. With your fingertips gently lift the jaw to open the airway and take care not to tilt the casualty's neck.

Key terms

Unconscious: a state lacking normal awareness of self or the environment

Over to you!

Practise taking your own pulse and check the rate and rhythm.

Compare the pulse at your wrist with the pulse in your neck (carotid pulse). Are they different in any way?

Compare your own pulse rate with that of others in your group.

Assessment and monitoring

If an infant or child is unresponsive but breathing normally, it is essential to assess and monitor their condition while you wait for the ambulance to arrive. See Figure 12.3.

Figure 12.3 The main points for assessing and monitoring the condition of an unresponsive casualty

What to check	How to assess and what to note
Airway	Make sure nothing is blocking the airway or obstructing breathing (e.g. vomit).
Breathing	Note the rate and depth of breathing and any changes (if the casualty stops breathing, be prepared to start CPR).
Circulation	Check the pulse at the neck (carotid pulse). Note the rate and strength of the pulse and any changes.
Responsiveness	Keep talking and asking questions; gentle shaking or pinching the skin to see if there is any response. Note any changes.
Changes in general condition	Check the colour of the skin and lips. Note any blueness or other changes. Check for the presence of any bleeding or complaints of pain from the casualty.

Practical Assessment Task   3.1   3.2

Ben is a trained first aider and works at a children's centre. He is called to attend to an incident in which a child has collapsed and is unconscious. Gemma, one of the nursery assistants, has placed the child in the recovery position by the time Ben arrives at the scene.

1. Explain why it is important for the child to be in the recovery position.

2. Describe how Ben should continue to assess and monitor the condition of the child.

3. Give examples of any changes in the child's condition that Ben should make a note of.

Keep your notes to help you with your assessment. Your assessor will need to assess your competence in demonstrating the recovery position in a realistic, simulated environment.

Be able to provide first aid for an infant and a child who is unresponsive and not breathing normally

What is CPR?

For life to be maintained, oxygen must be taken into the lungs and pumped through the body in the bloodstream. Any accident or injury that interferes with this process can result in a life-threatening situation, for example, if air cannot get into the lungs or if the heart stops beating. If the human body is deprived of oxygen, then vital organs can very quickly be affected and may result in death. The first aider therefore needs to act quickly and know exactly what to do.

CPR stands for cardiopulmonary resuscitation and involves the first aider performing the functions of both breathing and blood circulation for the casualty. It is important to have the correct training in order to carry out CPR as it is a vital life-saving procedure. The ABC rule will help you to identify these priorities:

A = an open **A**irway – gently tilt the casualty's head back and lift the chin.

B = adequate **B**reathing – breathe air into the casualty (even the air we breathe out contains 16% oxygen which is enough to resuscitate another person).

C = sufficient **C**irculation – give the casualty external chest compression to apply the pressure required to pump blood to the vital organs.

When to administer CPR to an unresponsive infant or child

As a general rule, CPR should only be administered by people who are trained in the technique. First aid organisations provide guidance for untrained bystanders in how to provide emergency resuscitation until trained help arrives. As a trained first aider, CPR should always be carried out if a casualty is unresponsive, is not breathing and has no pulse. The procedure should be followed even if you have doubts about its success and you should always carry on until help arrives.

CPR for infants and children

If possible, send someone else to call for an ambulance immediately, but if you are on your own, carry out CPR for one minute before calling. If there is any evidence of blood or other fluid around the child's mouth, then a disposable face shield should be used. See Figure 12.4.

Your assessment criteria:

4.1 Identify when to administer CPR to an unresponsive infant and an unresponsive child who is not breathing normally

4.2 Demonstrate how to administer CPR using an infant and a child manikin

Over to you!

▶ *Using the heel of your hand on the top of a desk, table or other firm surface, practise carrying out compressions at the rate of 100 per minute.*

▶ *With a partner, time each other and practise your rhythm for giving 30 compressions at a rate of 100 per minute.*

Figure 12.4 The CPR procedure for infants and children

CPR for infants (less than 1 year old)

1. Give five rescue breaths:

- Tilt the head back and lift the chin to open the airway.
- Seal your lips around the baby's mouth and nose.
- Blow gently into the lungs, looking along the chest as you breathe. Fill your cheeks with air and use this amount each time.
- As the chest rises, stop blowing and allow it to fall.
  Repeat four more times.

2. Give 30 chest compressions:

- Place the baby on a firm surface.
- Locate a position in the centre of the chest.
- Using two fingers, press down sharply to a third of the depth of the chest.
- Press 30 times, at a rate of 100 compressions per minute.
- After 30 compressions, give two rescue breaths.

3. Continue to resuscitate at 30 compressions to two rescue breaths until help arrives.

CPR for children (1–12 years old)

1. Give five rescue breaths:

- Tilt the head back and lift the chin to open the airway.
- Seal your lips around the child's mouth and pinch the nose.
- Blow gently and watch the chest as you breathe. Make sure your breathing is shallow and do not empty your lungs completely.
- As the chest rises, stop blowing and allow it to fall.
- Repeat four more times, then check the child's carotid pulse.

2. Give 30 chest compressions:

- Place one or two hands in the centre of the chest (depending on the size of the child).
- Use the heel of the hand with arms straight and press down to a third of the depth of the chest.
- Press 30 times, at a rate of 100 compressions per minute.
- After 30 compressions, give two rescue breaths.

3. Continue to resuscitate at 30 compressions to two rescue breaths until help arrives or the child recovers.

Seizures

A seizure (also known as a convulsion or fit) consists of involuntary contractions of muscles in the body. The condition is due to a disturbance in the electrical activity of the brain and seizures usually result in loss or impairment of consciousness. The most common causes are **epilepsy** or head injuries.

General signs of a seizure are:

▶ sudden unconsciousness

▶ rigidity and arching of the back

▶ convulsive, jerky movements.

In dealing with seizures, first aid treatment must always include maintaining an open airway and monitoring the infant or child's vital signs (their level of response, pulse and breathing). You will also need to protect the infant or child from further harm during a seizure and arrange appropriate aftercare once they have recovered. First aid treatment for a seizure includes:

▶ If you see the child falling, try to ease the fall.

▶ If possible, protect the infant or child's head by placing soft padding underneath it.

▶ Make space around them and if necessary, make sure other children move away.

▶ Remove dangerous items, such as hot drinks or sharp objects.

▶ Note the time when the seizure started.

▶ Loosen clothing around the infant or child's neck.

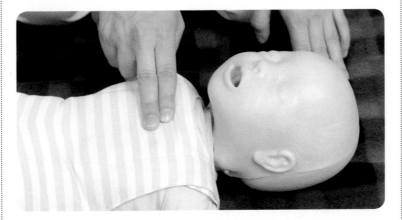

When the seizure has finished:

▶ Open the airway and check the infant or child's breathing.

▶ Be prepared to give CPR if necessary.

▶ Place the infant or child into the recovery position if they are unconscious but breathing normally.

Your assessment criteria:

4.1 Identify when to administer CPR to an unresponsive infant and an unresponsive child who is not breathing normally

4.2 Demonstrate how to administer CPR using an infant and a child manikin

4.3 Describe how to deal with an infant and a child who is experiencing a seizure

Key terms

Epilepsy: a disorder of the nervous system characterised by convulsions, which can result in a loss of consciousness

Over to you!

Investigate the condition of epilepsy at: www.epilepsy.org.uk/

Look at the 'Epilepsy policy for schools' information and make a list of the key principles that should be included in every school policy on epilepsy.

- ▶ Monitor and record vital signs (level of response, pulse and breathing).
- ▶ Make a note of how long the seizure lasted.

Do not move the infant or child unless they are in immediate danger.

Do not put anything in their mouth or use force to restrain them.

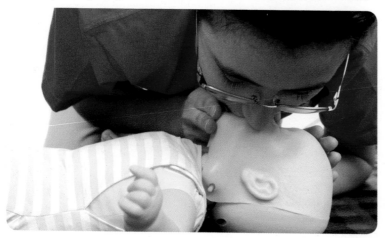

If any of the following apply, dial 999 for an ambulance:

- ▶ The infant or child is unconscious for more than 10 minutes.
- ▶ The seizure continues for more than 5 minutes.
- ▶ The infant or child is having repeated seizures or having a seizure for the first time.

Practical Assessment Task   4.1   4.2   4.3

Andy is a trained first aider and works at an out-of-school club. He is responsible for a small group of children aged 5–10 years who attend every day from 3.30 to 6pm. One of the children, Peter, aged 7 years, has epilepsy. All the staff at the club are aware of Peter's condition and know what to do if he has a seizure.

Andy is outside playing football with Peter and a small group of children. Suddenly, Peter falls to the ground and starts to have a seizure.

1. Describe what Andy's immediate first aid treatment should be.
2. Describe how Andy should monitor Peter's condition during and after the seizure.
3. Identify when Andy should commence CPR with Peter.

Keep your notes to help you with your assessment. Your tutor or assessor will need to assess your competence in performing CPR in a realistic, simulated environment, with both an infant and a child manikin.

Be able to provide first aid for an infant and a child who has a foreign body airway obstruction

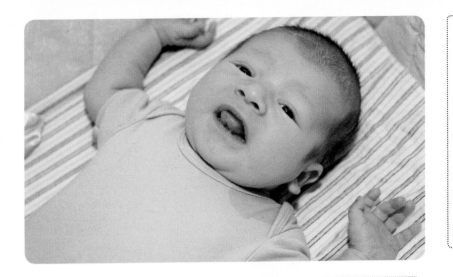

What is an airway obstruction?

Infants and young children are especially prone to choking. A child may choke on food, or put small objects into their mouth and cause a blockage of the airway.

If the blockage of the airway is mild, the casualty will be able to speak or cry and should usually be able to clear it by coughing. If it is severe, they will be very distressed and unable to cry, speak, cough, or breathe and will eventually lose consciousness.

First aid treatment for choking

Your aims are to remove the obstruction and to arrange urgent transport to hospital if necessary. See Figure 12.5.

Figure 12.5 First aid treatment for choking

Casualty	Mild obstruction	Severe obstruction
Infant	• Check the infant's mouth, remove any obvious obstructions. • Do not sweep your finger around in the mouth (this could push any obstruction further down the airway).	• Lay the infant face down along your forearm, with the head low. Support the back and head. • Give up to five back blows with the heel of your hand. • Check the infant's mouth, removing any obvious obstructions. • If the obstruction is still present, turn the infant onto their back and give up to five chest thrusts. (Using two fingers, push inwards and upwards towards the head against the infant's breastbone, one finger's breadth below the nipple line.)

continued...

Casualty	Mild obstruction	Severe obstruction
		• If the obstruction does not clear after three cycles, dial 999 for an ambulance. • Continue until help arrives. 
Child	• Encourage them to continue coughing. • Remove any obvious obstruction from the mouth.	• Give up to five back blows with the heel of your hand. • Check the mouth and remove any obvious obstruction. • If the obstruction is still present, give up to five abdominal thrusts. • Continue as for an infant. 

Practical Assessment Task 5.1 5.2 5.3

Sally is a trained first aider and works as a daily nanny. She has sole charge of two children, Poppy, aged 3 years, and Danny, aged 18 months. Both children enjoy being active and Sally plans lots of exciting play activities for them every day.

After lunch one day, Poppy asks Sally to help her make a necklace with some wooden beads. Sally and Poppy sit on the floor with the beads and Danny is playing with a shape sorter nearby. Poppy and Sally are totally absorbed in making necklaces with the beads, when suddenly Danny starts to cough and seems to be choking.

1. Describe how Sally could tell if Danny had a mild or severe airway obstruction.

2. Describe what Sally's first aid treatment should be.

3. Describe the procedure that Sally should follow after administering first aid treatment.

Keep your notes as evidence towards your assessment. Your assessor will need to assess your competence in treating choking in a realistic, simulated environment, with both an infant and a child manikin.

Be able to provide first aid to an infant and a child who is wounded and bleeding

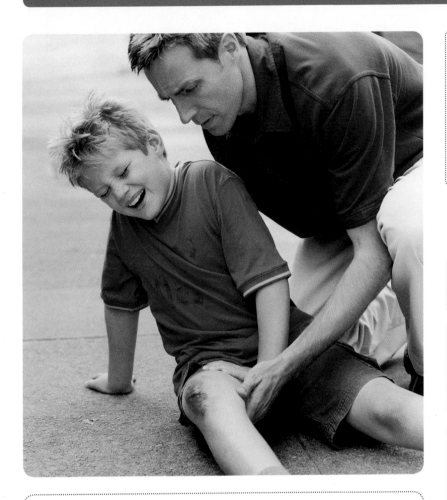

Your assessment criteria:

6.1 Describe common types of wounds

6.2 Describe the types and severity of bleeding and the effect that it has on an infant and a child

Key terms

Bacteria: microscopic organisms that can cause disease

External bleeding: bleeding that involves blood leaving the body (actual blood will always be visible)

Internal bleeding: bleeding occurring inside the body (actual blood is not usually visible)

Shock: a critical condition brought on by a sudden drop in blood flow through the body

Tetanus: a serious infection of the nervous system caused by bacterial infection of open wounds

What are the dangers from wounds and bleeding?

A wound is caused by any break in the surface of the skin. When this happens:

▶ blood and other body fluids can be lost causing **shock**

▶ **bacteria** can enter the body and cause infection.

If the bleeding is minor, the aim of the first aider is to prevent infection. With severe bleeding, the aim is to prevent further blood loss and minimise the shock that can be caused (see page 270).

Some injuries can result in **internal bleeding**, for example, following a fall. This can be more serious than **external bleeding** as the blood cannot escape from the body and may cause damage to vital organs.

If a wound has been caused by a dirty or rusty object or from an animal bite, then the child should always be treated at the hospital. An injection may be necessary to prevent **tetanus** infection.

Over to you!

▶ *Have you ever had an injury that resulted in bleeding? How severe was it and how was it treated?*

▶ *Share your experiences with others in the group.*

Types of wounds

There are several types of wounds that can result in bleeding:

- Incised: a clean cut, for example from a knife
- Lacerated: a jagged cut, for example from barbed wire
- Puncture: a penetrating wound, for example from a nail
- Graze: a surface wound, for example from a sliding fall
- Contused: a bruise, with bleeding under the skin

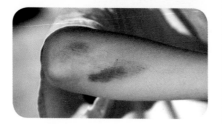

Types of bleeding

Bleeding can occur from any of the different blood vessels in the body. It can be external or internal and either major or minor as shown in Figure 12.6.

Over to you!

Using Figure 12.6, describe the type of bleeding and the risks in the following situations:

- *A 3 year old has cut her finger on a sharp, pointed object. The skin is broken and blood is trickling out.*
- *A 5 year old has fallen onto some glass and cut his leg. The skin is broken and blood is oozing out.*
- *A 9 year old has fallen from the top of a climbing frame and bumped his head. There is no sign of any blood, but he is complaining of pain and a bruise has started to appear on his forehead.*

Figure 12.6 Types of bleeding

Type of bleeding	Characteristics	Risks
Arterial (from an artery, a major blood vessel carrying oxygenated blood)	Blood is bright red and usually spurts out	Can result in extensive blood loss Danger of shock
Venous (from a vein, a blood vessel carrying deoxygenated blood)	Blood is dark red and oozes out	Can result in extensive blood loss Danger of shock
Capillary (from a very small blood vessel)	Usually only minor bleeding and blood trickles out	Minimal blood loss but still a risk of infection
Major	Extensive blood loss	First aid emergency Danger of shock and can be life threatening
Minor	Limited blood loss	Minimal blood loss but still a risk of infection
External	Skin is broken, blood escapes from the body	Risk of infection Danger of shock
Internal	Skin is not broken, blood collects inside the body Pain, swelling or bruising	Damage to internal organs Danger of shock

Treatment for major and minor external bleeding

Any open wound is at risk of becoming infected. It is very important to maintain good hygiene procedures to prevent infection between yourself and the injured infant or child. Always wear disposable gloves and make sure that any cuts on your own hands are covered. See Figure 12.7.

The most effective way of minimising blood loss from major bleeding is to apply direct pressure over the wound. If the injury is on an arm or a leg, raising the limb will slow down the blood flow and help to stop the bleeding.

Your assessment criteria:

6.1 Describe common types of wounds

6.2 Describe the types and severity of bleeding and the effect that it has on an infant and a child

6.3 Demonstrate the safe and effective management for the control of minor and major external bleeding

6.4 Describe how to administer first aid for minor injuries

Figure 12.7 First aid treatment for both major and minor external bleeding

Type of injury	First aid treatment
Minor bleeding 	• Wash and dry your own hands and put on disposable gloves. • Clean the cut, if dirty, under running water, and pat dry. • Cover the cut temporarily while you clean the surrounding skin with soap and water, and pat the skin dry. • Cover the cut completely with a sterile dressing or non-allergenic plaster.
Major bleeding 	• Wash and dry your own hands and put on disposable gloves. • Apply direct pressure to the wound with a pad or sterile dressing. • Raise and support (if the injury is on a limb). • Lay the casualty down to treat for shock (see page 270). • Bandage the pad or dressing firmly to control bleeding. • If bleeding seeps through the first bandage, cover with a second bandage.

Treatment for minor injuries

In most first aid situations with children, injuries are likely to be relatively minor, usually with very little blood loss. A common minor injury involving bleeding with children is a nosebleed. This usually occurs when tiny blood vessels inside the nostrils burst, either as a result of an injury to the nose, or from sneezing, picking or blowing the nose.

The first aid treatment for a nosebleed is as follows:

▶ Reassure the child and ask them to sit down.

▶ Advise them to tilt their head forwards.

▶ Tell the child to breathe through their mouth and to pinch the soft part of the nose (they may need help to do this).

▶ After 10 minutes, release the pressure from the nose. If the bleeding has not stopped, pinch the nose again for two further periods of 10 minutes.

▶ Once the bleeding has stopped, clean around the nose with lukewarm water.

▶ Tell the child not to blow or pick their nose for a few hours (because this may disturb blood clots that may have formed in the nose).

Do not let the child's head tip back as blood may run down the throat and cause choking.

If the nosebleed is severe, or if it lasts longer than 30 minutes, the child should be taken to hospital.

Practical Assessment Task | **6.1** | **6.2** | **6.3** | **6.4**

In each of the following situations, describe the type of wound, the types of bleeding and the appropriate first aid treatment:

1. Molly, aged 3 years, has been bitten on the hand by a dog. The skin is broken and blood is trickling out.

2. Kenny, aged 7 years, has fallen on a rusty barbed wire fence and cut his knee. The skin is broken and a lot of dark red blood is oozing out.

3. Jenny, aged 11 years, starts to have a nosebleed. There is a lot of blood and Jenny is panicking.

4. Hussein, aged 5 years, has fallen in the playground and grazed his knee. There is not much bleeding, but the wound is covered in dirt and grit.

Keep your notes to help you with your assessment. Your assessor will need to assess your competence in dealing with bleeding in a realistic, simulated environment.

Know how to provide first aid to an infant and a child who is suffering from shock

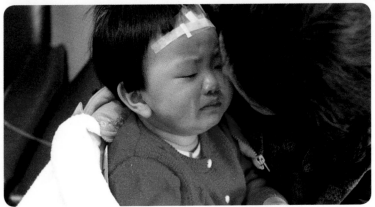

Your assessment criteria:

7.1 Describe how to recognise and manage an infant and a child who is suffering from shock

7.2 Describe how to recognise and manage an infant and a child who is suffering from anaphylactic shock

What is shock?

Shock is a life-threatening condition that occurs when the vital organs, such as the brain and heart are deprived of oxygen. The most common cause of shock is extreme blood loss but it can be caused by damage to the heart muscle, for example, by electrocution.

Recognising and treating shock

The main signs of shock are:

▶ pale, cold, clammy skin (lips could become blue in severe shock)

▶ sweating

▶ weakness and dizziness

▶ feeling sick and possibly vomiting

▶ feeling thirsty

▶ rapid, shallow breathing.

The main first aid treatment for shock is:

▶ Give lots of comfort and reassurance.

▶ Lay the casualty down, raise and support their legs.

▶ Use a coat or blanket to keep them comfortably warm.

▶ Do not give them anything to eat or drink.

▶ Check breathing and pulse frequently.

▶ If the child becomes unconscious, put them in the recovery position (see page 258).

▶ If breathing stops, follow the DRABC resuscitation sequence (see page 255).

Over to you!

Have you ever been in a situation where you have suffered from shock or experienced someone else in shock?

▶ *What caused it?*

▶ *What happened and what treatment was given?*

▶ *Compare your responses with others in the group.*

270

Anaphylactic shock

Anaphylactic shock is a severe allergic reaction which can be life-threatening. It is usually triggered by a substance to which the casualty is highly sensitive, for example, drugs such as penicillin, insect stings or food such as peanuts.

The main signs of anaphylactic shock are:

▶ difficulty in breathing, wheezing or gasping for air

▶ general signs of shock (see previous page)

▶ swelling of the tongue and throat

▶ puffiness around the eyes

▶ extreme anxiety.

The main first aid treatment for anaphylactic shock is:

▶ Send for an ambulance.

▶ Check whether the child has their own medication and help them to use it if trained to do so (see below).

▶ Reassure and comfort the child.

▶ Treat for shock (see previous page).

▶ If the child becomes unconscious, put them in the recovery position (see page 258).

▶ If breathing stops, follow the DRABC resuscitation sequence (see page 255).

Children who are known to suffer from anaphylaxis will usually carry their own medication with them at all times. This is usually in the form of an EpiPen® or similar device. An EpiPen® is easy to use, although special training should be undertaken and you should always check the policies and procedures in the setting.

Key terms

Anaphylactic shock: a severe and sometimes life-threatening allergic reaction

Knowledge Assessment Task   7.1   7.2

Design a leaflet or webpage for parents that provides information about recognising and managing shock and anaphylactic shock in infants and children. You can illustrate your work with suitable images.

Keep your work as evidence towards your assessment.

Are you ready for assessment?

AC	What do you know now?	Assessment task	✓
1.1	The responsibilities of a paediatric first aider	Page 251	
1.2	How to minimise the risk of infection to self and others	Page 251	
1.3	A description of suitable first aid equipment, including personal protection, and how it is used appropriately	Page 253	
1.4	The information that needs to be included in an accident/incident record and how to record it	Page 253	
1.5	The definition of an infant and a child for the purposes of first aid treatment	Page 251	

Your tutor or assessor will need to observe your competence in a realistic, simulated situation.

AC	What can you do now?	Assessment task	✓
2.1 2.2	Demonstrate how to conduct a scene survey and a primary survey on an infant and a child	Page 257	
2.3	Identify when and how to call for help	Page 257	
3.1	Demonstrate how to place an infant and a child into the appropriate recovery position	Page 259	
3.2	Describe how to continually assess and monitor an infant and a child while in your care	Page 259	
4.1 4.2	Identify when to administer CPR to an unresponsive infant and a child who is not breathing normally and demonstrate how to administer CPR using an infant and child manikin	Page 263	
4.3	Describe how to deal with an infant and a child who is experiencing a seizure	Page 263	
5.1	Differentiate between a mild and a severe airway obstruction	Page 265	
5.2 5.3	Demonstrate how to treat an infant and a child who is choking and describe the procedure to be followed after administering treatment	Page 265	
6.1	Describe common types of wounds	Page 269	
6.2	Describe the types and severity of bleeding and the effect it has on an infant and a child	Page 269	
6.3	Demonstrate the safe and effective management for the control of minor and major external bleeding	Page 269	
6.4	Describe how to administer first aid for minor injuries	Page 269	
7.1 7.2	Describe how to recognise and manage an infant and a child who is suffering from: shock or from anaphylactic shock	Page 271	

13 | Managing paediatric illness and injury (MPII 002)

Assessment of this unit

This unit is about dealing with a range of paediatric illnesses and injuries. It includes conditions such as fractures, burns and poisoning as well as medical conditions such as diabetes and asthma.

The assessment of this unit is partly knowledge based (things that you need to know about) and partly competence based (things that you need to be able to do in the real work environment or in your placement). Some of the practical assessment in this unit may be carried out in realistic, simulated situations. It is important to remember that illness and injuries to do with children can be life-threatening and so the assessment of this unit should be taken very seriously.

In order to successfully complete this unit, you will need to produce evidence of both your knowledge and your competence, as shown in the following charts. Your tutor or assessor will help you to prepare for your assessment, and the tasks suggested in this chapter will help you to create the evidence that you need.

AC	What you need to know
3.1	How to manage an infant and a child with foreign bodies in their eyes, ears and nose
3.2	How to recognise and manage common eye injuries
4.1 4.2	How to recognise and manage chronic medical conditions (including sickle cell anaemia, diabetes and asthma) and serious sudden illnesses (including meningitis and febrile convulsions)

5.1 5.2	How to recognise and treat the effects of extreme cold and heat for an infant and a child
6.1 6.2	How to safely manage an incident involving electricity and describe first aid treatments for electric shock incidents
7.1 7.2	How to recognise the severity of burns and scalds to an infant and a child and respond accordingly
8.1 8.3	How poisons enter the body and sources of information that provide procedures for treating those affected by poisonous substances
8.2	How to recognise and treat an infant and a child affected by common poisonous substances, including plants
9.1 9.2	How to recognise and treat the severity of bites and stings to an infant and a child and respond accordingly

AC	What you need to do
1.1	Describe the common types of fractures
1.2 1.3	Describe how to manage a fracture and a dislocation
1.4	Demonstrate the application of a support sling and an elevation sling
2.1	Describe how to recognise and manage head injuries including concussion, skull fracture and cerebral compression
2.2	Demonstrate how to manage a suspected spinal injury

This unit also links to some of the other mandatory units:

MU 2.4	Contribute to children and young people's health and safety
PEFAP 001	Paediatric emergency first aid
TDA 2.2	Safeguarding the welfare of children and young people

Some of your learning will be repeated in these units and give you the chance to review your knowledge and understanding.

What is a fracture?

A fracture is a broken or cracked bone, which can be caused by either direct or indirect force. The bones of infants and young children are very supple and can be surprisingly strong, but even young bones will split, bend or crack from the stress of an injury.

Types of fracture

There are two main types of fracture, closed and open. With a closed fracture, the bone is broken, but the surface of the skin remains intact. With an open fracture, the surface of the skin is broken and the fractured bone may stick out through the damaged skin.

Recognising fractures and dislocations

All suspected fracture injuries should be handled carefully as unnecessary movement may cause further damage. A fracture can generally be recognised by the following signs and symptoms:

▶ pain near the injury

▶ difficulty in moving

- ▶ swelling around the injury

- ▶ deformity of position (for example, twisting or unusual bending)

- ▶ sight of the actual bone protruding from the skin and bleeding (open fractures).

If the skin is broken, there is the danger of infection, so care should always be taken to prevent infection of an open fracture.

A dislocation is the displacement of one or more bones at a joint, for example, the shoulder.

The signs and symptoms of a dislocation are very similar to those of a fracture and if you are in any doubt, then treat the injury in the same way as a fracture. You should never attempt to replace dislocated bones in their normal positions as this can result in further damage to the surrounding tissues.

With an open fracture the surface of the skin is broken.

General treatment of fractures and dislocations

Children should be comforted with lots of reassurance as they may be very frightened. You should not move the casualty unless you have to. Your first aid treatment should be as follows:

- ▶ Steady and support the injury with your hands to stop any movement.

- ▶ If there is bleeding, use a clean pad to apply pressure and control the flow of blood, then bandage securely (see page 268).

- ▶ **Immobilise** the fracture by splinting, for example, apply padding, a sling, scarf or bandage.

- ▶ Dial 999 for an ambulance.

- ▶ Raise and support the injured limb, if it does not distress the casualty too much.

- ▶ Do not give the casualty anything to eat or drink (in case an operation is necessary).

- ▶ Observe the casualty for signs of shock and treat appropriately (see page 270).

Key terms

Immobilise: to prevent from moving

Practical Assessment Task   **1.1**   **1.2**   **1.3**   **1.4**

1. Prepare a short talk for parents about the different types of fractures and the first aid treatment for fractures and dislocations with infants and children.

2. Present your talk to the whole group.

Keep your notes from your talk to help you with your assessment. Your assessor will need to assess your competence in applying both a support sling and an elevation sling in a realistic, simulated situation.

Be able to provide first aid to an infant and a child with a head, a neck and a back injury

Your assessment criteria:

2.1 Describe how to recognise and manage head injuries including concussion, skull fracture and cerebral compression

What are the dangers of head, neck and back injuries?

All head, neck and back injuries are potentially serious and require proper assessment and careful handling. Injuries may be associated with damage to the brain or a skull fracture and can result in unconsciousness. See Figure 13.1.

A head injury may produce **concussion**, which is a brief period of unconsciousness, followed by complete recovery. Some head injuries may produce compression of the brain (**cerebral compression**), which is life-threatening. See Figure 13.2.

The first aid treatment of any casualty with a head injury should include an assessment of their responsiveness (AVPU code) as follows:

A – Is the casualty **alert**, eyes open and responding to questions?

V – Does the casualty respond to **voice** and obey simple commands?

P – Does the casualty respond to **pain** (e.g. eyes open or movement in response to being pinched)?

U – Is the casualty **unresponsive** (i.e. unconscious)?

If children experience any kind of head injury in the setting, even just bumping heads with another child, then a formal note like the one in Figure 13.2 should always be completed and sent home to the parents or carers. The note should clearly outline the symptoms that may develop, such as a headache or vomiting, which could indicate a more serious injury requiring medical attention.

Key terms

Cerebral compression: pressure on the brain caused by blood or other abnormality

Concussion: a mild brain injury usually caused by a blow to the head

Over to you!

▶ *How are children's head injuries dealt with in your placement or work setting?*

▶ *Why do you think it is important for head injury notes to be sent home to parents or carers when children have experienced a head injury?*

▶ *Share your experiences with others in the group.*

▶ *Investigate the head injury note that is used in your placement or work setting and keep a copy as evidence towards your assessment.*

Figure 13.1 Recognition and first aid management of different head injuries

Type of injury	Possible causes	Recognition	First aid management
Concussion (the brain is 'shaken' inside the skull)	Any blow to the head; a fall; sports injuries	• Brief period of unconsciousness • Dizziness • Mild headache	• Check level of responsiveness. • Monitor and record vital signs – level of response, breathing and pulse. • Arrange for the casualty to go to hospital, if they develop symptoms such as headache, vomiting, or blurred vision. • Complete a head injury note. • If the casualty does not recover fully, dial 999 for an ambulance.
Skull fracture (the bones of the skull are broken or cracked)	Any head injury (particularly resulting in unconsciousness)	• A wound or bruise on the head • Clear fluid or watery blood coming from the nose or an ear • Unconsciousness	If the casualty is conscious: • Help them to lie down. • Do not turn the head in case there is a neck injury. • Control any bleeding by applying pressure around the wound. • Dial 999 for an ambulance. • Monitor and record vital signs until medical help arrives. If the casualty is unconscious: • Open the airway using the jaw thrust method and check for breathing (see page 255). • Be prepared to give CPR if needed (see page 260). • Dial 999 for an ambulance. • Monitor and record vital signs until medical help arrives.
Cerebral compression (pressure on the brain from blood or other fluid)	Bleeding within the skull or swelling of the brain (caused by a head injury infection or medical condition)	• Intense headache • Noisy breathing becoming slow • Unequal pupil size • Drowsiness • Noticeable change in behaviour such as irritability • Unconsciousness	If the casualty is conscious: • Dial 999 for an ambulance. • Keep them supported in a comfortable position and reassure. • Monitor and record vital signs until medical help arrives. If the casualty is unconscious, follow procedure for a skull fracture.

Figure 13.2 Notification of head injury form

Notification of head injury

Date: Name of child:

Description of accident and/or injury:

If your child experiences any of the following symptoms, you should consult your doctor without delay:

- Headache
- Nausea or vomiting
- Dizziness
- Blurred vision

Signed:

Your assessment criteria:

2.1 Describe how to recognise and manage head injuries including concussion, skull fracture and cerebral compression

2.2 Demonstrate how to manage a suspected spinal injury

Key terms

Intervertebral discs: pads of cartilage between the vertebrae of the spine

Spinal injuries

Possible injuries to the spine include fractures, strains or displaced **intervertebral discs** ('slipped discs'). If you have any doubt about the nature of the injury, always treat it as a fracture. Take great care in handling the child because of the danger of damaging the spinal cord. The two most vulnerable areas of the spinal column are the neck and the lower back.

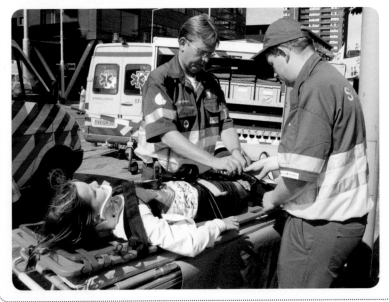

The first aid management of a suspected spinal injury is:

▶ Do not move the casualty unless it is an emergency (e.g. building on fire).

▶ Check ABC and consciousness (see page 255).

▶ Give CPR if necessary (see page 260).

▶ Reassure the casualty and stay calm.

▶ Place the casualty in the spinal injury recovery position (see page 258).

▶ Steady and support the head and neck by placing your hands over the casualty's ears.

▶ Dial 999 for an ambulance.

▶ Monitor the level of response, pulse and breathing until medical help arrives.

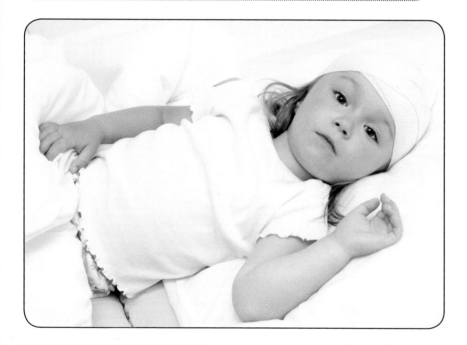

Practical Assessment Task   2.1   2.2

Design and create an illustrated poster, leaflet or webpage to provide information for trainee first aiders on how to recognise and manage:

1. concussion

2. a skull fracture

3. cerebral compression.

Keep your work to help you with your assessment. Your assessor will need to assess your competence in managing a suspected spinal injury in a realistic, simulated situation.

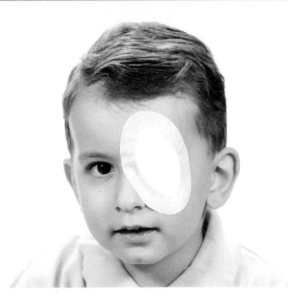

What is a 'foreign body'?

The term 'foreign body' is used in first aid to mean any object or matter that enters the body but should not be there. Foreign bodies can enter the body through any of the natural openings, for example, the mouth. They can also penetrate through the skin or the eyes.

Young children can easily push objects into their ears and nose, for example, beads or marbles. Great care should always be taken to make sure that small objects are never given to young children to play with (see Chapter 9 (CCLD MU 2.4) on page 190).

Management of foreign bodies

As a general rule, do not try to remove foreign bodies from the nose or ears, as you can cause more damage by pushing the object further in. Always remain calm, reassure the child and prevent them from poking at the object. You should arrange for the child to be taken to hospital for specialised medical help.

Foreign bodies can also enter the eyes and cause irritation and sometimes more serious damage. Particles of dust, grit or even loose eyelashes can cause children to rub their eyes, resulting in discomfort or further injury.

General first aid treatment for a foreign body in the eye or common eye injury would be:

▶ Try to stop the child from rubbing the eye.

▶ Sit the child in a chair and stand behind them.

▶ With clean hands, use your index finger and thumb to separate the affected eyelids.

▶ Ask the child to look right, left, up and down so you can examine every part of the eye.

▶ You may be able to remove the foreign body with the corner of a clean gauze pad.

▶ If you can see the foreign body, irrigate the eye using an eye irrigator and sterile water (if available).

▶ If this treatment is unsuccessful, cover the eye with a sterile eye pad and arrange for the child to be seen at the hospital.

Over to you!

▶ *Have you ever helped anyone with something in their eye?*

▶ *What happened and what did you do?*

▶ *Have you ever had anything stuck in your ears or nose, or do you know anyone who has?*

▶ *What happened?*

Compare your experiences with others in your group.

Knowledge Assessment Task   3.1   3.2

Describe how you would manage the following first aid situations:

1. Ruby, aged 18 months, has pushed a bead up her nose and is screaming

2. Hassan, aged 4 years, has pushed a small marble into his ear and is complaining that it hurts

3. Julia, aged 7 years, is complaining about having something in her eye. She has been rubbing her eye, which is now very red and watery.

Keep your notes as evidence towards your assessment.

Your assessment criteria:

4.1 Describe how to recognise and manage chronic medical conditions including sickle cell anaemia, diabetes and asthma

Key terms

Asthma: a non-infectious condition that can be triggered by allergic reactions and causes breathing difficulties

Asthma attack: a sudden worsening of asthma symptoms, with extreme wheezing, coughing and breathlessness

Diabetes: a disease with high levels of sugar in the blood

Nebuliser: a device used to dispense medication in the form of a mist inhaled directly into the lungs

Respiratory: relating to the process of breathing

Sickle cell anaemia: a blood disorder characterised by abnormal red blood cells

Spacer device: a specialised inhaler designed for very young children with asthma

What is a chronic medical condition?

A medical condition that requires ongoing treatment for a long period of time, or sometimes throughout a lifetime, is called a chronic condition. Examples of chronic medical conditions in infants and children include **asthma**, **diabetes** and **sickle cell anaemia**.

It is very important for anyone who works with children and young people to have an understanding of chronic medical conditions and know how to manage any symptoms should they arise. Children with chronic medical conditions can usually participate in all the normal activities in a setting, but there may be certain restrictions, for example, relating to exercise or diet, that practitioners need to be aware of. Chronic medical conditions can be aggravated by a variety of different triggers, which can lead to a sudden worsening of symptoms. This can result in a first aid emergency and it is very important to be able to recognise and manage these situations.

Asthma

Asthma is a **respiratory** disorder characterised by wheezing, coughing at night and episodes of difficult breathing. It is usually triggered by an allergy, for example, to pollen or animal fur.

Many children with asthma can manage their symptoms by using an inhaler on a regular basis. This can help to control the condition and prevent an **asthma attack** from occurring. Very young children may need to use a **spacer device** or a **nebuliser**.

Managing an asthma attack

Asthma attacks can be very frightening for children and it is important for the paediatric first aider to act quickly and calmly. See Figure 13.3.

Figure 13.3 Recognition and first aid management of an asthma attack

First aid emergency	Possible causes	Recognition	First aid management
Asthma attack	The air passages in the lungs become narrowed, go into spasm and breathing becomes difficult. Specific triggers can be: • an allergy • a cold • cigarette smoke • extremes of temperature • exercise.	• Difficulty in breathing and speaking • Wheezing as the casualty breathes out • Distress and anxiety • Coughing • Blueness of the lips	• Keep the casualty calm and reassure them. • If they have a blue 'reliever' inhaler, encourage them to use it (young children may have a spacer device). • Encourage the casualty to breathe slowly, sitting in a comfortable position, often leaning forward with their arms resting on a table. Do not lie the casualty down. • If the inhaler has no effect after 5 minutes then dial 999 to get medical help.

Over to you!

▶ *In your placement or work setting, do you have any children or young people who use an inhaler for asthma?*

▶ *How is this managed in the setting?*

▶ *How are staff informed about children's medical conditions in your placement or work setting?*

Compare your experiences with others in the group.

Diabetes

The most common type of diabetes that occurs in children and young people is called type 1 diabetes. Individuals with this condition are not able to regulate the level of sugar in their blood because the **pancreas** does not produce enough **insulin**. Without insulin, the blood cannot absorb sugar that the body needs for energy.

The management of type 1 diabetes usually involves monitoring the amount of sugar and carbohydrate in the diet and giving injections of insulin on a daily basis. Many children learn how to check their own blood sugar levels and to inject their own insulin from an early age.

Diabetic first aid emergencies

The blood sugar levels of children with diabetes can change rapidly and this can result in a first aid emergency with either **hypoglycaemia** or **hyperglycaemia**.

Figure 13.4 Recognition and first aid management of hypoglycaemia and hyperglycaemia

Your assessment criteria:

4.1 Describe how to recognise and manage chronic medical conditions including sickle cell anaemia, diabetes and asthma

First aid emergency	Possible causes	Recognition	First aid management
Hypoglycaemia (low blood sugar level)	A fall in the blood sugar level usually due to: • too much insulin • not enough carbohydrate • strenuous activity.	• Weakness, faintness, or hunger • The casualty may seem confused • Sweating and pale, cold, clammy skin • Rapid pulse • Deteriorating level of response	• Help the casualty to sit or lie down. • Give them a sugary drink, glucose sweets, chocolate or any other sweet food (not diet drinks as they don't have enough sugar in them). • The casualty should see their doctor even if they feel fully recovered. • If the casualty loses consciousness, don't give them anything to eat or drink as they may not be able to swallow and may choke. • Place them in the recovery position, (see page 258). • Monitor and record the levels of response, pulse and breathing. • Dial 999 for an ambulance.
Hyperglycaemia (high blood sugar level)	A high blood sugar level which can be caused by: • not enough insulin • too much carbohydrate.	• Warm, dry skin • Rapid pulse and breathing • Fruity or sweet smelling breath • Excessive thirst	• Dial 999 for an ambulance. • If the casualty loses consciousness, follow the procedure above.

Sickle cell anaemia

Sickle cell anaemia is an inherited, genetic condition characterised by having abnormal red blood cells. Normal red blood cells are flexible and can travel easily around the blood vessels, but the red blood cells of someone with sickle cell anaemia are more rigid and 'sickle-shaped'. This can cause blockages in the small blood vessels, preventing oxygen from getting through and causing severe pain.

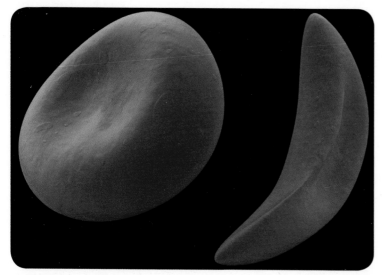

Sickle-shaped red blood cells are characteristic of sickle cell anaemia.

Key terms

Hyperglycaemia: abnormally high blood sugar level

Hypoglycaemia: abnormally low blood sugar level

Insulin: a hormone secreted by the pancreas which regulates the level of sugar in the blood

Pancreas: a digestive gland near the stomach which secretes insulin

Sickle cell crisis: a sudden worsening in the symptoms of sickle cell anaemia causing severe pain

Sickle cell crisis

Children with sickle cell anaemia can experience severe attacks known as a **sickle cell crisis**. This can be a life-threatening condition and the paediatric first aider should know how to respond. The first aid management of a sickle cell crisis is shown in Figure 13.5.

Figure 13.5 Recognition and first aid management of a sickle cell crisis

First aid emergency	Possible causes	Recognition	First aid management
Sickle cell crisis	Blockage of small blood vessels by sickle-shaped red blood cells. Can be triggered by an infection like flu, or very cold temperatures.	• Severe pain, especially in the bones • Difficulty breathing	• Reassure the child and keep them calm and comfortable. • Dial 999 for an ambulance. • If the casualty loses consciousness, place them in the recovery position (see page 258). • Monitor and record the levels of response, pulse and breathing.

Sudden illnesses

Some serious childhood illnesses can result in emergency situations and it is important that a paediatric first aider knows how to recognise and manage these conditions.

Meningitis

The main symptoms and treatment for meningitis are discussed in Unit TDA 2.2 (see Chapter 6, page 134). **Septicaemia** often occurs with meningitis and both conditions can be life-threatening. Meningitis and septicaemia can strike with little or no warning and the symptoms can be hard to recognise at first as they often appear like flu or other less serious illnesses. The symptoms in babies and young children do not present in any particular order, but knowing the symptoms and acting fast can save lives. Both meningitis and septicaemia can produce a rash, which does not fade under pressure. The best way to test this is by doing the 'glass test' (see the photograph on page 151 in Chapter 6). Press the side of a glass firmly against the rash. If it doesn't fade, it is important to get medical help immediately. See Figure 13.6 below.

Your assessment criteria:

4.1 Describe how to recognise and manage chronic medical conditions including sickle cell anaemia, diabetes and asthma

4.2 Describe how to recognise and manage serious sudden illnesses including meningitis and febrile convulsions

Key terms

Fontanelle: the soft spot on top of a baby's head

Septicaemia: blood poisoning caused by bacterial infection

Figure 13.6 Recognition and first aid management of meningitis and septicaemia

First aid emergency	Recognition	First aid management
Meningitis	<ul><li>Severe headache</li><li>High temperature (fever)</li><li>Vomiting</li><li>Very sleepy</li><li>Blotchy rash</li><li>Babies may have a high pitched cry, a bulging soft-spot (**fontanelle**) and not want to be fed or touched.</li></ul>	<ul><li>Dial 999 for an ambulance.</li><li>Reassure the child and keep them comfortable.</li><li>If the casualty loses consciousness, place them in the recovery position (see page 258).</li><li>Monitor and record the levels of response, pulse and breathing.</li><li>Be prepared to carry out CPR if necessary.</li></ul>
Septicaemia	All of the above symptoms plus:<ul><li>pale or mottled skin</li><li>pain in the joints</li><li>cold hands and feet</li><li>extreme shivering</li><li>breathless.</li></ul>	<ul><li>Follow the procedure for meningitis.</li><li>Septicaemia is a life-threatening condition and the child should be taken to hospital immediately.</li></ul>

Febrile convulsions

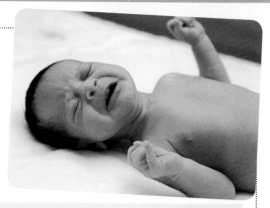

Febrile convulsions are seizures that occur in babies and young children when there is a rapid increase in body temperature to over 39°C. This often happens as a result of an infection and although febrile convulsions can be frightening, they are rarely serious. See Figure 13.7.

Figure 13.7 Recognition and first aid management of febrile convulsions

Recognition	First aid management
• The child loses consciousness, becomes stiff and stops breathing for up to 30 seconds. • The head is thrown backwards and the legs and arms begin to jerk. • The child's eyes roll upwards and the skin appears pale. • After a few minutes this stops, the child goes limp and regains consciousness. • The seizures are brief, usually lasting only a minute or two and never more than 5 minutes.	• Do not intervene while the convulsion is taking place, but make sure that the child is safe and cannot hurt themselves (e.g. remove toys from the cot). • Carefully turn the child's head to one side to prevent choking. • When the fit subsides, keep the child in the recovery position (see page 258). • Cool the child down by removing excess clothing or bedclothes. • Open a window or use a fan in the room. • Sponge the child down with cool (not cold) water. • Arrange for the child to be seen by a doctor. • If fits are prolonged or follow each other rapidly, call an ambulance. • The first time a child suffers febrile convulsions they should be admitted to hospital for investigations.

Knowledge Assessment Task   4.1   4.2

Choose one of the following conditions:

► sickle cell anaemia
► type 1 diabetes
► asthma
► meningitis
► febrile convulsions.

Write an article for a parenting magazine about the recognition and management of your chosen condition in infants and children. Include the signs and symptoms of the condition and the first aid treatment for emergency situations.

Share your articles in the group and keep your article as evidence towards your assessment.

Key terms

Febrile convulsion: a seizure (fit) caused by a significant rise in body temperature

What are the effects of extreme heat and cold?

The human body can usually regulate its own temperature very well, but can be affected by extremes of heat and cold. Sunburn and heatstroke can occur from overexposure to heat and **hypothermia** can result from extremely low temperatures.

Infants and very young children are particularly vulnerable to the extremes of heat and cold as they have difficulty in controlling their own body temperature.

First aid management

The recognition and first aid treatment of the effects of extreme heat and cold are described in Figure 13.8.

Figure 13.8 Recognition and first aid management of the effects of extreme heat and cold

First aid emergency	Recognition	First aid management
Sunburn	• Reddened skin • Blistering	• Remove the child from the sun (into the shade or preferably indoors). • Cool the skin by sponging with cool water. • For severe sunburn, extensive blistering or skin damage, seek medical help.
Heatstroke	• Headache, dizziness and confusion • Hot flushed and dry skin • A rapid deterioration in the level of response • A full bounding pulse • Body temperature above 40°C	• Quickly move the casualty to a cool place. • Dial 999 for an ambulance. • Wrap the casualty in a cold wet sheet or sponge them down with cold water. • Monitor and record the level of response, pulse and breathing rate until help arrives. • Be prepared to carry out CPR if necessary (see page 260). • If the casualty becomes unconscious, place them in the recovery position (see page 258).

continued...

First aid emergency	Recognition	First aid management
Hypothermia	• Body temperature below 35°C • Pale skin which is cold to the touch • **Note:** babies' cheeks may appear pink • Slow and shallow breathing • Sluggish and difficult to feed • Babies may have a feeble cry	• Place the casualty in a warm bed with warm bedding and clothing. • Cuddle infants to use skin to skin contact to transfer body heat. • Give the casualty a warm drink. • Remove any wet clothes. • Obtain medical help if the body temperature does not begin to rise.

Risks from overheating

Overheating is one of the factors associated with **sudden infant death syndrome** (cot death) in babies, particularly in the first year of life.

The Foundation for the Study of Infant Death recommends the following advice to reduce the risk of cot death:

▶ Always place a baby on their back to sleep and with their feet at the bottom of the cot.

▶ Don't smoke, either during pregnancy or in the same room as the baby.

▶ Don't let a baby become too hot, use layers of light bedding and keep the baby's room temperature between 16°C and 20°C.

Key terms

Hypothermia: an extremely low body temperature

Sudden infant death syndrome: the sudden and unexpected death of an apparently healthy infant during sleep

Knowledge Assessment Task   5.1   5.2

Vicky is a teenage mother and her baby, Amy, is 5 months old.

Vicky has spent an afternoon in the park with Amy and some of their friends. It was a hot, summer's day, with very little cloud. Amy was wearing a sunhat and was dressed in a cool, cotton dress with short sleeves.

As Vicky undresses Amy for her bath in the evening, she notices that Amy's arms are very red and puffy. Amy is more irritable than usual and cries when Vicky puts her in the bath.

1. Describe how Vicky should treat Amy's sunburn.
2. What signs would indicate that Vicky should get medical attention for Amy?
3. How could Vicky have prevented Amy from getting sunburned?

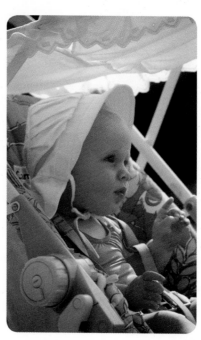

Know how to provide first aid to an infant and a child who has sustained an electric shock, burns or scalds

Your assessment criteria:

6.1 Describe how to safely manage an incident involving electricity

6.2 Describe first aid treatments for electric shock incidents

7.1 Describe how to recognise the severity of burns and scalds to an infant and a child and respond accordingly

7.2 Describe how to treat burns and scalds to an infant and a child

Key terms

Conduction: the transfer of electricity from one material to another by direct contact

What are the dangers of electrical injuries?

The passage of electricity through the body may result in serious and sometimes fatal injuries. Electricity can cause the heart to stop beating and can cause severe burns where the electricity enters the body. Young children are particularly at risk because they may try to play with switches, wires and plugs. Home safety with electrical equipment is extremely important and precautions should always be taken to protect children from electrocution (see Chapter 4 (MU 2.4) on page 86).

First aid treatment

An electric current can pass through a variety of different materials that allow the **conduction** of electricity, for example metal, water and the human body. Some materials do not allow the conduction of electricity (non-conductive), for example wood, rubber and plastic.

Over to you!

▶ *Think about the different ways children can experience electrical injuries in the home environment.*

▶ *Make a list of all the home safety equipment that is designed to protect children from electrical injuries.*

▶ *Share your ideas with others in the group.*

Whatever the cause of the electrical injury, it is important never to touch the casualty with your bare hands until you are sure that there is no danger to yourself from the electric current.

In dealing with any electrical injury, the aim of your first aid treatment is to:

▶ break the electric current safely (by switching off at the mains)

▶ remove the casualty from the electricity source

▶ check the casualty's level of responsiveness

▶ check breathing (if the casualty is unconscious) and be prepared to carry out CPR if necessary (see page 260)

▶ place the casualty in the recovery position (see page 258) and continue to monitor the level of response, pulse and breathing rate

▶ arrange for the casualty to be taken to hospital.

If you cannot break the current safely, stand on something that is non-conductive (for example, a wooden box or a thick stack of newspaper) and use a non-conductive object (for example, a wooden chair or stool) to help you move the casualty, or pull on the casualty's clothing. Never touch the casualty's flesh with your bare hands and never use anything metallic or damp to touch the casualty.

What is the difference between a burn and a scald?

Burns can be caused by extremes of temperature (heat or cold), from chemicals or radiation. Burns caused by 'wet' heat, such as steam or hot liquids are called scalds. For first aid purposes, the management of burns and scalds is the same.

The main dangers from burns and scalds are:

▶ infection as a result of damage to the protective skin layer

▶ shock due to loss of body fluid.

As with electrical injuries, the risk of burns and scalds with infants and young children is greater because they are less aware of the dangers involved. Safety precautions are very important to protect children from burns and scalds.

Severity of burns and scalds

The severity of a burn or a scald depends on how much of the body
it covers and how deep the injury goes.

Infants and young children are particularly at risk from burns and
scalds because their small body size means that a relatively large
area of their body can be damaged. See Figgure 13.9.

Figure 13.9 The three main levels of burning or scalding

Level of burn or scald	Characteristics
Superficial	Affects only the outer layers of the skin, resulting in redness, swelling and extreme tenderness
Intermediate	Involves the formation of blisters and surrounding redness
Deep	Affects all layers of the skin, resulting in damage to nerve endings and therefore relatively little pain

It is often difficult to distinguish between the different
levels, but a large burn will almost certainly involve all
three levels.

First aid treatment

The treatment of burns and scalds will depend on how
serious the injury is.

For minor burns and scalds:

- ▶ Stay calm and reassure the casualty.

- ▶ Hold the affected area under cold water for at
  least 10 minutes

- ▶ Gently remove any jewellery, shoes or other
  constricting items from the injured area (before
  it starts to swell).

- ▶ Cover the burn with clean, non-fluffy material
  to protect from infection (a clean plastic bag or
  kitchen film all make good dressings).

As a general rule, if a minor burn is larger than a postage stamp it
requires medical attention. See also Figure 13.10.

For severe burns and scalds:

▶ Stay calm and reassure the casualty.

▶ Start cooling the burn immediately under running water for at least 10 minutes.

▶ Dial 999 for an ambulance.

▶ Make the casualty as comfortable as possible.

▶ Continue to pour cold water over the burn for at least 10 minutes or until the pain is relieved.

▶ Put on disposable gloves and remove jewellery and any restricting clothing from the injured area, unless it is sticking to the skin.

▶ Cover the burn with clean, non-fluffy material to protect from infection.

▶ All deep burns of any size require urgent hospital treatment.

Figure 13.10 Rules for the first aid treatment of all burns

Do not...	Why?
use any lotions, ointments or creams.	This can introduce infection.
use adhesive dressings (plasters).	They will stick to the skin and cause more damage.
break blisters, remove any loose skin or try to remove any clothing that is stuck to the skin.	This can introduce infection and cause more damage to the injured area.

Clothing on fire

Most children's clothing is made from **non-flammable** material. However, clothing can still sometimes catch on fire and it is important to know exactly what to do in order to minimise injury or even save a life. First aid treatment should follow these steps:

▶ Stop the casualty panicking or running around as any movement or breeze will fan the flames.

▶ Lie the casualty down.

▶ If possible, wrap the casualty tightly in a coat, curtain or heavy blanket (not made from nylon) to smother the flames.

▶ Dial 999 for a ambulance and stay with the casualty until help arrives.

▶ Observe the casualty for signs of shock and treat as necessary (see page 270).

Over to you!

▶ *In your placement or work setting, what precautions are taken to protect babies and young children from sunburn?*

▶ *How is this managed in the setting?*

Compare your experiences with others in the group.

Key terms

Non-flammable: not able to burn easily

How do poisons enter the body?

A poison is any substance that may cause temporary or permanent damage if taken into the body in sufficient quantity. Once in the body, poisons can enter the bloodstream and be carried quickly to all organs and tissues. Depending on the poison, the effects can start to be seen immediately or over a longer period of time. Poisons can enter the body in any of the following ways:

▶ swallowed (e.g. medicines, plants or contaminated food)

▶ absorbed through the skin (e.g. poisonous sprays like pesticides)

▶ inhaled (e.g. breathing in poisonous gases or fumes)

▶ splashed into the eyes (e.g. acid)

▶ injected (e.g. by a syringe or a bite from a poisonous snake).

Recognising and treating poisoning

Once in the body, poisons act in different ways. Some poisons (such as sleeping tablets) affect the nervous system and can cause problems with breathing or heart function. Poisons that are swallowed can react directly with the food passages and cause vomiting and diarrhoea. Corrosive poisons (such as bleach) may severely burn the lips, mouth and stomach, causing intense pain. Young children are particularly at risk from poisoning and the **Child Accident Prevention Trust (CAPT)** estimates that more than 5000 children every year are admitted to hospital as a result of a poisoning incident.

The recognition of poisoning will vary depending on the poison, but the signs and symptoms may include:

▶ nausea or vomiting

▶ unconsciousness

▶ pain or burning sensation on the skin or in the mouth and throat

▶ empty containers nearby.

The aims of your first aid treatment should be to:

▶ Maintain the airway, breathing and circulation.

▶ Carry out CPR if required, using a face shield if necessary to protect yourself from contamination (see page 260).

▶ Stay calm and reassure the casualty.

▶ Remove any contaminated clothing.

▶ Identify the poison if possible, asking others for information if necessary.

Your assessment criteria:

8.1 Describe how poisons enter the body

8.2 Describe how to recognise and treat an infant and a child affected by common poisonous substances, including plants

8.3 Identify sources of information that provide procedures for treating those affected by poisonous substances

Key terms

Child Accident Prevention Trust (CAPT): a charity working to reduce the number of children and young people killed or injured as a result of accidents

▶ Arrange for urgent transport to hospital.

▶ Refrain from causing the casualty to vomit (this will cause more damage).

Poisonous plants and fungi

Many young children eat plant leaves or brightly coloured berries, but very few of these will actually result in serious poisoning. However, swallowing even small amounts of the **foxglove** plant can cause vomiting, and seizures may occur as a result of swallowing **laburnum** seeds. Serious poisoning from eating mushrooms is rare, but expert advice should always be taken before eating any wild mushrooms as some can be fatal.

The outdoor areas in any setting should be checked for poisonous plants and if plants are kept inside, they should be identified as non-poisonous.

Information sources on poisoning

Many organisations offer information about poisoning and guidance on procedures for treating individuals who are affected by poisonous substances. These organisations include:

St John Ambulance: www.sja.org.uk

British Red Cross: http://childrenfirstaid.redcross.org.uk/

Health Protection Agency: www.hpa.org.uk

National Health Service: www.nhs.uk/conditions/food-poisoning
www.nhsdirect.nhs.uk

Over to you!

▶ *In small groups, make a list of all the poisonous substances you can think of in a home environment that could be dangerous to infants or young children. Make sure you consider all the rooms in the house as well as the garden, garage and shed.*

Compare your list with other groups.

Key terms

Foxglove: a common garden plant with distinctive bell-shaped flowers, usually purple in colour

Laburnum: a flowering shrub or tree with bright yellow flowers

Over to you!

▶ *In pairs or small groups, investigate the work of some of the organisations listed above and their advice and guidance on treating poisoning.*

▶ *Share your findings with others in the group.*

Knowledge Assessment Task	7.2	6.1	6.2	7.1
		8.1	8.2	8.3

Plan and produce a display focusing on the first aid management of electrical injuries, burns and scalds and poisoning incidents with infants and children. Your display should include information about:

▶ how to safely manage an incident involving electricity

▶ how to recognise the severity of burns and scalds

▶ how poisons enter the body

▶ first aid treatment for electric shock, burns and scalds and poisoning

▶ sources of information about treating those affected by poisonous substances.

Take photographs of your display and keep your notes as evidence towards your assessment.

What are the dangers of bites or stings?

A sting from a bee, wasp or hornet is not usually serious and is often more painful than dangerous. However, with any insect bite or sting it is important to look for signs of an allergic reaction. Some children are allergic to insect stings and may experience anaphylactic shock (see page 271). A bite from an animal that causes a break in the skin will always need prompt attention because of the risk of infection. This may be complicated by tetanus and, in very rare cases, by **rabies.** Although poisonous snakes are very unusual in this country, some people keep poisonous snakes as pets and a snake bite can result in a dangerous injury. Young children sometimes bite each other and human bites can also cause serious injuries requiring first aid treatment.

Key terms

Rabies: a serious disease of the nervous system spread by the bite of infected animals such as dogs and foxes

A bite from a dog can be complicated by tetanus infection.

First aid management

The treatment of bites and stings depends on the severity of the injury. Some of the main points to consider are outlined in Figure 11.3.

Figure 13.11 Recognition and first aid management of bites and stings

Injury	Recognition	First aid treatment
Minor sting	Pain, swelling and redness around the site of the sting	• Stay calm and reassure the casualty. • Don't use tweezers to try to remove the sting as you risk squeezing more poison into the wound. • Apply an ice pack or cold compress for at least ten minutes, and if possible raise the affected part. • If swelling and pain persist, advise the casualty to go to their doctor.
Serious sting	Stings to the mouth and throat can be dangerous. There may be severe swelling, which could cause the airway to become blocked.	• Sucking on an ice cube, an ice lollipop, or sipping cold water will help to prevent any swelling in the mouth or throat. • If breathing becomes difficult or if there is any swelling to the face, neck, tongue, mouth or lips or any signs of a rash, then arrange for medical help immediately (see page 271 for signs of anaphylactic shock).
Minor bite	Puncture wound with slight bleeding, or indentations in the skin	• Wash with soap and water and cover the wound with a sterile dressing. • Seek medical help. • Tetanus injection may be necessary.
Serious bite	Several lacerations with extensive tissue damage and bleeding	• Apply direct pressure to control the bleeding (see page 268). • Cover the wound with a sterile dressing and bandage securely. • Observe for signs of shock and treat appropriately (see page 270). • Arrange transport to hospital.

Knowledge Assessment Task   9.1   9.2

Produce an information fact sheet for your placement or work setting about dealing with bites or stings with children when going out on visits. Your fact sheet will be a useful guide for the paediatric first aider and for parent helpers. It should include information about how to recognise the severity of bites and stings and details of the first aid treatment.

Keep your fact sheet as evidence towards your assessment.

Are you ready for assessment?

AC	What do you know now?	Assessment task	✓
3.1	How to manage an infant and a child with foreign bodies in their eyes, ears and nose	Page 283	
3.2	How to recognise and manage common eye injuries	Page 283	
4.1 4.2	How to recognise and manage chronic medical conditions (including sickle cell anaemia, diabetes and asthma) and serious sudden illnesses (including meningitis and febrile convulsions)	Page 289	
5.1 5.2	How to recognise and treat the effects of extreme cold and heat for an infant and a child	Page 291	
6.1 6.2	How to safely manage an incident involving electricity and describe first aid treatments for electric shock incidents	Page 297	
7.1 7.2	How to recognise the severity of burns and scalds to an infant and a child and respond accordingly	Page 297	
8.1 8.3	How poisons enter the body and sources of information that provide procedures for treating those affected by poisonous substances.	Page 297	
8.2	How to recognise and treat an infant and a child affected by common poisonous substances, including plants	Page 297	
9.1 9.2	How to recognise and treat the severity of bites and stings to an infant and a child and respond accordingly	Page 297	

Your tutor or assessor will need to observe your competence in a realistic, simulated situation.

AC	What can you do now?	Assessment task	✓
1.1	Describe the common types of fractures	Page 277	
1.2 1.3	Describe how to manage a fracture and a dislocation	Page 277	
1.4	Demonstrate the application of a support sling and an elevation sling	Page 277	
2.1	Describe how to recognise and manage head injuries including concussion, skull fracture and cerebral compression	Page 281	
2.2	Demonstrate how to manage a suspected spinal injury	Page 281	

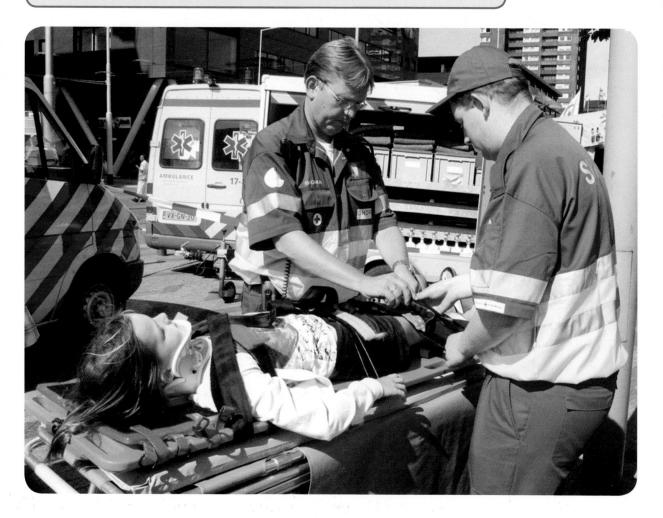

Index

ABC (Airway, Breathing, Circulation) rule 260
abstract ideas 126
accidents 88, 104, 152
    bleeding/wounds 266–9
    reporting 108–9, 252–3
    see also first aid
acronyms 23
active listening 26, 160
activities 181, 212–14
acute illnesses 105, 116
ADHD (Attention Deficit Hyperactivity Disorder) 187, 232
advice 20, 52–5
agencies 142–3
Airway, Breathing, Circulation rule 255, 260
airway obstruction 264–5
'alert, voice, pain, unresponsive' code 278
allergic reactions 106, 107, 223, 252, 271, 298–9
anaphylactic shock 106, 107, 271
animal bites 266, 298
antenatal factors 128
anti-discriminatory practice 42–7, 49–51
appraisals 69, 81
aptitude 61
ASD *see* autistic spectrum disorder
assertiveness 136
assessments, child development 192–5
asthma 106, 150, 151, 284, 285
Attention Deficit Hyperactivity Disorder (ADHD) 187, 232
audio recording 195
autistic spectrum disorder (ASD) 187, 233
AVPU (alert, voice, pain, unresponsive) code 278

babies 158, 159, 225
back injuries 278, 280–1
bacteria 110, 250, 266
badges 103
barriers to communication 22–7
baselines 74
beaches 98
behavioural development 122–7, 193
behavioural problems 131, 184–7
bilingual children 159
biometrics 140
bites 266, 298–9
bleeding injuries 266–9
blood sugar levels 286
body products, waste disposal 114
bone fractures/dislocations 276–7
breathing problems 260–3, 264–5, 284, 285
bruising 267
bullying 137, 142, 144, 148
burn injuries 293–5

CAMS (Child and Adolescent Mental Health) 187
CAPT (Child Accident Prevention Trust) 296
cardiopulmonary resuscitation (CPR) 255, 260–1
Care Quality Commission 44
carers 240–3
Care Standards Act (2000) 44
care workers 143
casualties 248
    assessment/monitoring 255–7, 259
    responsiveness 258–63, 278
    signs/symptoms 256–7
cerebral compression 278, 279
charts 183

checklists 195
child abuse 144–9
Child Accident Prevention Trust (CAPT) 296
Child and Adolescent Mental Health (CAMS) team 187
Child Convention, Rights of the 43
child development
    0 to 3 years 123
    3 to 5 years 124
    5 to 8 years 125
    8 to 12 years 126
    12 to 19 years 127
child development 120–33
    assessments 192–5
    concerns 129
    influences 128–9
    stages 122–7
    supporting 190–205
    transitions 130–1, 198–9
childminders 231
Children Acts (1989 & 2004) 44, 66, 138
choices, encouraging 165, 181
choking 264–5
chronic illnesses 106, 284–7
circle time 167
clarification, communication 26
clinical waste 114
clothing 111, 114, 295
clothing on fire 295
codes of practice 42, 47
cognitive development 122–7, 193
collaboration 60, 61
colleagues
    advice/support 53
    communication 10–11
    feedback from 81
communication 2–31
    advice 20

approach 24

assistance 27

barriers 22–7

child development 22, 122–7, 129, 193

with children/young people 9, 12, 15, 22, 158–61, 164

clarification 26

colleagues 10–11

confidentiality 10, 28–9

cultural differences 22

cycle 5

definition 4

dialects 23

with disabled children 12, 15, 22

distress 23

effectiveness checking 26

electronic devices 25

emotional difficulties 23

environmental factors 22, 24

feedback 12

health problems 23

importance 4–13

interaction 166–7

jargon use 23

language differences 22

language needs 14–21

listening skills 26

meeting needs 14–21

methods 18–19

non-verbal feedback 12

pace 24

with parents 10, 79

partnership working 241

reasons for 6–7

relationships 6

repeating 26

services context 236–9

slang use 23

specialist devices 25

special needs 15

speed 24

support 24, 27

through play 160–1

types 4, 16–17

understanding 161

work impact 8–11

work setting 4–13

competence requirements 60–7

concepts 123

concussion 278, 279

conduction 292

confidentiality 10, 28–9, 140, 192

conflict 170–1

consent, medication administration 116

consequences of choices 165

consistency 178, 181

Convention on the Rights of the Child (1989) 43

conversations, group 167

convulsions 106, 152, 262–3, 289

cot death 291

covert discrimination 36, 39

CPR (cardiopulmonary resuscitation) 255, 260–1

Criminal Records Bureau (CRB) 44, 139

criminal services 143

cultural practices 22, 223

curriculum vitae (CV) 82

cyber-bullying 137, 142, 148

Danger, Response, Airway, Breathing, Circulation (DRABC) 255

Data Protection Act (1998) 238

definitive lists 54

depression 131

descriptions, free 195

diabetes 106, 116, 220, 284, 286

dialects 23

diaries 70

diet 220–5

    allergies 223

    cultural/religious practices 223

    healthy eating 220–2

    nutrients 221, 222

Disability Discrimination Act (1995) 46

disabled children see special needs children

disclosures 146

discrimination 36–9, 49–51

dislocation injuries 276–7

disposal of waste 114

distress 23

diversity 34, 52–5, 168, 169

doctors 142, 233

dogs 113, 298

Down's syndrome 128, 129, 232

DRABC (Danger, Response, Airway, Breathing, Circulation) 255

drinks 225

duties, work role 60

ear injuries 282

Early Years Foundation Stage (EYFS)

    hazards 89

    health and safety 90–1

    national standards 63

    positive environments 208, 209

    positive relationships 162

    standards 63

    welfare requirements 139, 209

early years workers 233

eating disorders 131

'eatwell plate' 222

Education Acts (1981, 1993 & 1996) 47

educational psychologists 187, 233

Education Inspectorate (Scotland) 208

education services 143

egocentric thinking 168

electrical injuries 292–3

electronic communication devices 25

Elliot, Jane 37

email 19

emergencies, 999 calls 101, 105, 256, 263, 295

emergencies 100–3, 153

    fire procedures 101, 295

    getting help 101, 105, 256, 263, 295

hyperglycaemia 106, 286

hypoglycaemia 106, 286

meningitis 288

missing children 102

reporting procedure 108–9

security incidents 102–3

septicaemia 288

services 101, 105, 256, 263, 295

sickle cell crisis 287

staff role 106

sudden illnesses 288–9

see also first aid

emotional abuse 144

emotional development 122–7, 129, 193

emotional difficulties 23

empathy 8, 26, 168–9

employees/employers, health and safety responsibilities 64, 90

encouragement 215, 241

environmental factors 22, 24

epilepsy 106, 262

equality 32–57

advice 52–5

importance 34–41

information sources 52–5

of opportunity 34

promotion strategies 40–1

Equality Act (2006) 46

equipment

first aid 250, 252

play 92

E-safety 148

ethnic diversity 35

event samples 195

Every Child Matters programme 44, 138, 208

evidence, personal development 83

external bleeding 266, 267

eye colour experiment 37

eye contact 17

eye irritation/injuries 282–3

EYFS *see* Early Years Foundation Stage

face shields, first aid 260

face-to-face communication 18

facial expression 17, 159

failure to thrive 144, 145

fairness 170, 178

family doctors 142, 233

family support workers 143, 233

febrile convulsions 289

feedback 12, 80–1

feelings 7, 199

fine motor skills 122

fire emergencies 101, 295

fire safety 92

first aid, 999 emergency calls 101, 105, 256, 263, 295

first aid 246–301

ABC rule 260

accident reports 252–3

airway obstruction 264–5

animal bites 266, 298

assessment/monitoring of casualties 254–7, 259

asthma attacks 284, 285

back injuries 258, 278, 280–1

bites 298–9

bleeding 266–9

breathing problems 260–3, 264–5

burns 293–5

calling for help 101, 105, 256, 263, 295

cardiopulmonary resuscitation 255, 260–1

casualty assessment/monitoring 254–7, 259

casualty signs/symptoms 256–7

cerebral compression 278, 279

choking 264–5

chronic illnesses 284–7

clothing on fire 295

cold extremes 291

concussion 278, 279

convulsions 262–3, 289

definition 248

diabetic emergencies 286

dislocations 276–7

ear injuries 282

electrical injuries 292–3

emergency assessment/action 254–7, 259

emergency calls 101, 105, 256, 263, 295

equipment 250, 252

eye irritation/injuries 282–3

face shields, resuscitation 260

febrile convulsions 289

first aider role 101, 152, 248–53

fitting 262–3, 289

foreign body obstruction/penetration 264–5, 282

fractures 276–7

head injuries 278–80

heatstroke 290

hepatitis 250

human immunodeficiency virus 250

hygiene 250, 268

hypothermia 291

incident reports 252–3

infection risk 250

insect bites/stings 298–9

jaw thrust technique 258

kits 250, 252

meningitis 288

minor injuries 269

neck injuries 278

nosebleeds 269

nose injuries 269, 282

overheating 290, 291

poisoning 296–7

primary surveys 255–7

recovery position 258

reporting accidents/incidents 252–3

resuscitation 255, 260–1

scalds 293–5

scene surveys 254–5

seizures 262–3, 289

septicaemia 288

shock 266, 267, 270–1

sickle cell crisis 287

signs/symptoms of casualties 256–7

skull fracture 279

spinal injuries 258, 280–1

stings 298–9

sudden illnesses 288–9

sunburn 290

surveys 254–7

symptoms of casualties 256–7

temperature extremes 290–1

unconscious casualties 258–63

wounds 266–9

fitting (seizures) 106, 152, 262–3, 289

fontanelles 288

food additives 223

food poisoning 297

food safety 224–5

Food Standards Agency 222

foreign body obstruction/penetration 264–5, 282

formal appraisals 81

formula feeds 225

foxglove 297

fractures 276–7

free descriptions 195

fungi poisoning 297

gastroenteritis 224

general practitioners (GPs) 142, 233

gestures 17

GPs (general practitioners) 142, 233

grommets 25

gross motor skills 122

group conversations 167

hair care 216

halal dietary law 223

hand-eye co-ordination 193

hand-washing 112, 224

hazards 88–9, 98

head injuries 278–80

health

    child development 128

and communication 23

diet 220–3

see also illness

health and safety 86–119

    legislation 64–5, 92–3

    off-site visits 98–9

    policies/procedures 88–93

    reporting procedure 91

    responsibilities 90–1

    safe environments 96–7

    work setting policies 88–93

Health and Safety at Work Act (1974) 64, 92–3

Health Safety at Work Regulations (1999) 94–5

Health and Safety Executive (HSE) 94

health services 142

health visitors 232, 233

healthy eating 220–2

hearing impaired children 15

heatstroke 290

hepatitis 250

Her Majesty's Inspectorate of Education (Scotland) 208

HIV (human immunodeficiency virus) 250

HMIE (Her Majesty's Inspectorate of Education) 208

hobbies 193

holistic development 122, 194, 230

honesty 199

housing conditions 128

HSE (Health and Safety Executive) 94

human immunodeficiency virus (HIV) 250

hygiene 110, 112, 216, 224, 268

hyperactivity disorder 187, 232

hyperglycaemia 106, 286

hypoglycaemia 106, 286

hypothermia 291

ideas, expressing 7

identity badges 103

illness

communication barriers 23

dealing with 152

procedures 104–7, 108–9

signs/symptoms 150–1

see also health

immobilisation of fractures 277

immunity 110

inappropriate behaviour 184–7

incidents

    definition 88

    reporting procedures 107, 108–9, 252–3

    reviewing 107

inclusion 32–57

    advice 52–5

    environments 211

    importance 34–41

    information sources 52–5

    promotion strategies 40–1

    working practices 42–51

inclusive environments 211

Independent Safeguarding Authority (ISA) 44, 138–9

induction 62

induction loops 24

infection control 110–15, 250

infectious illnesses 151

information-sharing 6–7, 236–9, 241

information sources

    colleagues 53

    equality/inclusion 52–5

    parents 53

    written resources 53

information storage 238–9

inhalers 284, 285

injuries

    bleeding/wounds 266–9

    dealing with 152

    procedures 104–7

    see also first aid

insect bites/stings 298–9

inspections 208

insulin 116, 286

integrated children's services 138

integrated working 230

intellectual development 122–7, 193

interaction 6, 48, 166–7

interests, children's 193

internal bleeding 266, 267

internal policies/procedures 63

internet 137, 148

intervertebral discs 280

interviews 61

intruders 102, 103

ISA (Independent Safeguarding Authority) 44, 138–9

jargon 23

jaw thrust technique 258

job descriptions 60

journals 70

key persons 162

Kidscape 142, 177

knowledge development 78–83

laburnum 297

language differences 22

language needs 14–21

language therapists 233

learning activities 78

learning support 72–3

legal services 143

legislation
  anti-discrimination 42–7
  health and safety 64–5, 92–3
  inclusive practice 42–7
  safeguarding children 138–9

lifestyles 242

linen 114

listening skills 26, 160, 199

literacy skills 129

literal thinking 161

Local Safeguarding Children Boards 146

logical thought 125

lost children 102

Makaton 159

Management of Health Safety at Work Regulations (1999) 94–5

Manual Handling Operations Regulations (1992) 93

maturation 122

medical incidents 104–7

medicines 116–17, 252

meningitis 150, 151, 152, 288

mentors 81

microwave ovens 225

minor injuries 269

missing children 102

mobile phones 148

motor skills 122

multi-agency working 230

mushroom poisoning 297

mutism, selective 131, 187

mutual respect 240

narrative descriptions 195

National Occupation Standards (NOS) 66

nebulisers 284, 285

neck injuries 278

needs, expressing 7

neglect 144

non-flammable material 295

non-infectious illnesses 151

non-medical incidents 100–3
  fire procedures 101
  getting help 101
  missing children 102
  security incidents 102–3

non-verbal communication 4, 6, 12, 16–17, 19, 158, 159

norovirus 111

nosebleeds 269

nose injuries 269, 282

NOS (National Occupation Standards) 66

note-keeping 203

nursery rhymes 39

nutrients 221, 222

nutrition see diet

obesity 220

objectives 72

observation 184, 192–7

off-site visits 98–9

Ofsted (Office for Standards in Education) 208

online safety 148

ovens 225

overheating 290, 291

overt discrimination 36, 38

paediatric emergency first aid see first aid

paediatric illness/injury see first aid

pancreas 287

paramount needs 44

parentese 158

parents
  accident/incident reporting 109
  communicating with 10, 79, 109
  encouragement 241
  expertise resource 241
  information source 53
  partnership working 240–3
  special needs children 241

parks 98

partnership working 228–45
  barriers 235
  carers 240–3
  characteristics 234
  difficulties 242
  parents 240–3
  services context 230–5

pastimes 193

performance standards 69, 80–1

persona dolls 168

personal care needs 216–19

personal development 58–85
  evidence 83
  feedback 80–1
  knowledge 78–83
  personal views 67
  plans 72–7

recording 82–3

reflection process 68–71, 79

skills 78–83

standards 63–6

support 72–3

understanding 78–83

work role 60–6

personal hygiene 110, 112, 216, 224

personal protective clothing 111

personal views 67

person specifications 60

photographs 195

physical abuse 144

physical development 122–7, 193

physical gestures 17

pictures 161, 183

plans, personal development 72–7

plants, poisonous 297

play 92, 160–1, 168

poisoning 296–7

police 143

policies

definition 42

health and safety 88–93

information-sharing 236–7

medication administration 117

positive behaviour 176–9

safeguarding 140

work role 62, 63

population 35

portfolios 82

positive behaviour

definition 180

policies/procedures 176–9

rewarding 181–3

supporting 174–89, 200–1

positive environments

factors 212

individual needs 210–15

personal care needs 216–19

regulatory requirements 208–9

supporting 206–27

positive reinforcement 177, 181, 182, 185

praise 182, 183, 215

preferences, expressing 7

prejudice 36–7

premature babies 128, 129

primary surveys, first aid 255–7

probation officers 143

procedures

definition 42

health and safety 88–93

information-sharing 236–7

medication administration 117

positive behaviour 176–9

safeguarding 140

work role 62, 63

professional responsibility 149

progress see personal development

protective clothing 111

proximity, communication 17

psychologists 187, 233

puberty 126, 127

public environments 98

Public Order Act (1986) 45

public parks 98

public transport 98

puppets 168

qualifications 82

questionnaires 81

rabies 298

Race Relations Acts (1976 & 2000) 45

racial discrimination 45

Racial and Religious Hatred Act (2006) 45

record keeping 238

recovery position 258

recyclable waste 114

referral process 186–7, 232–3

reflection 68–71, 202–3

diaries/journals 70

process 70

purpose 68–9

question types 70

self-improvement 79

regression 131

regulations

health and safety at work 94–5

manual handling operations 93

regulatory bodies 63

relationships

communication 6

developing 162–5

supporting 166–71

trust 162, 164

religion 223

repeating, communication 26

reporting

accidents/incidents 107, 108–9, 252–3

health and safety 91

residential care workers 143

resilience 136

resources 212–13

respect 48, 240

respiratory disorders 284

responsibilities

employees 64

employers 64

first aiders 248–53

health and safety 90–1

safeguarding issues 146, 149

students 65

work role 60

responsiveness of casualties 278

resuscitation 255, 260–1

resuscitation (CPR) 255, 260–1

retail areas 98

Rights of the Child Convention (1989) 43

risk assessment

issues 96

planning 96, 98–9

questions to ask 96

stages 95

work setting 94–9

risks 88–9, 97

role models 181

routines 218

rubbish disposal 114

safeguarding 44, 66, 134–55

    agencies 142–3

    concerns 146

    guidelines 138–9

    legislation 138–9

    policies/procedures 140

    professional responsibility 149

    purpose 136–7

    responding to concerns 146

safety *see* health and safety

sample recording 195

sanctions 185

scald injuries 293–5

scene surveys, first aid 254–5

school inspections 208

Scotland 208

security incidents 102–3

seizures 106, 152, 262–3, 289

selective mutism 131, 187

self-development *see* personal
    development

self-evaluation 68, 69

self-harming behaviour 131, 187

SENCOs (Special Educational Needs
    Co-ordinators) 14, 53, 187

senses 214

sensory activities 214

septicaemia 288

serious accidents/incidents 108–9

sexual abuse 144

sexualised behaviour 187

sharps, waste disposal 114

shock 266, 267, 270–1

sickle cell anaemia 284, 287

sickle cell crisis 106, 107, 287

sign language 158–9

signs of illness/injury 104, 150–1,
    256–7

simulations 257

skills 61, 78–83

skin care 216, 217

skull fracture 279

slang 23

sleep disturbances 131

'slipped discs' 280

SMART objectives 74–5

snake bites 298

social development 122–7,
    129, 193

social inclusion 35

social networking 137

social services 142–3

social workers 142, 233

soiling incidents 115

spacer devices 284

spatial awareness 127

special communication needs 15

Special Educational Needs Co-
    ordinators (SENCOs) 14, 53, 187

Special Educational Needs and
    Disability Act (2001) 46

specialist communication devices 25

special needs children

    communication 12, 15, 22

    non-verbal communication 12

    parents 241

    personal care needs 216–17

    positive environments 211

speech problems 131

speech therapists 233

spinal injuries 258, 280–1

staff meetings 73

standards, work role 63–6, 80–1

statutory requirements 139, 209

stereotypes 39, 40

stigmatisation 48

stimulating activities 181, 214

students 65

sudden infant death syndrome 291

sunburn 290

support

    communication 7, 24, 27

    learning 72–3

personal development 72–3

    when to seek 54

support workers 143, 233

surveys, first aid 254–7

swimming pools 98

symptoms of illness/injury 104,
    150–1, 256–7

tactile stimulation 214

tantrums 186

teachers 143, 233

teamworking 61

teeth-brushing 216

telephone communication 18

temper tantrums 186

tetanus 266, 298

text messages 19

therapists, speech 233

thinking skills 122–7, 193

thoughts, expressing 7

'time out' strategy 185

time samples 195

touch 17

towels 114

toys 92

training folders 82

training opportunities 73

transient lifestyles 242

transitions 130–1, 198–9

treasure baskets 214

triggers 184

trusting relationships 162, 164

unconscious casualties 258–9

unco-operative behaviour 187

understanding

    personal development 78–83

    work role 60–2

United Kingdom (UK) 35

vegan diet 223

vegetarian diet 223

verbal communication 4, 16, 158–9

video 195

violent behaviour 187

viruses 110

visitor badges 103

visually impaired children 12, 15

visual prompts 161, 183

voluntary services 143

vomiting virus 111

vulnerable children 136

waste disposal 114

water 225

welfare requirements 66, 209

wellbeing 66

'winter vomiting virus' 111

wishes, expressing 7

work role

appraisals 69

aptitude 61

competence requirements 60–7

duties 60

emergencies 106

induction phase 62

internal policies/procedures 63

performance standards 69

personal views 67

policies/procedures 62, 63

reflection process 68–71

responsibilities 60

self-evaluation 69

skills 61

standards 63–6

starting a new job 62

understanding 60–2

work setting

child development support 190–205

medication management 116–17

relationship support 166–71

risk assessment 94–9

safeguarding policies 140

wounds, first aid 266–9

written communication 18–19

written records 195

written resources 53

young person development *see* child development

youth workers 233

Notes